'*Streets Ahead* lives up to its name. It is one of the most all-encompassing books ever written on property investing in Australia. Chock-full of practical information, ideas and case studies, it should be required reading for anyone contemplating taking the plunge into real estate investing. Australians may love property but still find it very difficult to get unbiased advice. The financial planning industry is not interested because the real estate sector does not generate the high levels of ongoing fees available from funds managers. Educating people on benefits of bricks and mortar investment has mainly been left to the marketeers, who are much more interested in enriching themselves than their clients. *Streets Ahead* will certainly help to fill the education gap and Monique and Richard Wakelin should be congratulated for it.'

Pam Walkley, Editor, Money magazine

Streets Ahead

How to Make Money from Residential Property

Monique Wakelin & Richard Wakelin
contributing author, Fiona Marsden

To our parents – John, Elisabeth, Henry and Lola.

> *Streets Ahead represents the professional opinions and expertise of the authors. It is intended as general information only and must not be substituted for individual financial and/or property investment advice. Whilst all care has been taken in compiling the data and information contained herein, no warranties or guarantees are given in relation to their accuracy. Neither the authors nor the publisher, the editor or their respective employees ofr agents can be held responsible for any loss or claim arising out of the use, or misuse, of the suggestions made in this book. All the client case study stories in this book are true and unaltered. Personal and identifying details have been changed to protect the privacy of the individuals concerned.*

Universal Press, the publisher of the maps found within this publication, disclaims any responsibility or duty of care towards any person for loss or damage suffered from any use of these maps for whatever purpose and in whatever manner. Whilst considerable care has been taken by this publisher in researching and compiling the maps, the publishers accept no responsibility for errors or omissions. No person should rely upon this directory for the purposes of making any business, investment or real estate decision.

Published by:

Wilkinson Publishing Pty Ltd   ACN 006 042 173
Level 4, 2 Collins Street
Melbourne, Vic 3000

Tel: 03 9654 5446   www.wilkinsonpublishing.com.au

Copyright © 2007 Monique Wakelin and Richard Wakelin

All rights reserved. No part of this publication may be reproduced, stored in a retrieval system or transmitted in any form by any means without the prior permission of the copyright owner. Enquiries should be made to the publisher.

Every effort has been made to ensure that this book is free from error or omissions. However, the Publisher, the Author, the Editor or their respective employees or agents, shall not accept responsibility for injury, loss or damage occasioned to any person acting or refraining from action as a result of material in this book whether or not such injury, loss or damage is in any way due to any negligent act or omission, breach of duty or default on the part of the Publisher, the Author, the Editor, or their respective employees or agents.

National Library of Australia Cataloguing-in-Publication data:

    Wakelin, Monique.

    Streets ahead : how to make money from residential property.

    Includes index.

    ISBN 9781921332104.

    1. Residential real estate - Australia. 2. Real estate investment - Australia. I. Marsden, Fiona. II. Wakelin, Richard. III. Title.

    333.33220994

Contents

About the Authors ix
Acknowledgments xi
Introduction xiii

PART ONE
What All Property Investors Must Know 1

Chapter One
Why Invest in Property?
    Pluses and pitfalls: comparing apples with apples 3

Chapter Two
Property Investment Advice
    Trick or treat? 18

Chapter Three
External influences on residential property
    Economics and other denizens of the deep and meaningful 34

Chapter Four
What is an Investment Property?
    And why your home doesn't always qualify! 68

PART TWO
Laying the Groundwork   83

Chapter Five
Making a Start
    Why your first investment property is the most important   85

Chapter Six
Where to Buy
    Location, location, and then some!   97

Chapter Seven
What to Buy
    Why 'any old property' really won't do!   122

Chapter Eight
Organising Finance
    Looking after your bottom line   146

PART THREE
Leaving No Stone Unturned   167

Chapter Nine
The Nuts and Bolts of Getting Your House in Order
    Building inspections, conveyancing, insurance and other lesser evils   169

Chapter Ten
Tax and Residential Property
    Fighting the demons without creating a nightmare!   184

Chapter Eleven
Mastering the Skills of Searching and Negotiation
    Pounding the pavement for profit   196

PART FOUR
Keeping the Good Times Rolling   217

Chapter Twelve
Managing Your Investment Property
    Forfeiting the illusion of control   219

Chapter Thirteen
Evaluating the Success of Your Investment
    What to do with what you've got   237

Chapter Fourteen
Adding Value
    A sense of adventure   258

Appendix A
Glossary of Property Investment Terms   280

Appendix B
Useful Contacts   285

Index   292

About the Authors

Richard Wakelin has 30 years' experience in residential property.

After working in property management, he gained comprehensive experience in residential and commercial property. Early on in his property career, Richard identified a growing need among residential property purchasers for independent advice and representation, in an industry very much geared towards representing *sellers*.

By the early 1980s he was working with organisations that were developing specialist services in property investment advice. During this time he also became well known as a property commentator with regular media appearances—a role he considers critical to ensuring that authentic advice is freely available to the public.

In March 1995 he struck out on his own, establishing Wakelin Property Advisory with his business and life partner Monique Wakelin.

Richard holds an Advanced Certificate in Real Estate and is a Member of the Real Estate Institute of Victoria.

Monique Wakelin has enjoyed a diverse career spanning performing arts, education and corporate communications. Since the mid-1990s she has combined her communications expertise with her role as a property adviser, working with her business and life partner Richard Wakelin.

Monique is an experienced presenter and media commentator on property issues. She has appeared in some of the country's best known print and electronic media including *The Australian*, *The Age*, *The Herald Sun*, *The Australian Financial Review*, *The Bulletin*, *Money* and *A Current Affair*. She co-hosts a popular property investment talkback segment on Melbourne ABC radio, and is a sought after presenter on business and property related topics.

Monique holds a Bachelor of Education, is an Affiliate of the Real Estate Institute of Victoria and a Member of the Public Relations Institute of Australia.

Acknowledgements

We would like to extend our appreciation to the people who have been so generous with their time and expertise:

Our sincere thanks to contributing author Fiona Marsden for her tireless efforts and those endless blocks of chocolate that kept all three of us firing through many late nights!

We are indebted to our colleagues at Wakelin Property Advisory, particularly Paul Nugent for his expert technical input and ability to mentally calculate almost any mathematical equation instantaneously at any hour of the day or night.

Our heartfelt thanks to Saul Eslake, Chief Economist, ANZ Bank, for his almost saintly patience and expert guidance on economic content for Chapter Three. Thanks are also due to Phil Anderson of Economic Indicator Services, for general information on business and investment cycles.

Our 'Medal for Good Humour' and appreciation for her expert technical advice on taxation-related material goes to Melanie Cassy of Melanie Cassy and Associates.

We also wish to thank senior staff from professional bodies and research organisations including:

Daryl Smeaton, CEO, and David Wesney, Real Estate Institute of Australia

Carmel McCormack and Grant Aldous of the Real Estate Institute of Victoria

Brodie Johnson, from Residex

Jonathan Doheny and Lloyd Howlett from UBD

Fiona Bergin from the REIQ

As for the team at Hodder Headline Australia, it doesn't get much better than these guys!

Most importantly, we thank our individual and institutional investor clients, whose questions, comments and trust in our professional expertise over so many years have provided ample inspiration for this book.

Richard Wakelin and Monique Wakelin

Introduction

It's no secret that we Australians love our residential property!

Here, finally, is the step by step practical guide that will help you understand what drives property markets and how to choose investment properties that will put you in control of your financial destiny. And for most of us, gaining control over our financial destiny is rarely just about money; it's really about funding our hopes and dreams!

The principles and practices you're about to read have been developed, tried and tested by us as professional property advisers for over 20 years. They've made thousands of clients hundreds of thousands of dollars within very realistic timeframes. This formula works! What's more it's as low risk as any strategy can be given that there's no such thing as a completely *risk free* investment.

Go ahead and treat this book like the working tool that we've designed it to be. Write all over it and note your experiences and discoveries—because a journey of discovery is most assuredly what this book is all about!

And whilst we're on the subject of discovery, consider the opportunity before you if you have school-aged children in your life. The lack of practical education provided to young people on financial matters is an increasing concern given that for the last ten years, government policies are clearly steering us towards a self-funded retirement. And this is not about to change! Share your investment journey and this book with your own children, nieces, nephews, a younger sibling, cousins or simply a family friend. They will learn with you how it feels to succeed in building independence and attaining the freedom it confers. Perhaps more importantly, they will also learn how to avoid making the same mistake twice! Your time and genuine interest in their future welfare will be one of the most valuable gifts you can give. Our schools should take up the call and include this important knowledge in their core curriculum.

As a totally independent property advisory company committed to helping our clients gain control over their financial destiny, we believe it's about time every Australian who wants to invest in residential property profitably and without undue risk was given the tools and information to do so without any vested interests colouring that advice.

Have a look at the Contents page before you start reading and consider it your road map. You'll get the most out of the book by reading it from cover to cover, in sequence, especially the first time around. Once you've done that, you'll find it easy to dip back into any chapter at any time and in any order that fits in with your property investment strategy, to fill gaps in your knowledge, or just to refresh your memory on certain concepts.

You'll reap the rewards of owning this book if you want to:

- discover the benefits of sensible, well-researched residential property investment as part of an *overall* strategy to help you retire comfortably without undue sacrifice along the way;

- select investment property that provides *superior long-term capital growth* above all else;

- understand the basics of other issues associated with successful investing—financing, building inspections, insurance, conveyancing, property management and more; and

- objectively evaluate the ongoing success of your investment, so you can keep progressing towards your personal and financial goals.

However we won't try to:

- convince you that residential property is superior to other forms of investment, and that it provides the sole solution to all your financial needs;

- provide financial planning information or advise you on the suitability of other asset classes;

- promote tax minimisation as the key purpose of investing;

- confuse you with laborious explanations of impossible concepts like 'timing the market'.

So, are you still with us? Then read on, and join us on a journey with one clearly defined goal—to help you on the way to financial independence through property decisions that really will get you 'Streets Ahead'!

Warm regards,
Monique Wakelin and Richard Wakelin
March 2002

PART ONE
What All Property Investors Must Know

CHAPTER ONE

Why Invest in Property?

PLUSES AND PITFALLS: COMPARING APPLES WITH APPLES

Well, *why* property, indeed? When we're faced with the tall task of providing for our financial future across an ever-lengthening lifespan, the mere thought of investing in property—or indeed any kind of investment vehicle outside our everyday bank accounts and compulsory superannuation funds—can be enough to freeze many of us into permanent inaction.

In our experience, from speaking with thousands of Australians through public education programs, face-to-face-interviews and radio talkback segments, this reluctance to act almost always stems from mis-information, fear or ignorance of the investment alternatives available, rather than a lack of motivation to look after our own best interests.

Most of us, for instance, have heard the warnings from financial commentators: Australians are living longer and having fewer children. In the middle of the post-war baby boom in 1954, a male child could expect to live to around 67 years, and his female counterpart to nearly 73. Members of Generation X fared better. Males born in 1971, for example, could expect to live about 68 years, and females around 75. Today's children have the longest life expectancy of all. Males born in

1998 can reasonably expect to achieve the ripe old age of 76, and females almost 81.

Over a mere half century, that's a whopping life expectancy increase of almost ten years for men and nine years for women. But who will fund these increased lifespans? Well, it is not likely to be Australia's taxpayers. With more life choices than their forebears, many women are opting to delay childbirth, have fewer children or elect not to have children at all. The birthrate is now below replacement level (Source: ABS). The result? A shrinking population of working-age Australians, and less taxpayer funds available to support an increasing number of retirees via the aged pension.

This gives present and future federal governments two options: (a) raise tax levels to compensate for the decline in our working population and keep pensions at current levels; or (b) keep tax levels on a relatively even keel, peg back the pension and encourage us to fund our own retirements. Considering the concerted efforts and incentives governments have made in recent years to encourage retirement savings through vehicles such as superannuation, and the likely political fallout from tax increases, you don't have to be Einstein to work out which option governments will find the most attractive!

In short, those of us who think we will be able to rely on the aged pension to fund our lifestyles in retirement will be in for a very nasty shock.

'Well, that's why I have super, isn't it?' we hear you say. Absolutely—but will it be enough? Someone on today's average earnings (around $40 000 pa), who contributes at prevailing superannuation guarantee rates for 30 years, then combines this with the aged pension in retirement, will have around $20 000 per year to live on in today's terms. Hardly the stuff of which comfortable retirements are made—not to mention precious little reward for all those years of working hard and paying bucketloads of tax!

So where to from here?

When it comes down to it, all most of us want is enough money to live comfortably throughout our retirement—to enjoy our later years and share them with friends and family, without having to scrimp and save. To do this, we need income-producing assets—investments that provide a source of funds over and above our regular wage or salary.

If the pension and super won't be enough, we're forced to look further afield. Broadly speaking, there are four investment alternatives: cash, fixed interest, property and shares. This is where the waters get muddied and our brains go into overdrive! 'How does each asset class work? Are some more secure, or more risky, than others? What kinds of products are there? How much do I need to invest? Do I invest in one asset class, or across the whole lot?' Since few, if any of us, learned the principles of investment at school or university, these are all eminently reasonable questions. And when we don't know a blue chip share from a managed fund or a government bond, answering the question, 'Why property?' may seem a long way off.

So, to help make sense of things for you, we'll take a look at the characteristics of property in relation to other asset classes. Note that while Table 1.1 (p. 6) is not proffered in any way as general financial advice (we are not financial planners or licensed securities dealers), it does help put the characteristics of property into their correct perspective.

Table 1.1: Comparison of Investment Asset Classes

Characteristic	Cash	Fixed interest	Direct property	Shares
Relative risk level/volatility	Low	Low/moderate	Moderate	High
Return potential	Income only	Income only	Capital growth (and loss); regular rental income	Capital growth (and loss); irregular income via distributions/dividends
Taxation status	Income taxed at marginal rate	Income taxed at marginal rate	*Advantage:* negative gearing, depreciation *Liability:* capital gains tax	*Advantage:* imputation credits or similar (company pays tax before you do) *Liability:* capital gains tax
Leveraging potential (capacity to borrow on the value to fund other investments)	High	High	High (can borrow up to 95% of value of property in many cases)	Moderate (can borrow up to 80% of value of shares in many cases)
Liquidity (how quickly and easily you can sell/redeem)	High	Moderate	Low	High
Personal/ psychological control	High Psychological familiarity of 'money in the bank'	High (if self-managed) Psychological security of relatively stable income	High (can add value, buy, sell, gift, will) 'Real asset' security of a basic commodity—people need a place to live	High (if self-managed) Notional, intangible—based on decisions and performance of companies

Source: Financial Planning Association of Australia
Macquarie Investment Management
Suncorp Metway
ANZ Bank
Commonwealth Bank
Bank of Melbourne
National Australia Bank
Vanguard Investments

From the table you can see that each asset class has a wide variety of characteristics. Some assets grow in value; others provide only income. Some can be sold or accessed quickly; others take longer. Some are relatively low risk and provide equally modest returns; others are higher risk but offer the possibility of higher returns (and losses). Therefore, each of the four asset classes can play an important and valid role in creating financial independence.

The pros and cons of investment property

Property, like any other asset class, can never be the 'perfect' investment. It can't provide you with low risk, high return, high liquidity and big tax breaks all rolled into one. If it was that simple and that fabulous, every Australian would be investing in property from the time they were old enough to open up a Monopoly board!

So, what does property really have to offer, and what are its shortcomings?

1. CAPITAL GROWTH AND RENTAL INCOME

The number-one advantage of residential property—provided it's carefully chosen—is the potential for excellent long-term capital growth.

Capital growth will increase your equity or 'net worth' (what you own, not what you owe) more quickly than could be achieved simply through loan repayments. It is capital growth and steadily increasing equity that will enable you to acquire further assets, generate as much income as you need and ultimately achieve financial independence.

Long-term capital growth potential is the single most important consideration in selecting investment property, because it gives you leverage.

Ever been to the bank for a loan of any description? One of the first things any lender will ask for is security or collateral. Residential property, because of its intrinsic and tangible value, is number one on their list—giving you the greatest degree of borrowing power. Most banks will lend the highest 'loan to value ratio', or LVR—the proportion of the asset's value the bank will lend—on property, often up to 95 per cent. By contrast, shares attract an LVR of up to 80 per cent, although many lenders will only lend 50–60% of the value of the shares because lenders view them as less tangible and more volatile. The higher your property's rate of capital growth, the greater your ability to use the accumulating equity to purchase further income-producing assets.

Streetwise

Top performing residential investment property—the kind this book shows you how to identify and purchase—must double in value at least every seven to ten years. To do this, it must grow in capital value by an average of at least 7 to 8 per cent per annum ahead of the prevailing inflation rate.

Residential property can also produce regular passive income, through rent—income you don't earn through your own exertions. While you are still working, rent helps offset running costs such as loan repayments, insurance and rates, so you can put more of your salary or business income into other areas of life. In retirement, rent replaces your working income and reduces, or eliminates, your reliance on the pension and superannuation.

Of course, property also has its downsides. Along with the potential for capital growth comes the potential for capital loss or stagnation. Over the years we've met hundreds of property investors who thought they were 'on a sure thing', simply because property as a whole goes up in value over time, only to find that their cherished moneymaker was, in fact, a dead duck! What they didn't realise when they purchased was that, from a capital growth perspective, when you've seen one property, you definitely haven't seen them all! Capital growth varies substantially from city to city, suburb to suburb, street to street and property to property.

Rental income, too, can fluctuate along with changes in supply and demand, in turn affecting vacancy periods between tenancies. However, provided you choose the right asset, set reasonable rent levels and choose your tenants wisely, you can minimise market variations and vacancies and maintain a smooth flow of income.

Furthermore, unlike the capital worth of a property, rental income increases more or less uniformly across property types and geographical locations. This is because capital worth and rental incomes are driven by very different factors. Purchasers have a financial stake in the properties they own. In the case of home-buyers, they also have

Choosing the right type and location of property is crucial.

an emotional stake. This means they will often pay a premium to secure their property of choice. Accordingly, values can rise strongly.

In contrast, tenants do not have a financial (nor usually an emotional) stake in the properties they rent, and therefore won't sustain rental increases of the same calibre or frequency. This means supply and demand work differently in the rental market. When would-be first home buyers become active, usually as a result of government grants or a reduction in interest rates, rental vacancies rise and rental values can moderate. As property values rise and first home buyers are priced out of the market, many return to renting, creating a resurgence of demand and a corresponding rise in rental values.

A word about 'returns'

From our discussions so far, you can see that capital growth and rental income are two very different creatures, yet many investors confuse them, often to their considerable disadvantage.

How many times have you seen advertisements for new property developments promising 'guaranteed returns'? It's vital to realise that these 'returns' actually refer to rental income, not capital growth. What these properties provide is a consistent rental amount for a limited timeframe, to help establish their credentials as 'premium' investments. This amount may be higher than the property's true rental value. At the expiration of the guarantee period, the rent reverts to the true market rate as influenced by supply and demand.

Few investors realise that, when the property industry talks about 'rental returns', they're not talking about the dollar amount that comes to you and helps fund holding costs. They're talking about the rental income as a percentage of capital value. This looks fantastic on paper, but the reality is quite different. A rental return is only 'high' when the true capital value—and capital growth potential—are correspondingly low! This stymies, not accelerates, your ability to accumulate net equity (the proportion of an asset that is free of debt) and leverage to purchase further assets.

Conversely, when you see a property with a low rental return, remember that this return is only low in relation to the capital value. The actual rental dollar amount may well be appropriate for that location and style of property.

Given that rental income increases at a different rate from capital value, and that low rental returns can indicate high capital value and high capital growth potential, it follows that **the very best investment properties will grow in capital value more quickly than they grow in rental value**.

Bet this flies in the face of everything you've been led to believe about property investment! *But if you can master this concept, you've won half the battle!*

To illustrate, let's look at Table 1.2's two hypothetical investment properties and see how the figures stack up. Investor A focused primarily on rental return when selecting the asset, while Investor B focused on capital growth.

From a rental perspective, Investor A's property appears superior because its rental income as a dollar amount and a percentage of capital value is higher. But in terms of capital growth—the tool that gives you

Table 1.2: Rental Returns

This table depicts two common scenarios. They are not based on median values statistics, but rather on real examples that are observed in a wide variety of marketplaces.

	Investor A Low capital growth, 'high' rental return	Investor B High capital growth,* 'low' rental return
Purchase price (in today's dollars)	$200 000	$200 000
Gross rental income at purchase**	$14 000 (7% of capital value)	$11 000 (5.5% of capital value)
Average capital growth***	5% pa	10% pa
Average rental income growth****	5% pa	5% pa
Gross rental income pa		
After 5 years	$17 868	$14 039
After 10 years	$22 805	$17 918
After 20 years	$37 146	$29 187
Capital value		
After 5 years	$255 256	$322 102
After 10 years	$325 779	$518 748
After 20 years	$530 659	$1 345 500

*   Remember: 'high capital growth' means growth at least 7 to 8 per cent above the prevailing inflation rate.
** This is the gross rental amount; you can generally expect to spend around 25 per cent of the gross rental income on holding and running costs, excluding interest on loan repayments.
*** These figures are illustrative only. They include average annual inflation of 2 per cent over 20 years. In reality, inflation rates vary over time. The key point here is that low capital growth seriously hampers the ability to leverage and accumulate a substantial asset base.
**** For illustration's sake we have assumed an annual average rental increase of 5 per cent. In reality, rental increases will fluctuate according to market conditions.

leverage to purchase further assets and increases your net worth—Investor B's property is way ahead.

This gives Investor B a dual advantage:

After 20 years the property will be worth $1 345 500, and will of itself generate gross rental income of $29 187 (approximately $560 per week).

Furthermore, with a substantial amount of equity, Investor B can leverage to purchase additional assets—significantly enhancing their income-producing capacity.

Compare this with the plight of Investor A. While they have generated more rental income than Investor B from one single asset, their relative lack of equity through limited capital growth severely hampers their ability to leverage and purchase additional income-producing assets.

What would you rather own—one property commanding $37 146 in rental income, or several properties each commanding $29 187! It's the combined income from all your assets, not the income from any one asset, that really counts.

But wait, there's more!

High capital growth property gives you another major advantage. By building equity quickly, your debt will comprise an increasingly smaller proportion of the asset's overall value. This means that you own much more than you owe—putting you in the driver's seat.

By contrast, low capital growth makes you much more reliant on active debt reduction to create equity—not only will you need to make additional loan repayments over and above the minimum amount, but you will have to do it from your after-tax wage or salary. If you are like many investors, equity built through capital growth from astutely selected residential property will far outstrip the rate at which you can find extra funds from your hip pocket.

Choosing low-capital-growth property puts the pressure on you, the individual, to build equity right throughout the ownership period. Why would you do this when you can choose a high-growth property at the outset, then step back and allow other people, through the forces of supply and demand, to do it all for you!

2. TAX BENEFITS

To save you more money, property also offers tax advantages in three key forms:

- ***negative gearing*** of borrowings and outgoings;
- ***deductions*** for certain expenses; and
- ***depreciation*** on fixtures, fittings and, for newer property, the building itself.

There is no doubt that these advantages can significantly lessen the sting of all the outgoings involved in holding investment property. But the tax department's generous treatment only goes so far. On the downside, because investment property has the potential for capital growth, it is also subject to:

- capital gains tax (CGT) on your capital gain (profit) if and when you sell the asset;
- goods and services tax (GST), payable on the purchase price of new property and on renovations, improvements and repairs to established property; and
- state-based taxes such as stamp duty and land tax.

It is probably fair to say that the tax advantages of property are promoted more effectively by government and industry and are better understood by investors than the tax liabilities. Little wonder, then, that many investors view property primarily as a tax-reduction vehicle and very often part with huge sums of money to builders and developers promising massive tax savings to effectively 'write off' the cost of the investment.

Never buy a property for tax reasons alone.

Why? Because property purchased primarily for tax reasons, and with tax-oriented benefits such as stamp duty savings and building depreciation allowances, all too frequently lacks the characteristics required for sustainable capital growth and rental income. If you buy such a property, you risk saying goodbye to more money in lost growth than you'll save in tax deductions!

If you are really serious about property investment, the main aim must be to increase what you own outright, not just reduce what you owe the government in tax, so you can eventually forget about making money and *enjoy* life. If that leaves you with a 'tax problem'—which is really a 'wealth problem'—then the only problems you really have are (a) the opportunity to buy another wealth-building asset; and (b) finding a very good accountant!

3. PERSONAL CONTROL

Investing in direct property, as distinct from property trusts via managed funds, gives you a high degree of personal control. Not only can you sell, bequeath or lease the property depending on your needs, but you can implement well-conceived and executed improvements to add substantially to its capital value.

4. REAL ASSET SECURITY

For those of us who like to see what we are investing in, one of the most attractive aspects of owning property is its real asset security—the fact that a property's intrinsic value, the land on which it sits, cannot be destroyed. Even the value of units is underpinned by the value of the land they occupy. So if your property burns to the ground you are relatively well positioned to recover from the loss, provided you have adequate insurance.

On the flipside of this comes illiquidity. Unlike shares, managed funds or fixed interest investments, you can't sell off property in portions when needed.

This is why it pays to have highly liquid assets, such as cash, on hand to cover unforeseen situations particularly in the first three to five years of the investment when you're paying off more interest than principal. As time goes on, however, you'll reduce debt *and* begin to see substantial capital growth. At this point you'll be able to borrow against that equity, subject to advice from your accountant and financier.

5. PERPETUAL DEMAND

Finally, at the risk of stating the obvious, we all need somewhere to live! Residential property is a basic commodity so there will always be a baseline level of demand. In their younger years not everyone can afford, or even wants, to buy their own home. And because personal circumstances change, some people move between home ownership and renting several times throughout their lives.

Table 1.3: Percentage of rental households 1947–99

	1947	1954	1961	1966	1971	1976
% Renting	44.0	34.3	27.6	26.7	27.9	25.9
% Change	–	–9.7	–6.7	–0.9	+1.2	–2

	1981	1986	1991	1996	1997–98	1999
% Renting	25.7	25.7	26.6	28.7	26	27.3
% Change	–0.2	Nil	+0.9	+2.1	–2.7	+1.3

Source: Australian Bureau of Statistics Australia Housing Survey catalogue no. 4182.0

Statistics from the Australian Bureau of Statistics (Table 1.3) tell us that at any point approximately 30 per cent of the population rents. Despite rapid changes in Australia's economic and social fabric, this figure has remained pretty much constant since the post-war prosperity of the 1960s and 1970s. So within the context of normal rental market fluctuations, there will usually be a relatively reliable supply of tenants to occupy your investment.

FAQ: What's more important—rental income or capital growth?

Capital growth is the most important consideration. It is what builds equity and enables you to leverage to purchase further investments. Rental income on the other hand helps fund holding costs, loan repayments, municipal rates and maintenance.

In other words, rental income helps you hold on to your investment property, while capital growth helps you make money from it. After you retire, however, rental income takes on a more important role as it replaces your working wage or salary.

The more assets you are able to acquire, the better your ability to generate a plentiful, well-diversified source of retirement income. Building equity through capital growth is the best way to achieve this.

CHAPTER TWO
Property Investment Advice

TRICK OR TREAT?

Now that we've put investment property as an asset class under the microscope, let's take a look at the range of 'advice' available—from those who sing the praises of investment property, to those who are somewhat less enamoured. Why do they say the things they say? And how can you tell the good advice from the bad and the downright ugly?

Picture this ... you approach a doctor or dentist for a professional opinion on a potentially serious condition, only to be confronted with a smorgasbord of 'special deals':

- '10 Per Cent Discount on all Heart Surgery, This Month Only'
- 'Free Consultation for a Child when Accompanied by a Paying Adult'
- 'Grand Opening Special—Hip Replacements—Buy One, Get One Free!'

You'd run a mile wouldn't you?

When you're choosing a healthcare provider, substance is more important than style. Skills, qualifications, training and experience are what count. The same goes for other professionals who deal in highly specialised areas, such as accountants and lawyers.

So why, when it comes to a major life decision like buying an investment property, are so many people willing to buy an asset purely on the basis of glossy incentives—guaranteed 12 months' rent, massive tax savings, immediate positive cash flow?

Given Australians' relative familiarity with property and debt management through home ownership, why would we put so much money on the line without firmly establishing the asset's long-term investment potential, and the adviser's independence, credentials and motives?

A large part of the problem is that when it comes to property, the inborn ability to tell the difference between being **advised** and being **sold to**, which works so well in other areas of our lives, is led up a thousand blind alleys. Slick marketing campaigns with glossy brochures, inviting commercials and immaculate display suites are carefully crafted to intensify the emotions that property inevitably excites.

How on earth does the average would-be investor work out which advice is valid and which stems from self-interest—let alone how to apply it in the kind of property investment strategy that will help, not hinder, them along the path to financial independence?

The solution is almost unbelievably straightforward.

If property investment advisers *sell* property, or receive substantial payments from a third party to promote particular products or developments, *they are not giving you reliable, independent advice.*

> **There is no such thing as free advice or bargains when it comes to investing in property.**

Similarly, when you hear anti-property sentiments, financial incentives may be behind them. Many financial advisers have maligned residential property as an investment asset class. They may tell you that:

- 'There's no growth in property.'
- 'Property only grows at the rate of inflation.'
- 'If you have your own home, you're already "overweight" in property as an asset class.'
- 'Shares consistently outperform property.'

… and so on.

In many instances the people who make such statements have no reason to tell you the truth about property as an asset class, because their financial interests lie elsewhere. They make their money through initial and ongoing payments called 'trailing commissions' that they receive from the companies who provide the products they have recommended. So, even though legislation mandates full disclosure of these commissions, this does not necessarily mean a product has been recommended with the investor's best interests in mind, or that it's the most appropriate one for their needs.

Are property investment courses useful?

If you are contemplating an investment property purchase you may think you'd like to attend a course or two as part of your natural learning curve. Let's look at some of the pitfalls.

No doubt you have seen ads for seminars that promise you 'instant wealth' presented by 'Aussie battlers' who started out broke but now control an empire worth millions of dollars. They will tell you they have no property qualifications and are not licensed to advise you; they say they are just ordinary people sharing their experiences.

Their initial seminar is offered in large venues at a relatively low cost, so hundreds of people come along to see what it's all about. After watching a passionate presentation, participants are encouraged to attend a more 'intensive' course or seminar, often at considerable cost. Because this seminar material contains multiple disclaimers, the presenters are effectively saying, 'I'm happy to tell you what I did and what I learned, but don't expect me to be accountable to you because I'm not *advising* you. I'm just *sharing* my experiences.'

If you're considering attending such an event, ask whether it makes sense to pay thousands of dollars to people with no property advisory qualifications and no experience in advising or being accountable to clients in a one-on-one situation.

Of even greater concern is that, while many of these courses espouse generally sound selection principles, the objective is often to sell property—such as house and land packages, townhouses or units in high-rise complexes. Frequently, the presenter or an affiliated organisation has been directly involved in these developments and may encourage you to purchase a property in which they have a financial interest.

So when you see advertisements for courses promising 'financial independence through property investment', find out whether these educators are, in fact, selling something else!

The role of estate agents

It's probably timely to clarify the role of traditional estate agents who sell property. Selling agents are not qualified to give general financial

Streetwise

Recently, the property advice industry has seen the emergence of property education companies or 'research institutes'. Many of their names bear a striking resemblance to those of Australian and overseas universities—even though they are not affiliated with them! In reality, these companies are often involved in developing or selling property, or may be financially aligned with those who do.

You have probably seen their CDs and cassettes available free of charge in retail outlets as diverse as petrol stations, milk bars and fish and chip shops. Ask yourself whether a company truly dedicated to genuine property advisory work would choose to source clients through these avenues, and provide valuable information at no cost.

advice. They are employed and paid by vendors to market their properties to best advantage and obtain the very highest sale price. While they must be fair and reasonable in their dealings with purchasers, their key avenue of accountability lies with the vendor. Be wary of estate agents who offer to advise you free of charge, and then recommend that you purchase a property one of their vendor clients is paying them to sell!

In some instances real estate companies offer introductions to finance sources, or may have their own finance or financial planning division. If this is the case, and you're considering doing business with them, make sure you probe and uncover all sources of their remuneration as part of your due diligence.

Selling agents sometimes also offer to assist purchasers by bidding or negotiating on another agency's property. While this is quite legitimate, be aware that it may be offered as a sweetener if the agent knows you have a property to sell.

Estate agents who are properly licensed, do not sell property and are exclusively involved in representing purchasers may be qualified to advise you on property investment.

But when even the training programs and qualifications offered by peak property industry bodies don't distinguish between genuine purchaser advisers and traditional estate agents, investors can find it difficult to tell the genuine article from the mere replica. Given the increasing number and profile of buyer advocates, there is an urgent need for real estate institutes and other training bodies to develop dedicated courses leading to qualifications that recognise and enhance the specialist skills required for this highly complex area of property investment advice.

So until the property industry addresses these issues, the onus is on you to give anyone purporting to advise or educate you about property investment a mighty good grilling! The following questions will provide a good start.

How much experience do you have in advising purchasers on property acquisition?

There is a vast difference between selling property and advising on a purchase. Look for an adviser with specific, long-standing experience and a solid track record of advising *purchasers*.

How much experience do you have in advising purchasers on *direct* residential property?

Direct residential property works quite differently from other property investment options such as direct commercial property and property trusts, because each is subject to different market conditions, management strategies and risk levels. What applies to one style of investment may not necessarily hold true for another.

Are you and your company suitably licensed?

Companies and individuals providing property advice must be qualified and/or licensed in accordance with the current requirements of the relevant state or territory government authority.

What formal qualifications do you and your staff hold?

Professional or tertiary qualifications can demonstrate practical knowledge, a long-standing commitment to property advice and a disciplined business approach.

Do you have unrestricted access to the property market?

Ensure your adviser is free to access and inspect the full range of geographical areas and properties. Restricted access may indicate an inability to give you truly unbiased, comprehensive information and guidance.

How are you and your company remunerated?

To help ensure truly independent advice when buying a property, professional fees should come from *you, the investor*. If they come from other sources, you may not receive impartial advice. Similarly, if your adviser is paid only on completion of the assignment, they may be under pressure to 'close the deal' quickly and move on to the next client, leaving insufficient incentive to negotiate a competitive purchase price and terms on your behalf.

Either way, be sure your adviser's remuneration is structured to protect your interests exclusively. Requesting full disclosure of all financial affiliations held by the company, its directors and advisers can help reveal any potential conflicts of interest.

Be sceptical of advice that's 'free', or focuses on tax savings or guaranteed rental income with little or no mention of capital growth.

What research is your advice based on?

The company should undertake or access credible, broad-based research on a regular basis to enhance their market knowledge and provide you with relevant advice.

What ongoing professional education do your directors and advisers undertake?

Participation in industry-specific and broad skill-based training throughout their career demonstrates an adviser's commitment to providing clients with the latest in market knowledge and business practice.

What ongoing services can your company offer after I've made a purchase?

Because residential property is a long-term investment, it is essential that your adviser offers ongoing advice on, and regular reviews of, your property's overall performance. It's also useful if the adviser has a broad network of contacts in related industries and can act as a first point of contact for referral to services such as conveyancing, property management and building repairs or maintenance. Be sure to ask for

Capital growth is the key investment objective.

full disclosure of any financial affiliations the company has with these third parties.

How will you make yourself accountable to me as a client?

Your adviser should be available and fully accountable to you during and after the acquisition process. In particular, they should:

- Update you regularly on the progress of the assignment in particular and market conditions in general.

- Represent you fully during negotiations.

- Provide systematic follow-through by liaising with other service providers during and following settlement.

- Contact you regularly in the months following the purchase to check that all is running smoothly and provide any necessary additional assistance.

- Review your portfolio at regular intervals to ensure it is achieving the desired results.

Above all, seek a number of opinions before engaging a property adviser. In the long term, it will be time very well spent.

The arguments against property—fact or fiction?

Having said how careful you need to be about choosing advisers when investing in residential property, it's time to look at the key assertions of commentators who advise against it.

PROPERTY VS SHARES—THE 'GREAT DEBATE' THAT'S REALLY A NON-STARTER

Almost everyone reading this book may, at some stage, have asked whether they are better off investing in property or in shares. They often see it as an 'either/or' proposition. Usually, this stems not from their own concerns, but from exposure through the media to the opinions of some financial commentators.

In fact, the property vs shares issue has become something of a great debate in financial circles, with proponents on either side constructing all kinds of arguments, graphs, tables and flowcharts to persuade investors that one asset class is inherently 'superior' to the other.

'Shares outperform residential property over the long term' vs 'Good property skyrockets in value.'

'You can always sell your shares to get quick access to funds, but you can't sell half a house!' vs 'There's nothing like bricks and mortar security—you need an investment you can see!'

At face value, the property vs shares comparison is understandable. From Table 1.1 in chapter one (p. 6) you can see that the two asset classes have many of the same characteristics—capital growth, income potential, tax advantages and leveraging capability. But look a little deeper and you'll find that the debate has fundamental flaws.

First of all, people who argue passionately for one asset class over another very often have a vested interest in doing so. Regardless of their area of specialisation, a truly unbiased adviser will acknowledge

case study

How Margot and Jim slipped on their Super... and what they did next!

When it comes to investing in property it's great if you can start relatively early in life. But what happens if you can't start as early as you'd like, or you simply believe what many people still do—that superannuation alone will do the trick and provide a comfortable retirement?

Margot, an administrator, and Jim, a university lecturer, both in their late 50s raised their two kids and diligently contributed to their respective industry superannuation funds believing exactly what they were told—that their payout would total several million dollars when they retired at age 65. After almost 25 years of ploughing money in to both funds (and, occasionally, dabbling in the stock market and property in coastal resort towns with very mixed results on both fronts), a 1997 assessment of their future super payout told a less than rosy story. Far from the projected 'several million' Margot and Jim would receive a combined total of around $400 000. Enough said.

They now had to make the most of their good income whilst it was still available to them and fast-track a worthwhile investment strategy. They went headlong into the books, the seminar circuit and the financial services sector and came away from that process feeling like many people do. Confused. As part of their rounds they came to one of our courses. They were still understandably wary but cognisant that 'at least a property in a sought after inner suburb wouldn't halve in value overnight'. In 1997, they bought two properties both within five kilometres of a major capital city. The first was a two-bedroom house purchased for $227 000 in the inner north and the second was a $237 000 two-bedroom house in the inner east.

> The dual purchase meant that diversifying their investment strategy was an important strategic consideration.
>
> Over the next four years, Margot and Jim were astounded to see their two investment properties virtually double in value. What's more Jim confirmed that they didn't have to make undue sacrifices to fund the difference between the rental income and holding costs. 'We still enjoyed eating out and going on holidays every year. Our lifestyle didn't suffer at all,' he said. Best of all, the capital growth was the effect of supply and demand operating in locations that have demonstrated consistent long-term performance in the marketplace. They didn't spend any money on improvements during those four years beyond routine maintenance. Aside from the increase in their properties' value, they also benefited from the tax savings of negatively gearing both the properties.
>
> Margot and Jim plan to buy two further investment properties and invest in Australian and international shares through a reputable managed fund. Within five years, they plan to sell their current home and semi-retire to a coastal location. By this time their properties and share portfolio will be providing the majority of their retirement income while continuing to grow in value.
>
> case study

that all asset classes can make a valuable contribution to your portfolio. The trick is to accurately identify the very best examples within each asset class.

Second, the arguments used to sway investors towards property or shares can be highly inaccurate. For example, property and shares might inhabit some common ground, but that's where the similarity ends. Property is solid and three-dimensional—you can walk through it, inspect it, lease it, renovate it, insure it, even demolish it and build something new in its place. Conversely, it can also be vandalised, burned down, flooded or just plain neglected. Shares, however, are notional—a way of dividing up a company's performance and profits into smaller portions that investors buy, injecting capital to fund the company's activities.

Property is also a highly individualised asset—each property within a street or locality is unique in some way, even if it has several characteristics in common with its neighbours. Yet every Telstra share, for example, is identical to every other. What *does* vary is the performance of the company concerned and the level of interest from investors.

Furthermore, property and shares are influenced by very different factors. Residential property values are driven primarily by supply and demand. Since everyone needs somewhere to live and the amount of land available is finite, property has an intrinsic value. You may be able to build more housing, but you can't create more land.

Certainly, supply and demand plays a significant part in determining the value of shares; investors usually pay more per share when there is a limited number to go around. But if the company's directors want to raise more capital, they can always issue more shares, which is certainly easier than building more property. However, because shares are notional, highly liquid parcels of a company, their value is primarily determined by company performance and market sentiment. When a company is performing well and investors are confident about the general economic outlook, share prices generally rise. When a company is performing badly and/or investors are nervous about the state of the economy or the performance of the relevant industry, share prices tend to fall.

Finally, the performance of property and shares is measured in different ways. 'Median values' measure the performance of residential property. The relevant authority in each state and territory—usually the Real Estate Institute or Valuer-General—collects sale prices of properties sold in a particular city, suburb or municipality. These values are placed in ascending order. The sale price that lies midway along the list becomes the 'median value'. Median values can be recorded for houses, units or a combination of both. And, because the value of property doesn't change overnight, they are charted on a quarterly or annual basis.

The All Ordinaries Index measures the performance of Australian shares. The 'All Ords', as it's commonly known, comprises the share prices of around 500 of Australia's largest companies, weighted according to the total market value of their shares. Because the value of shares fluctuates rapidly according to company performance and investor activity or confidence, the Index is constantly updated throughout each business day.

The only similarity between median values and the All Ordinaries Index is that each gives a broad picture of the overall trends in each asset class. But this won't help you compare one asset class with the other.

PROPERTY AND THE INFLATION MYTH

You may well have heard the assertion that to achieve high capital growth from property, there *must* be high inflation. This assumes that

Streetwise

If not 'property or shares', what question should we be asking? There can only be one answer: 'What kind of properties, and what kind of shares; and how do I make the most of both asset classes to create financial independence?'

---

capital growth follows inflation in a slavish and linear fashion—when inflation goes up or down, property automatically follows. This is not necessarily the case.

Think back to the 1960s and early 1970s: inflation remained low, yet property values rose steadily. There was a similar phenomenon in the second half of the 1990s and early 2000s when significant capital growth occurred during a low-inflation climate.

It is also true that property will be more expensive during times of high inflation, (see Table 13.2 on page 247) but this is because inflation will cause all of life's essentials to be more expensive as well, so property values will reflect this overall phenomenon.

Generally speaking, the problem with inflation driven rather than demand driven capital growth is that it is much more difficult to distinguish between high quality assets and 'lemons'. The best quality properties in all price categories grow irrespective of the inflation climate. They will hold their value and continue to grow during times of lower inflation whereas your proverbial 'lemons' will languish, or worse, show a substantial drop in value. 'Lemons' *need* inflation to prop up their value. Furthermore, because high inflation usually goes hand in hand with high interest rates, capital growth needs to be proportionally higher in order to justify the much higher borrowing and holding costs. Everything operates in proportion and in context, and investment property is no exception!

PROPERTY, CGT AND INDEXATION—MOUNTAIN OR MOLEHILL?

When you sell an investment property, or any kind of investment, you generally have to pay tax on any capital gain (capital growth) the asset has achieved during the time you've owned it. The capital gain is added to your other sources of income, for example wages or salary, and the total amount is taxed at your marginal rate.

Following reforms in 1999 to the capital gains tax (CGT), individual investors (not institutional investors or trusts) were entitled to receive a 50 per cent reduction, meaning that, while they still paid CGT at their marginal rate, only half the capital gain was taxed. As a trade-off, the government removed what were known as indexation benefits, which helped investors reduce their CGT liability by subtracting the proportion of capital gain that could be attributed to inflation.

Some advisers and commentators say that because investors can no longer reduce their CGT liability through indexation benefits, property is a less attractive investment.

If inflation rose substantially, the removal of indexation may well disadvantage property investors. However, as long as inflation remains within government targets, the effects of indexation removal should be minimal.

CHAPTER THREE

External Influences on Residential Property

ECONOMICS AND OTHER DENIZENS OF THE DEEP AND MEANINGFUL

Picture this: You wake up bleary eyed, stumble outside to get the papers or log on to your favourite website and settle down to read the morning's news over breakfast. Your spirits soar. Unemployment is down, the economy is roaring along and interest rates are low, too.

'Great!' you think, and toy with the idea of adding to your investment portfolio.

But hang on—two pages later you read about looming inflation. Inflation ... the evil spectre that makes virtually everything cost more 'overnight'. You read about wage claims, rising commodity prices, consumer debt and the lacklustre Australian dollar. There are calls for the Reserve Bank to support the dollar and slow the economy down by raising interest rates. 'Hmmm,' you think, 'maybe I should just sit tight for a while.'

In time, the Reserve Bank does step in and curb the inflationary pressure by raising interest rates several notches over the ensuing 12 to 18 months. As time goes on, you start to read about a projected economic slowdown. While the more optimistic commentators predict a 'soft landing', the dreaded 'R word' (that's 'recession') slips back into the vernacular of the more pessimistic ones. 'Whoa!' you muse, 'just as well I didn't invest, let alone borrow money. Looks like we're in for a bumpy ride.' And for a while, things do get a little scary.

But lo and behold, a year or so on, the Reserve Bank steps in yet again and begins to ease interest rates. Things begin to stabilise, the demand for real estate picks up where it left off and that terrific little property you could have bought for $250 000 would now fetch close to $290 000—you know this because an identical one a few streets away just sold for $288 000.

Granted, this is a deliberately simplistic representation of a very complex cycle of events. But it *does* illustrate how easily investor confidence is spooked by even minor economic ups and downs.

Interestingly, while buyers' demand for commercial property ebbs and flows with changes in the economy in general and monetary policy in particular, residential property is the least economically sensitive sector of the property market. Housing is a basic commodity—so it is the safest and best entry point into property investment.

The performance of commercial property—offices, shops and factories and the like—is more directly affected by local and national economic conditions. Values are largely dependent on the ongoing success, direction and sustainability of the tenant's business, as well as the terms and structure of the lease that is sold as part of the freehold. This makes commercial property more immediately reactive to a drop in business confidence and/or an economic downturn.

The big picture—a step back in time

In the eighteenth century and into the nineteenth century, money, food and basic commodities were generated **largely** through our own exertions. We made our own clothes, grew our own food, and generated an income or swapped goods and services largely through agricultural activity and cottage industries.

During the twentieth century, tools, machinery and time- and labour-saving gadgets revolutionised our everyday life, increasing our ability to produce food, clothing and other items quickly, inexpensively and in large quantities. We even built machines that allowed us to leave our own world and visit other worlds. All this created enormous economies of scale and unprecedented international trading opportunities that dramatically increased the amount of money flowing through the world's economies. The industrial age was the beginning of commercial enterprise as we know it today.

In the twenty-first century our focus is shifting again. Our early glimpses of the communication age are characterised by a move away from making products. We increasingly 'make' information and services through research and development, particularly in biotechnology and information technology.

Increasingly, running an economy has become somewhat like running a modern-day business. In a business you have an owner or manager directing the flow of resources and income. In an economy, you have the government, a Reserve Bank and other agencies supervising, regulating and influencing the activities of businesses, employees, consumers and taxpayers.

The viability of a business or an economy is determined by:

- the demand for its products and services;
- the financial health of clients, consumers or trading partners;
- the number of competitors in the marketplace; and
- the cost of the products, services and labour that keep the business or the economy ticking over.

Businesses and economies also need to balance the needs and welfare of their staff or stakeholders in the overall scheme of things.

When correctly structured and managed, a business makes a profit. A well-run economy delivers buoyant, affordable and sustainable conditions for the population as well as healthy trading opportunities. It also has to produce goods and services of a significant marketable value.

The most commonly used measure of the total marketable value of the products and services produced by an economy is known as gross domestic product, or GDP. While GDP is by no means a perfect measure—it doesn't, for example, include unpaid work done by family members in their own home—it is the only relatively comprehensive measure of economic activity derived in a consistent manner in many different countries. The amount of income-producing activity generated by a country or city has a direct impact on the underlying demand for key economic indicators such as housing and employment.

What goes around . . .

Within this very large framework, each country's and city's economy and marketplace move in fairly predictable cycles. In Australia, business and economic cycles last an average of ten to 12 years (Figure 3.1).

Figure 3.1: Economic Clock

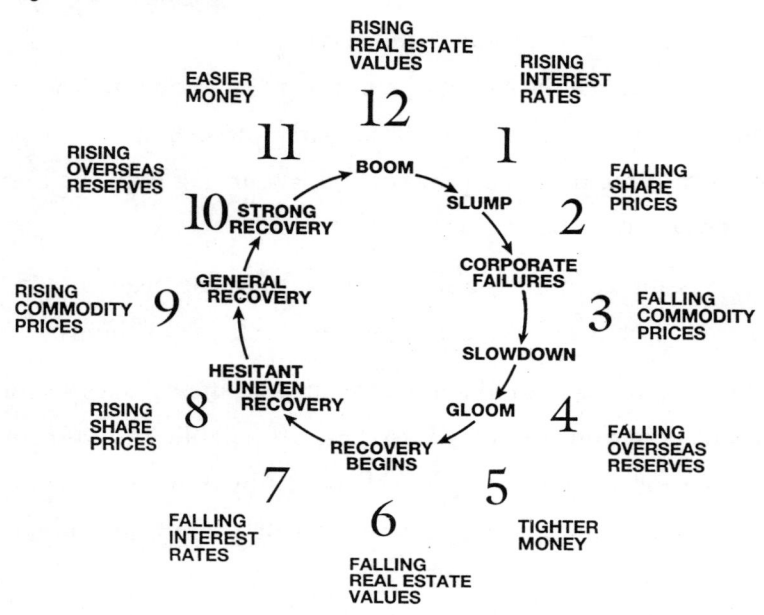

```
                    RISING
                    REAL ESTATE
        EASIER      VALUES        RISING
        MONEY                     INTEREST
                      12          RATES
              11                1
    RISING            BOOM                    FALLING
    OVERSEAS                    SLUMP         SHARE
    RESERVES    10 STRONG              2      PRICES
                   RECOVERY
                                   CORPORATE
    RISING         GENERAL         FAILURES    FALLING
    COMMODITY  9   RECOVERY             3      COMMODITY
    PRICES                                     PRICES
                                  SLOWDOWN
                 HESITANT
                 UNEVEN
    RISING    8  RECOVERY      GLOOM  4
    SHARE                                      FALLING
    PRICES        RECOVERY                     OVERSEAS
                  BEGINS                       RESERVES
                 7       6        5
    FALLING                         TIGHTER
    INTEREST                        MONEY
    RATES        FALLING
                 REAL ESTATE
                 VALUES
```

Source: London Evening Standard Bankers Trust Australia ltd
The Economic Clock depicts a typical sequence of 'landmark events' within an economic investment cycle. Naturally, however, individual cycles can, and do, vary.

We had a 12-year cycle between 1961 and 1973, a seven-year cycle between 1975 and 1982 and another seven-year cycle between 1983 and 1990. The most recent cycle began in 1991. In Australia, the end of a cycle is commonly marked by two or more consecutive quarters of negative GDP growth.

Residential property cycles exist within the wider economic cycles and are influenced by several major economic factors:

- domestic supply and demand;
- domestic inflation and interest rates (influenced by global trends); and
- employment growth and opportunities.

Let's look at each in turn.

Supply and demand has the biggest and most direct influence. The more people want to own real estate in a particular area, and the fewer properties available for sale, the more expensive it becomes. Simple, isn't it! The relative balance of supply and demand differs within and between cities, suburbs and precincts, so property values—and capital growth potential—vary accordingly.

Inflation and interest rates also have a pretty big influence on residential property—and don't the headlines love to talk it up! As you'd expect, however, the raising or lowering of rates is influenced by a very complex series of factors.

Interest rates, or, more accurately, cash rates, are set independently of the government by the Reserve Bank of Australia (RBA). This is the rate at which the major players in the financial markets, like the banks, will lend money 'at call' to one another. The cash rate serves as a benchmark for other important interest rates, especially the standard variable mortgage rate for home and investment loans.

In setting the cash rate, the RBA seeks to achieve its inflation target, as measured by the Consumer Price Index or CPI. The CPI measures

> **FAQ: Is now a good time to buy?**
>
> 'Timing the market' is one of the great myths of residential property investment, because you never know when the market has peaked or troughed, until *after* it has happened and you have missed the boat! A far more effective strategy is to buy the best possible quality asset you can afford, when you can afford it.

the affordability of goods and services typically bought by households. These days the inflation target is set at 2 to 3 per cent, by agreement between the Treasurer and the Governor of the Reserve Bank.

Streetwise

If the RBA thinks inflation is likely to exceed its target range in 12 to 18 months' time, perhaps because the economy is growing strongly and there are signs of pressure on prices and labour costs, it's likely to raise the cash rate. If the RBA believes inflation is likely to fall below the target in 12 to 18 months because, for example, it is concerned about a weaker economic outlook, it will be inclined to cut the cash rate.

This forward-looking approach is important because changes to interest rates do not affect the economy overnight, or even (usually) within a few months. The RBA needs to make a carefully considered judgement on how the economy and financial market participants will respond when making any changes to interest rates. Their decisions have a significant impact on consumer and investment spending, demand and general confidence in the economy.

Typically, interest rates on property loans increase or decrease almost immediately following a change in the RBA's cash rate.

As you can see, interest rates and inflation work hand in hand in an ever-changing and continuous cycle. When interest rates are low, consumers and businesses borrow more, so the nation's overall spending increases. And when people borrow more money, then spend it, greater demand puts pressure on the cost of living and therefore, inflation. When the RBA thinks inflation is getting too high, it steps in and raises interest rates. When national spending subsequently declines, the RBA cuts interest rates to boost spending and the cycle starts again.

The aim of all this tinkering with monetary policy and the maintenance of an inflation target is that the economy is steadied by checks and balances—making for greater stability and a better time to be had by all! If spending rose or declined and remained unchecked by interest rate changes, the result would be a volatile 'boom and bust' economy similar to that of the 1980s, when employment, spending power and living costs teetered from one extreme to another. And who needs that, when life's complicated enough!

More stable economic decisions and a substantial decline in interest rates since the early 1990s are by-products of this attention to monetary policy. As a result, carrying debt has become a much more affordable proposition for a wider section of the population. For example, many people who could not afford mortgages in the 1980s, when interest rates averaged around 14 per cent, became property owners in the 1990s when interest rates were far lower. Innovations such as loyalty programs offering perks such as frequent flyer points have encouraged a greater use of credit cards. So, relative to household income, the value of household debt has roughly doubled since 1990. As a result, even though today's interest rates are historically low, households are far more sensitive to interest rate movements than in the past. That's why even a small rise in interest rates causes angst in the community.

Another reason for this angst may be that many people don't make the distinction between credit-card driven consumer debt, which is used to fund items that usually *depreciate* in value, and debt that helps them buy income or growth-generating assets that *appreciate* in value, such as correctly selected investment property.

Going global

In recent decades globalisation has made its mark on interest rates, and therefore the residential property market. Since 1983, when the Australian dollar was floated to ensure we kept pace with an increasingly global economic environment, there has been a progressively closer connection between Australian and US interest rate cycles. The gap between the timing of movements in the two cycles has narrowed, bringing the structure of the two economies closer together.

In recent years data has been collected that shows just how closely the Australian economy, and therefore interest rate movements, mirror that of the US (extraordinary world events aside).

This similarity in economic fortunes means that as far as property is concerned, the activities of purchasers in the US have an indirect impact on our own purchasing activities. If the US economy is growing quickly and consumers are feeling confident, they'll borrow more money to buy property, shares and other assets. At some point, the US Federal Reserve will raise interest rates to rein in spending. Because Australia's Reserve Bank looks at US interest rate decisions as well as our own domestic conditions when assessing whether or not to change our own interest rates, a fall in US rates is often followed by a fall in ours. So next time you jump for joy when your mortgage payments

External Influences on Residential Property

Figure 3.2: Australian and US Real Gross Domestic Product

Historically, a downturn in the US economy has nearly always been mirrored in Australia with only a few exceptions

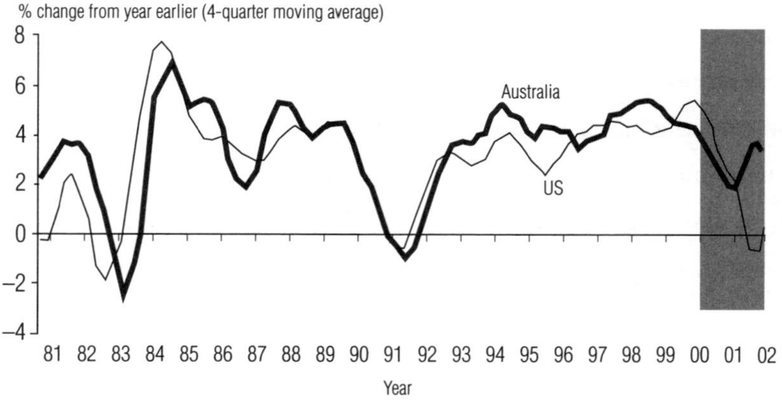

Sources: Australian Bureau of Statistics; US Department of Commerce; Economics@ANZ forecasts

drop, you may have the spending habits of your American counterparts to thank, at least in part!

INFLATION AND PROPERTY

Globalisation has also affected inflation in recent years. Later in this chapter we'll look at how it affects *property values*. Historically, the major contributors to inflation have been:

- *The cost of labour and wages relative to productivity*—if wages rise in circumstances where productivity is growing, this should not create inflationary pressure. If wages go up significantly ahead of productivity, we end up with rising inflation.
- *The $A–$US exchange rate*—when the value of the Aussie dollar goes down, the cost of imported goods goes up. If this cost rise is passed on to consumers, inflation will also rise over time.

43

- *The price of oil/petrol*—because of the worldwide dependence on oil across so many industries and applications, a significant rise in oil prices usually creates inflationary pressure.

Over the last decade or so, however, globalisation, trade liberalisation and the need for increased international competitiveness have made it more difficult for businesses to pass their own cost increases on to consumers. Therefore falls in the Australian dollar and increased oil prices no longer have as big an impact on inflation as they used to.

However, regardless of changes in the factors contributing to inflation, property values will continue to be influenced, though not wholly *dictated by*, inflation trends.

In the recent past, Australia has weathered domestic and global economic ups and downs surprisingly well. Low inflation in the late 1990s and early 2000s enabled the RBA to allow our dollar to fall, in order to shore up international competitiveness and offset the impact of the Asian financial crisis and the US economic downturn. It also helped protect consumer, investor and business confidence by keeping interest rates low.

The underlying stability, strength and tight supervision of Australia's banking and financial system have also been instrumental in shielding us from a more severe fallout. These conditions have supported interest and confidence in home ownership and residential property investment, notwithstanding turbulence in the new home sector caused by the introduction of the GST in 2000.

Another word on residential property and inflation ...

Chapter one touched on the misconception that property values rise and fall only according to changes in inflation levels. This is such a damaging myth that it's worth closer inspection.

Residential property is a basic commodity, therefore property values can reflect inflation levels. When badly chosen, a property may indeed depend largely on inflation to drive up its value. When inflation drops dramatically, though, this seemingly wonderful capital growth rate can all but disappear.

As we've pointed out, Australia has experienced sustained periods in which property prices have risen substantially against a background of low inflation. For example, when our economy stabilised in the second half of the 1990s and into the early 2000s, inflation remained low. Yet property values in some major capital cities rose sharply. Just ask anyone who's tried to buy property in Sydney or Melbourne in recent years! In Melbourne, the median house value rose from $160 500 in the June quarter of 1997 to $313 000 in the September quarter of 2001—an increase of 95% per cent. In Sydney, the median house value rose from $223 300 in the June quarter of 1997 to $315 000 in the September quarter of 2001—a 41 per cent increase (source: REIA, REIV).

In both cities, strongly accelerating demand for established property, particularly in the inner suburbs, coupled with a limited availability of land on which to build or redevelop, drove price growth—irrespective of the prevailing inflation rate.

Values in some other capital cities have been less spectacular in recent years, which is due to local relationships between supply and demand, employment and population trends—not to the inflation rate, which is a nationwide phenomenon.

If governments and regulators continue to manage the economy sensibly, it is reasonable to expect that inflation will stay at acceptable levels, minimising the possibility of inflation-driven price booms followed by severe downturns. This makes it easier for investors to distinguish second-rate investment property, which relies too much on inflation to drive capital growth, from 'the real McCoy', which grows in value because ongoing demand outweighs supply.

So when commentators say inflation is the primary force behind property values, or that property is a poor investment because 'values only increase in a high inflation environment', it's fair to question their understanding of property as an asset class!

Streetwise

While the Reserve Bank will cut interest rates to cushion the blow of an economy in possible decline, in doing so they're also providing a springboard for its subsequent upward climb.

Three myths on property and the economy

Many Australians—lay people and specialist commentators alike—believe that a softening economy spells disaster for the residential property market. Why is this? The following are commonly held myths about the relationship between property values and the economy.

MYTH 1: PROPERTY AND THE ECONOMY ARE SLAVISHLY INTERDEPENDENT

Housing activity, representing property's demand side, is a key indicator of the nation's economic health. The main reason is that housing activity typically leads the economy. Just like a weathervane indicates wind direction, it foreshadows what lies just ahead, economically speaking. It also has crucial links with other sectors of the economy. As we move up the 'food chain' it links into the manufacturing sector—for example, companies that produce building materials and manufacture everyday items. As we move down the 'food chain' it links in with retailing—for example, shops where you, as a consumer, go to buy your tapware or kitchen appliances. Therefore, as well as contributing to the demand for life's basics, housing activity contributes to both short- and long-term employment.

Property is also important to the economy because it accounts for a significant proportion of our overall wealth. The value of land and dwellings owned by Australian households as at 30 June 2000 was around $1.25 trillion, accounting for almost half our total household wealth. With figures like these, it is easy to see why property prices are such a major influence on our general confidence and willingness to spend.

FAQ: Do I need high inflation to achieve high capital growth from property?

No! If you choose a well located property with architectural scarcity and/or timelessness, ongoing market demand will help ensure strong, consistent capital growth, irrespective of the prevailing inflation rate.

However, the fact that residential property and the economy are strongly linked doesn't mean that the fortunes of one are identical to the fortunes of the other. The property market benefits from a softening economy because its fortunes revolve around supply and demand. When the economy slows, interest rates usually drop and buyers become more active, stimulating the property market.

Furthermore, as discussed in chapter one, property always enjoys an underlying minimum level of demand, regardless of the state of the economy, because everyone needs somewhere to live. Therefore this demand is influenced, but not solely dictated, by interest rate decreases in a slowing economic environment.

Given the huge financial contribution residential property makes to the economy and the fact that property values often thrive when the economy is softening, it's probably fair to say that the economy needs the housing sector more than the housing sector needs the economy!

MYTH 2: THE PROPERTY MARKET IS HOMOGENEOUS

While the residential property market as a whole benefits when the economy softens via interest rate cuts, not all purchasers are equally affected.

First home buyers feel the greatest impact of a softening economy and usually respond before other purchasers. Often aged in their 20s and 30s, they are in the early stages of their career and earning capacity. This means they have a small deposit and little, if any, equity in other assets. The size of their borrowings and the value of the property they buy are usually much greater than their income.

Lower interest rates combined with government grants for first home buyers may encourage these buyers to borrow more for a larger or more desirable property than they could otherwise have afforded. It also means that a larger portion of their loan will go into paying off the principal—enabling them to build equity more quickly.

As these buyers advance in their careers and increase their earnings, they also build up considerable equity in their first home. And as their lifestyle changes (e.g. having children and/or wanting to live in a more appealing environment), they use this equity to buy a second home. While the value of this home is often much higher, the equity from the first property reduces their borrowings. The gap between their income and borrowings begins to narrow, while their equity continues to grow.

Because lifestyle factors are the primary determinants of home-buying decisions for these purchasers, minor interest rate movements are of relatively little consequence to them. Unless rates change dramatically, activity in this sector remains fairly consistent.

Streetwise

One of the advantages of investing in residential property is that the supply and demand principle works across the whole market. If you're an investor, the value of your property is influenced not just by demand from other would-be investors, but from all the home buyers, too. This means that strong ongoing demand along with relative affordability and availability makes the mid-priced sector the backbone of Australia's residential property market—and the one that gives the most reliable investment performance.

By the time these buyers reach the top end of the housing market, however, a softening economic context again has a strong impact on their purchasing decisions. Now at the peak of their careers and possibly commanding a high income, they're likely to have significant equity in assets besides their home. Their home is no longer a key wealth-building vehicle.

These buyers know that the Reserve Bank adopts a highly proactive approach to monetary policy and managing the economy by anticipating and heading off 'booms' and 'busts' before they actually occur, rather than waiting until it is too late. They understand that when the RBA raises interest rates, it is because they want to avert inflationary pressures and promote sustainable growth. They know rate rises aren't designed to induce recessions and aren't a sign of imminent doom! So, when interest rates drop again, these buyers grow in confidence and are more likely to borrow to buy an even larger or more prestigious home in a highly sought-after area.

In turn, their increased confidence flows down through to the middle and entry levels of the market, pushing up property values across the board.

MYTH 3: A DROP IN MEDIAN VALUES EQUALS A PROPERTY MARKET DOWNTURN

Once the economy softens and interest rates drop, so, often, do well-known indicators of property market movements such as median values. This is when commentators typically say that the property market is on the decline. In fact, the opposite often proves true!

As first home buyer activity increases in the wake of lower interest rates and government grants, so does the number of sales at the lower end of the market and, as a result, the proportion of these sales relative to the market as a whole. Because median values cover all reported sales in a particular locality, they don't distinguish between different sectors of the market. When first-home-buyer activity increases, medians do indeed drop temporarily. But this is a sign of a stabilising economy and a healthy property market that's about to rise again.

As the economic cycle moves to its next, upward stage and interest rates stabilise or increase, first-home-buyer activity also abates—reducing the skewing of median values towards the lower end of the market. Median values are once again restored to their exalted, if somewhat misplaced, status as an accurate guide to the state of the property market in a given locality. Peace reigns ... until the tide turns and the economy changes once again.

And in our own backyard ...

So far, we have discussed how globalisation influences Australia's *general* economic and residential property market conditions. Let's take a look at how this operates in a specific market—Australia's most 'international' city, Sydney.

A relatively high proportion of Sydney's workforce is concentrated in globalised industries such as information technology, entertainment and financial services. Many people working in these industries are paid internationally competitive salaries in relative terms. When times are good and profits are up, their salaries and spending power grow. When the gears shift down a few notches, demand and prices react accordingly. As a result, property values have a tendency to take on 'international' proportions, especially in the upper price brackets.

In inner suburban Sydney, the relative scarcity of land and the desirability of water access, elevation and harbour views mean that a higher proportion of properties occupy the million-dollar-plus price range. Sydney property values are therefore higher, but more volatile and reactive to the international business climate, than those of other Australian cities.

As Australia's economy becomes more 'international', residential property values in other capitals, particularly Melbourne, may become more sensitive to fluctuations in overseas economies in the medium to long term. However, because housing is such a basic commodity, it is highly unlikely that residential property *as a whole* will ever display as much volatility as asset classes such as commercial property or the stockmarket.

The great folly of timing an investment

One of the most common questions investors ask us is, 'Should I buy now or wait till the market changes?' Many people think timing is a key factor in the success or failure of residential investment property. It isn't!

> ***'Time in the market' not 'timing the market' counts most.***

As we have discussed, the residential property market is cyclical—responding to the ebb and flow of supply and demand, as influenced by economic conditions and personal choices. In theory this means that if you buy at the bottom of the market, when prices are low, you'll not only save money on the initial purchase price, but optimise your capital growth when the market turns up. Surest way to make a fortune, right?

Well, it probably would be, except that no one, not even the experts, knows when the market has really bottomed until after the event, when it's on the way up again.

If you subscribe to this 'buy low' theory, you may also think you should sell when the market peaks to lock in your capital gain. But here you hit the same problem—if you can't pick the bottom of the market until it's on the way up again, you won't be able to pick the top of the market either until it's on the way down!

Furthermore, locking in your capital gain by selling when the market appears to be peaking fails to recognise a key characteristic of residential property. See Figure 3.3, which shows median house prices in

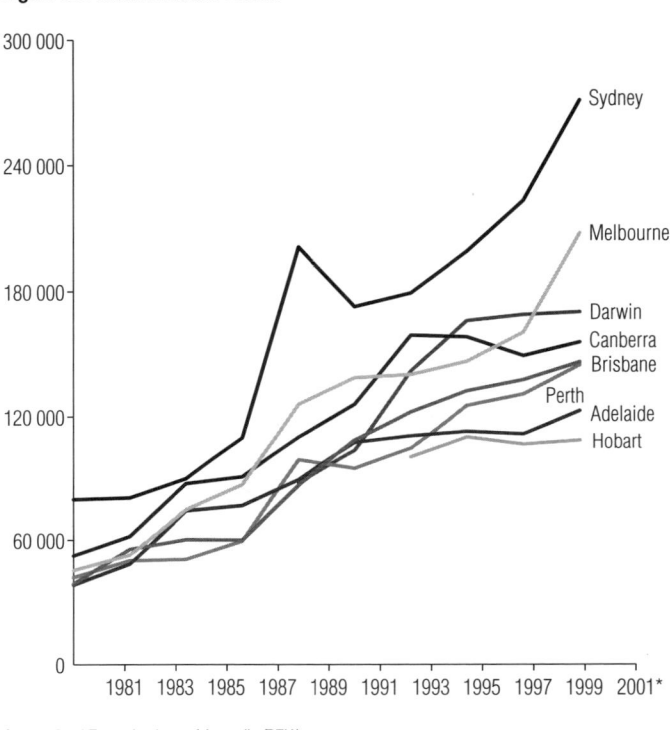

Figure 3.3: Median House Prices

Source: Real Estate Institute of Australia (REIA)
* Preliminary figure

the Australian residential property market. You'll see that, while the market rises and falls in accordance with various prevailing economic conditions affecting the market that we discussed earlier, it moves upwards over the longer term.

So, if you sell, you might avoid the next downturn . . . but you'll also miss out on future capital growth once the market steadies and improves. This approach seriously undermines your capacity to accumulate net wealth, leverage it to purchase further investments and ultimately achieve financial independence. Some of your profit will also be lost through CGT, professional fees and associated expenses, rather than being retained in the asset where it will do you the most good!

Note that Figure 3.3 only shows *median* increases; top-performing assets perform well in excess of these levels. If you have a property like this and sell it when you think it has reached its peak, you'll do yourself an even bigger disservice, as the gap between the sale price and the property's longer-term capital growth potential grows wider and wider.

Other investors adopt the opposite timing strategy. The minute they think property prices are slowing they run for cover, only to re-emerge to purchase if and when prices rise dramatically during a property boom. Not realising that dramatic price increases over a short period could be due to inflation and not natural, demand-driven capital growth, they think 'all growth is good growth' and pay little heed to the correct choice of asset.

Unable to sustain repayments because of the high interest rates that usually go hand in hand with high inflation, many of these investors end up having to sell. And by the time they do, the market drops again. If they've purchased an inferior investment they may find that it hasn't held its value in a lower inflation environment, and are forced to sell at a loss—a vicious cycle!

So what happens? They may become disillusioned and start questioning the validity of property as an asset class, rather than examining and modifying their own investment strategy.

Instead of timing their purchase to coincide with external factors over which they have no control, astute investors focus on finding the very best quality asset they can afford, holding it for the long term and letting time and natural capital growth do the work for them.

Streetwise

As long as you choose the right asset type and location, and your intention is to hold the asset indefinitely, it matters little when you buy.

City trends

As you'd expect, each capital city in Australia responds to economic conditions in different ways, at different times. Table 3.1 shows median values for each capital city since the late 1980s, when high inflation had a marked impact on sale prices.

SYDNEY

Because it has our biggest population and business centre, Sydney is the first to experience the effects of major economic changes and therefore leads the national property cycle. In combination with factors such as the desirability of the city's lifestyle and population trends, Sydney's international business climate also fuels higher property values, helping create a characteristically extreme property cycle.

When the economy is buoyant and investor/home-buyer confidence is high, Sydney usually experiences a sharp upturn in activity and property values. However, it only takes a slight fall in conditions for the market to turn down. Table 3.1 shows that Sydney's median property

Table 3.1: Median House and Unit Values Australian Capital Cities, 1989–2000

	1989	1990	1991	1992	1993	1994	1995	1996	1997	1998	1999	2000	Average % capital growth pa 1989-2000
Sydney													
Houses	$206 000	$184 300	$172 800	$179 800	$179 300	$182 800	$199 300	$203 700	$223 300	$248 500	$271 100	$309 500	4.0
Units	$137 100	$138 300	$134 200	$138 400	$139 400	$148 600	$154 800	$161 600	$188 900	$208 500	$227 200	$252 400	5.8
Melbourne													
Houses	$126 400	$140 000	$138 800	$136 500	$140 300	$144 300	$146 600	$146 300	$160 500	$189 500	$208 000	$250 000	6.6
Units	$91 700	$111 200	$113 400	$105 600	$107 800	$111 400	$114 100	$113 600	$119 700	$140 400	$158 300	$192 000	7.3
Brisbane													
Houses	$86 100	$103 000	$108 500	$118 500	$122 300	$127 300	$132 500	$133 800	$137 800	$141 800	$146 300	$149 000	5.2
Units	$78 800	$88 500	$91 300	$98 000	$100 400	$101 400	$107 000	$116 900	$128 300	$133 000	$147 500	$149 300	6.0
Adelaide													
Houses	$88 800	$100 500	$107 300	$107 800	$110 600	$112 400	$112 800	$110 200	$111 500	$116 600	$122 900	$132 600	3.8
Units	$69 900	$77 500	$82 800	$85 100	$94 100	$92 000	$92 600	$92 400	$89 700	$93 500	$89 000	$94 600	2.9
Perth													
Houses	$98 500	$97 500	$94 300	$97 500	$104 300	$118 900	$125 400	$127 100	$130 900	$140 000	$144 900	$155 600	4.3
Units	$69 800	$76 800	$75 800	$75 200	$77 700	$82 000	$87 900	$86 700	$90 100	$95 200	$102 800	$114 200	4.7
Canberra													
Houses	$110 000	$114 500	$126 000	$147 500	$159 100	$160 500	$158 300	$155 500	$149 300	$156 800	$155 800	$172 300	4.3
Units	$88 500	$95 600	$97 500	$119 400	$129 700	$129 300	$129 500	$123 700	$119 300	$125 000	$126 600	$136 100	4.1
Hobart													
Houses	$77 900	$84 800	$88 900	$91 500	$99 600	$107 500	$110 800	$108 000	$108 800	$109 900	$107 700	$118 000	3.9
Units	$66 400	$74 200	$72 600	$74 800	$79 300	$83 800	$86 500	$86 400	$78 100	$78 100	$84 800	$89 600	2.9
Darwin													
Houses	$87 300	$97 400	$103 200	$120 300	$142 100	$150 100	$166 100	$162 400	$169 000	$177 000	$170 300	$182 200	7.1
Units	n/a	$72 500	$81 400	$86 500	$97 000	$108 700	$117 700	$126 600	$131 200	$125 700	$155 600	$146 500	7.6

Source: State and national real estate institutes. Note: 'n/a' = 'not available'.

value dropped noticeably in the early 1990s, then rose significantly when inflation dropped and the national economy moved out of the 'recession we had to have'.

Additionally, Sydney has a greater concentration of more expensive property than other capital cities, especially in the million-dollar-plus range. A rise or drop in value of, say, 10 per cent, will therefore affect Sydney's overall median value more than it would in a city where the greatest volume of transactions occur at more moderate levels.

If you're investing in Sydney the entry price for a worthwhile investment is probably the highest in the country, and while the overall performance of a quality investment will be excellent, it's likely there'll be many ups and downs along the way. Adopting a long-term, buy-and-hold strategy is particularly important when investing in a comparatively volatile market, to smooth out the highs and lows.

MELBOURNE

Though it is Australia's second largest business centre, with a reasonably high exposure to the fluctuations of the wider economy, Melbourne exhibits a steadier pattern of price movements. This is because the greatest number of transactions occurs in the middle level of the market.

The Melbourne market typically follows Sydney's overall pattern, with a lag of anywhere between a few months to a year, sometimes longer. Melbourne investors therefore get more notice of price trends and movements than their Sydney counterparts, plus the advantage of observing how another city handles the shifting economic sands before they have to.

Table 3.1 shows that while median property values in Melbourne slowed considerably during much of the 1990s as the effects of the national recession were exacerbated by Victoria's own financial difficulties, they rebounded significantly in 1997 and began to reach levels few people expected. Upgrades to inner-urban infrastructure and a significant urban population drift point to a solid future for investors who know how to choose high-quality assets.

CANBERRA

Canberra seems to display a cycle all its own and, predictably enough, its economic and property cycles are closely related to its political climate. When the rest of Australia felt the full effects of a recession in the early 1990s, Canberra's property values rose as the city prospered as a result of robust government spending and a full-strength public sector. The private sector also flourished, deriving considerable business from the public sector.

With the advent of government spending cutbacks in the mid-1990s the public sector shrank and private sector activity suffered. Property values followed suit, only to increase once more as the political climate steadied.

If you live in Canberra and want to invest there, be sure to choose the most desirable precincts, such as those close to Civic and Lake Burley Griffin. Be aware too that property ownership in the ACT is restricted to a 99-year lease—you don't actually own a freehold title.

BRISBANE

Brisbane's property prices exhibit a reasonably predictable pattern of moderate growth due to the city's smaller population base and smaller economy relative to Sydney and Melbourne. However, local residents who know their home town intimately and take the trouble to flush out the best locations may reap rewards over time.

Interestingly, Brisbane is the only capital city where median unit values outperformed median house values at some stage during the period covered by Table 3.1. This is mainly due to recent inner-city residential development characterised by multi-unit towers sold at premium prices set by the developer, rather than by market forces.

In the nearby Gold Coast market, prices have been lacklustre for some time. Despite the area's strong, tourism-based economy and the periodic interstate migration that typically occurs during periods of economic gloom—remember all those Victorians who high-tailed it to the warmer climes in the early 1990s?—the quantity of new construction consistently exceeds demand and has created a considerable oversupply. This became especially evident in the second half of the 1990s when migration slowed and many Victorians who had gone north to escape the recession returned home.

DARWIN

Darwin has been an interesting performer and median values have shown a steady increase over the long term. The strength of Darwin's market is closely associated with tourism, the significant redevelopment of the inner suburbs and the city's expansion and rebuilding since Cyclone Tracy in 1974.

When there is a high concentration of construction and redevelopment in a relatively small population centre that incurs high costs associated with transporting materials and products, prices tend to demonstrate a steady rise.

PERTH

Median values in Perth have performed consistently since the mid-1990s after faltering briefly during the national recession in the early 1990s. Once again, this is primarily due to increasing local economic activity, the high number of new dwellings that have mushroomed over the last ten years and the rapid expansion of the city's suburbs and related infrastructure. Growth in the demand for, and therefore value of, quality established housing in city fringe locations and along the Swan River has also contributed to this consistent performance.

ADELAIDE AND HOBART

Adelaide and Hobart, while eminently affordable and very attractive from a lifestyle perspective, have lacked the investment strength and price growth of other capital cities. Whether this is due to their relatively small local economies as a proportion of Australia's GDP, their subdued population growth or comparatively lower underlying demand for property, is difficult to say. However, if you intend purchasing an investment property in either city, you'll need to be extremely careful to buy into only the highest quality locations close to the CBD with a high level of local amenity. This should include good schools, shops and transport facilities. Buildings will need to exhibit a timeless quality and be strictly limited in supply.

A very social creature—how demographics affect residential property

Economic cycles have a significant impact on the property market, but if you try to track residential property cycles purely in economic terms, you'll always be behind the eight ball.

Because property is an essential commodity and housing trends closely reflect our financial and life needs and choices, property trends change as our needs and choices do. Even though the property cycle is influenced by the wider business and economic cycle, it generally moves at a faster rate. In fact, we often see two or three property cycles within a single economic cycle. Remember that property is usually the first sector of the economy to go into a slowdown, and the first to emerge.

To gain a more complete picture of what influences residential property cycles and prices, you need to consider social variables as well as economic ones. Specifically, these are:

- population density and composition;
- infrastructure development;
- new technologies and their impact on the workplace; and
- subsequent consumer behaviour.

Luckily, you don't have to search endlessly to dig up this kind of information. The Australian Bureau of Statistics (ABS) gathers key demographic data during, and sometimes between, every national census. Demographics is the study of population. Specifically, it examines population numbers and structure relative to migration, lifestyle trends, geography and existing infrastructure. Analysts take the raw ABS data, then group and interpret it alongside pre-existing data to establish long-range patterns of social change. This helps governments and civic authorities predict how and where we might live, and then plan for those eventualities.

Streetwise

It is possible to buy well in any economic climate. The best advice we can offer is to invest whenever your finances allow—provided that you only ever buy the highest quality assets and never borrow more than you can comfortably repay.

Demographic data can also help *you* gain a perspective on which locations and property styles will be most enduringly sought after and demonstrate the best long-term investment performance. However, don't become a slave to statistics. Because demographic data is broad ranging and takes a long time to gather, interpret and distribute, most of it is not specific or current enough to be a foolproof analytical tool. The property market in each city and suburb exhibits unique characteristics and you should not attempt to invest without getting to know them first.

Let's look at some key demographic trends and their impact on property trends and values.

POPULATION SIZE AND DENSITY

You may be familiar with the oft-touted theory that population size and density are directly responsible for supply and demand, and therefore property values. To some degree, this is true. Sydney and Melbourne are Australia's largest cities, with around 40 per cent of the nation's population. They also have the highest property values and have experienced the most substantial overall long-term capital growth. Their densely populated inner suburbs and precincts, for example, have also demonstrated high overall property values and capital growth.

However, there are plenty of exceptions to the rule. Just because a city has a large population doesn't mean that every one of its suburbs and properties attracts the same level of demand. Even in more densely populated precincts, many properties lack the position, architectural style and/or scarcity value that drive optimum long-term capital growth.

Interestingly, the population density argument in particular is often touted by developers who need to sell properties in a particular location. Melbourne's inner city Southbank and Docklands precincts are good examples of vested interests using demographic trends to bolster buyer confidence in residential property—almost always new, multi-unit developments. It's a kind of self-fulfilling prophecy—supply is the driving force behind property values in these areas, creating an artificial demand that may not be sustainable in the longer term.

URBAN DRIFT

There is an identifiable pattern in the way cities and municipalities across the world develop, mature and then undergo a renaissance. In Australian cities that date back to early settlement, the original housing stock close to the CBD usually consists of smaller dwellings, with the odd grander property built in the nineteenth century.

As the population rose during the twentieth century, the housing stock began to drift outwards to accommodate increasingly affluent families who wanted more living space—something not usually available immediately next to the CBD. This phenomenon was particularly pronounced during the 1950s, 1960s and 1970s. In the 1960s we saw the subsequent emergence of satellite commercial precincts and shopping centres such as Chadstone in Melbourne, Indooroopilly in Brisbane and Parramatta in Sydney.

While this pattern of outward expansion has continued, in more recent years it is being balanced by a trend towards CBD and inner urban consolidation. This is occurring alongside unprecedented redevelopment and reassignment of land. Buildings previously used for industrial and commercial purposes are being converted to residential accommodation and leisure and entertainment facilities.

What is fuelling these momentous changes to our lifestyle choices and taking inner urban property values upwards?

Technology, far from affording us *more* leisure time as predicted ten to 15 years ago, has created enormous pressure to work longer and harder; to produce better results, more quickly.

These increased expectations and tighter deadlines are affecting our choice of lifestyle and leisure pursuits. It is no longer as desirable to

FAQ: What do you think about inner-city, high-rise units as an investment?

Generally speaking, properties in multi-unit developments (MUDs) do not make good investments. The sheer number of almost identical units within and across ever-burgeoning apartment blocks means they lack the scarcity value that plays a major role in driving capital growth. Additionally, their purchase price includes a significant premium that reflects the developer's profit goals, rather than the true market value.

spend hours commuting from middle and outer suburbs. More and more of us want to be within quick striking distance of head office and clients, with ready access to restaurants and entertainment—and we're not as keen to spend precious leisure time taming our little piece of suburban wilderness!

Here's where the population-based property theories do make *some* sense. Since a substantial number of service-related jobs are located in the CBD and surrounds, established inner suburbs attract a consistently high level of younger residents with high disposable incomes. While they may change jobs more often than their parents did, they tend to live in the same geographical area for a significant proportion of their adult lives. This underpins ongoing demand for housing, infrastructure, lifestyle and leisure facilities—offering the best long-term growth in property values.

Governments are encouraging the current urban drift, with almost all infrastructure spending focused on improving accessibility to and around the CBD. Naturally, this has resulted in dramatically increased demand for inner suburban housing, and property values have risen accordingly.

Examples of suburbs that have undergone this kind of change in recent years include Newtown in Sydney, Richmond in Melbourne and New Farm in Brisbane. Built during the cities' earliest formation, these areas had established infrastructure and a predominance of period-style housing. The influx of younger, affluent residents has seen a substantial number of renovations and new developments, bringing a considerable increase in property values.

Richmond, for example, 3 km from Melbourne's CBD, is characterised by modest period cottages originally built to house workers in the manufacturing industry. During the 1960s and 1970s, many privately owned units were also built at a relatively low cost. Government statistics show that in 1986, when low-income residents made up more than one-third of the suburb's population and traditional nuclear families accounted for around one-quarter of households, the median house value was $92 000. By 1996, when the proportion of high-income residents had almost doubled and there were almost as many young couples as nuclear families, the median value increased to $172 500. By 2000, in the wake of this population shift, substantial redevelopment and infrastructure upgrades, the median shot up to $310 000.

New Farm, next to the Brisbane River and 2 km from the CBD, is a similar example. As younger people moved in towards the CBD and riverside living in established precincts became more popular, the median house value rose from $175 000 in 1993 to $285 000 in 2000.

However, it's important to distinguish between established inner suburban precincts with a limited supply of housing and a degree of 'green space', and city fringe areas with thousands of new residences in multi-storey developments. Because the nature of our work is increasingly service oriented and needs little physical space compared with manufacturing and industry, property development companies have jumped on the urban consolidation bandwagon, creating a proliferation of apartment blocks in areas where obsolete industrial estates offer relatively large parcels of land for redevelopment at comparatively low prices.

The trouble is, that while these developments are close to workplaces and leisure precincts and may hold initial appeal for tenants, they don't necessarily make a good investment. The sheer number of projects being marketed off-the-plan, currently under construction or nearing completion makes correct selection extremely confusing, even difficult for seasoned investors.

Furthermore, even at night, high noise levels—caused by public transport, private vehicles, rubbish and delivery trucks, street sweepers and so on—are the trade-off residents pay for the convenience and excitement of city living. In this kind of environment, a block that has been built to maximise profit for developers at the expense of quality construction will have a perennially mobile and dissatisfied population. This is hardly the recipe for solid, long-term asset performance.

Streetwise

How well Australia weathers economic and demographic changes depends to a large extent on the fortunes of major world economies and our government's willingness to implement pre-emptive strategies to manage the impact of these dynamic forces, without inducing a recession.

It's important for you, the individual investor, to understand the effects of these dynamics on the property market. Be aware, however, that placing too much emphasis on them is a perfect recipe for procrastination. And procrastination is the biggest thief of time!

CHAPTER FOUR
What is an Investment Property?

AND WHY YOUR HOME DOESN'T ALWAYS QUALIFY!

If property is fundamental to Australians, both as a source of shelter and equity, it seems logical enough that the best kind of investment property is the one right under your nose—the one you live in and love—or something very similar. Not necessarily ...

The great paradox of residential investment property is that, because many would-be investors already have first-hand experience of it as home owners ('Of course I know about property; after all, I live in one!'), they think that the kind of property they like to live in is the same kind of property that makes a good investment.

Ever known someone who bought an investment property because they fell in love with it, or it was just around the corner from their own home and they could keep a close eye on the tenants? Or someone who bought a property thinking that it didn't really matter where it was or what it looked like, because anything with a roof and four walls would be a worthwhile financial proposition? What about someone who lived in a home for a few years, renovated it and expected to make an automatic profit by selling the improved version? (Maybe that 'someone' was you!)

In each case, these people confused the characteristics of property—tangible, three-dimensional, and therefore emotive—with the reason they were buying it (to make money). They failed to understand that buying an investment property differs from buying a home in one fundamental way.

Buying property is a business decision, so emotions and personal tastes must be left out of the equation.

Every day across Australia, many people replicate these mistakes, often creating considerable personal and financial difficulties. Why?

1. We see property as a reflection of ourselves.

Even if we're on a tight budget, our homes are a reflection of how we see ourselves and possibly even how we would like others to see us. Why have rulers throughout history built pyramids, palaces, official residences, Taj Mahals and so on? To create monuments to their ancestors and to themselves!

People today are no different—we gravitate to properties that we find personally appealing; properties that convey an image we are comfortable with or aspire to. The trouble is, 'love' is often blind! It's vital to realise that emotional value and financial value are not always the same.

2. We think of our home as the chief source of wealth.

Australians' enduring attachment to home ownership has become an indelible part of our national psyche. Before World War Two, renting was an accepted way of life for a significant proportion of Australians. Families would often rent the same home for a generation or more.

However, in the post-war years when governments began encouraging home ownership to 'rebuild' our nation, the three-bedroom brick veneer or weatherboard home on a standard quarter-acre block became synonymous with the popularised ideal that everyone was entitled to their very own 'little piece of Australia'. By the 1960s, over 70 per cent of Australians were home owners. Even today, with an increasingly global economy, diverse investment opportunities and a consumer-savvy climate, the home ownership ideal holds true for the great majority of Australians.

The idea of the home as the chief source of wealth—and a form of superannuation to see us into retirement or pass on to our children—flowed naturally from this mindset. Australians were encouraged to buy a home, live in it for years and pay off the debt to build equity. The idea of capital growth as opposed to debt reduction as an equity builder didn't enter the equation (that's what shares were for, and not too many of us had those!). The result was that the vast majority, if not all, of our assets were tied up in the family home—small wonder so many of us confuse home-buying with investing.

3. We equate 'spending' with 'investing'.

Because of the role the family home has traditionally played in our asset base and in our way of thinking, many Australians assume that the very act of spending money on a property automatically makes it an investment.

This assumption arose during the 1950s, 1960s and 1970s, when improved economic conditions led to greater affluence in the community. With more money to spend and the desire for a broader, more varied lifestyle, we developed larger, contemporary-style houses in what are now middle-ring suburbs. This injection of capital into previously undeveloped areas meant that values rose dramatically from a low base. As a result, property values were relatively uniform throughout a given city. In some cities it was quite realistic, for example, to think you could pay a similar price for a three-bedroom house in the outer suburbs as a three-bedroom house a few kilometres from the CBD.

Today, however, property is not a homogeneous asset class. The emergence of the inner suburbs as desirable places to live, along with the development of new and pseudo-revivalist architectural styles, means properties vary considerably in terms of location, style and size—and therefore the level of demand they enjoy among buyers and tenants. The level of supply relative to demand is now the key factor influencing the purchase price of property, and its ongoing capital growth—and it is capital growth that primarily determines an asset's investment potential.

This explains why there is a growing gap between many of today's middle-ring suburbs and their inner suburban counterparts. Many of the properties that were considered cutting edge in the 1960s and 1970s have now become dated architecturally. Where it is not viable to renovate them to a more timeless style, buyers may tend to look in other areas—particularly inner suburbs with more appealing architectural styles and close proximity to the CBD's employment and entertainment opportunities.

With urban consolidation here to stay, there's no going back to the way things were—demand for housing in certain areas will always be stronger than in others. So take a deep breath—it's time to bid fond

Australians already own too much property—the plaintive refrain of the uninformed!

One of the reasons Australians have trouble distinguishing between property as a home and property as a true investment is that we're constantly exposed to the view that, because so many of us own homes, we're overcommitted in property as an asset class. Many commentators advise against investment property in favour of other assets such as shares or managed funds. In making this assertion, these commentators fail to apply the 'purpose test'—that is, what is all this property being used for? In the majority of cases—around 70 to 75 per cent—it's occupied by the people who own it. But what about the other 25 to 30 per cent? If they're occupied by tenants, they must be owned by investors—people who are:

- making money from the property through rental income and, hopefully, capital growth;
- contributing to the amount and variety of private rental accommodation, reducing the onus on governments to provide public housing;
- building wealth to facilitate their financial independence before and after retirement; and
- being recognised by governments for these efforts through tax concessions for the entire time they hold the investment!

By contrast, the family home attracts no tax benefits during the holding period, just an exemption from CGT at the time of sale. This indicates that even the government, which relies on tax revenue to implement its policies, regards the home primarily as a source of personal security rather than a true investment.

farewell to any lingering preconceptions. To survive and thrive as a property investor in today's market, you need to separate matters of the mind from matters of the heart. We're asking you to approach the task of buying an emotion-laden asset with an emotion-free mindset!

Your home can be a financial springboard

Your home is *not* an investment. But if some properties yield higher capital growth than others, you might feel it is possible to find a home you can live in and enjoy, as well as make money from.

There are two ways your home can kick-start you along the road to financial independence.

1. If you are a first home buyer, you may choose to adopt what is primarily an investor's mindset—that is, you are prepared to compromise in the short term and sacrifice some of the things on your personal wish list to achieve more rapid capital growth. This is the only instance where it may be desirable to combine a financial objective with a lifestyle focus.

    If this is what you want to do, you need to choose a property that is within your budget but still of a style, and in a location, that produces consistent capital growth. You cannot compromise on this part of the equation. But when it comes to your personal wish list, you will need to make a few tough choices about what you must have, as distinct from what you'd like to have but can really live without.

    When buying your second home several years down the track, all that equity will put you in a stronger financial position, enabling you to buy a home for love alone, and maybe even an investment property as well. Not a bad result after just a few years of compromise!

2. If you already have your own home and are paying it off or own it outright, you can use the equity as collateral to fund the purchase of an investment property.

Even if your home hasn't achieved spectacular capital growth, it can still be an excellent springboard to buying a true investment property. The longer you own it, the more equity you'll accumulate through the principal component of your loan repayments—giving you leverage to purchase properties that will deliver a real investment performance.

FAQ: ***Can I use my home as an investment?***

Your home is not an investment property, because it doesn't produce rental income, and you can't claim holding costs as tax deductions. Most importantly, it may not have the correct location or building style to generate strong consistent capital growth. However, the equity in your home can provide a useful source of *leverage* from which to purchase a true investment property.

Home or investment—at a glance?

To help you clearly determine the difference between a home and an investment, let's take a more detailed look at the 'purpose test' we mentioned earlier.

When you buy a home, you're looking to satisfy personal considerations, such as:

- Relative affordability—how many bedrooms and what level of renovation/appearance/mod cons can you buy for your money?
- Enough accommodation and amenities—bedrooms, bathrooms, living/work space—to meet your immediate and medium-term needs.
- Décor, architectural style and location that you find appealing, or which at least can be *made* appealing, within the constraints of your budget and local town planning laws.
- A floor plan that meets your specific needs, though you may have to make a few changes for certain purposes, for example hobbies or a home office.
- A stimulating/peaceful/social/rural/urban environment, depending on your desired lifestyle.
- Reasonable proximity to educational facilities if you have children, major roads, freeways and/or public transport.
- Reasonable proximity to work, shops, friends, family, social venues, places of worship or amenities that enable you to pursue a favourite hobby or just relax!

When you first buy a home, **lifestyle** and **value for money** are your prime concerns. And once you settle into the area and find your favourite medico, restaurant, gym, parks and so on, these initial personal considerations become long-term emotional attachments and it's usually pretty hard to leave.

But when you're looking for a true investment property, it's a whole new ball game. Instead of thinking about whether you could live in the property, ask yourself whether it will appeal to the wider market for years to come. Why would other buyers want this property? Why would tenants in general want to live there? You don't need to like or fall in love with it—remember, you'll never have to live in it, and not case study

How Dougal and Joan chose a home with a headstart

Dougal and Joan's property investment history goes back to 1983, when they bought their first home. Their story is a great example of how choosing a home with an eye to the future can give you a financial advantage...

A couple truly ahead of their time, Dougal and Joan decided to buy a first home they were fairly sure would go up in value relatively quickly so that they could use the equity to acquire investment property. In order to achieve this objective, they were prepared to compromise on the number of bedrooms (they settled for two rather than three), and the level of cosmetic renovation (basic rather than 'drop dead gorgeous').

Their single fronted 1890s timber cottage, five kilometres from a major capital city was purchased at auction amid gasps from the assembled crowd. At the time, the property's technical value was around $58 000. They paid $67 000, quite a bit more in percentage terms and certainly a princely sum at the time. Their $45 000 home loan was considered astronomical at the time!

Whilst it's never a good idea to overpay, Dougal and Joan saw all the signs that augur well for capital growth in this property. It was in sound structural order, was of a timeless and increasingly popular architectural style, young people were moving into the street and renovating and the property was close to all services and facilities. Local values had been rising steadily for some time. In paying the extra amount and taking out a slightly bigger mortgage, they took what they considered a 'calculated' risk. For the first two years they 'made do' and focused on reducing their mortgage.

In 1985, they repainted the house inside and out, recarpeted the bedrooms and polished the floorboards elsewhere. Skylights were installed to brighten things up and the kitchen and bathroom were retiled. Outside, there was a new picket fence and the seemingly endless concrete was ripped up and a cottage garden was planted. All in all it was a modest renovation project, but one that focused on cosmetic work that would enhance their lifestyle and add significantly to the property's value.

By 1988 Dougal and Joan were ready to move on to a home more in keeping with their desire to live in a bigger home further away from the city. They were well aware that capital growth on a new house wouldn't match that of the first one and what's more it didn't matter! Now they had the luxury of making lifestyle their priority. Based on directly comparable market transactions, their little cottage had almost trebled in value in the space of five years growing from $67 000 to around $195 000. Dougal and Joan sold their cottage in order to buy their new home for cash. They were now well and truly on their way to building their investment portfolio.

After more debt reduction on their new home, investment property number one was secured in 1994. Since building equity through capital growth was the sole objective, and because they had limited funds to invest, they opted for a one-bedroom unit with off-street parking and two courtyard gardens on title for $115 000. When it comes to quality units in the inner suburbs of cities, the presence of land and off-street parking on title is a relatively rare and prized commodity. By 1996, the one-bedroom unit was worth $135 000. Equity in their home continued to mount as they kept reducing their loan balance.

As their overall equity continued to grow, Dougal and Joan added two further investment properties to their portfolio in 1996. Further purchases were made in 1998, and 2000. In addition to investing in property, Dougal and Joan also began investing in shares in 1999. Today, they enjoy an excellent quality of life and control an investment portfolio in excess of two million dollars.

▶

> (It's interesting to note how the effect of compounding capital growth on high quality property makes loans such as Joan and Dougal's original $45 000 loan increasingly insignificant over time. Consider that in 2002, Dougal and Joan's original home is worth in the vicinity of $420 000, more than six times or $353 000 more than what they paid for it 20 years ago!)
>
> Dougal and Joan have achieved significant financial security primarily through the capital growth that astute asset selection brings. Whilst their incomes have grown too, they remain relatively modest. It's the quality of their investments and their financial discipline that have won the day.
>
> case study

all your tenants will share your personal tastes. In fact, to maintain the necessary emotional distance, it's probably better if you *don't* like it!

What are the hallmarks of a true investment property?

Now it's time to get technical. Because buying investment property is a business decision and buying a home is a personal one, the factors that make a good investment property are clearer than the factors that make a good home.

LONG-TERM, HIGH CAPITAL GROWTH POTENTIAL

Far and away above anything else, top-quality investment property must have the potential to double in value at least every seven to ten years. Let this be your rule of thumb, and henceforth your mantra, for selecting investment property!

True capital growth means that the value of the asset grows because demand consistently outstrips supply. It also means you don't have to add value via improvements or renovations. If you do renovate, true capital growth also means that the improvements must add genuine value—that is, value greater than their original cost—within a reasonable timeframe of around three to five years, or less.

The recession of the early 1990s provided an excellent environment to demonstrate the true strength of prime investment property. As property advisers, we would attend auctions or negotiate private sales to secure high-quality assets on behalf of clients and watch as property after property was keenly contested, selling for higher prices than last transacted. In many cases those last transactions had taken place during the boom of the late 1980s, when prices were generally *higher* than during the recession.

COMPETITIVE, SUSTAINABLE RENTAL INCOME

A top-performing investment property must supply an optimum, yet sustainable, source of rental income to:

- help offset holding costs;
- qualify you for investment-related tax concessions; and
- replace your wage or salary after you decide to stop working.

These are all very important considerations; without rental income, buying investment property would be a far less desirable and viable option. But it must be kept in perspective. So many Australians make the mistake of thinking that because rental income is something they can *see*, something they receive on a regular basis, that it's the most important consideration when buying investment property. This is not the case.

It is vital to understand that while rental income provides a tangible and significant reward for holding a very tangible asset, it must always be secondary to capital growth when you're weighing up a property's investment potential—because it is capital growth that enables you to build equity and purchase further investments.

Having said this, it is important to know what constitutes a reasonable rental return for a quality investment property. As explained in chapter one, it is the dollar value of rent that counts, not the return as a percentage of capital value because, generally speaking, the higher a property's capital value the lower the percentage return. If you still doubt this, just ask the tax department—when they look at your tax return, they are only interested in the dollar value of your rent, because this is what constitutes income, which in turn is what can be taxed on the one hand and reimbursed through concessions on the other.

Look for a property that commands rental income in the upper range of what can be achieved for directly comparable property in the same locality on today's market. If you set the rent too high, you'll find it hard to attract tenants, resulting in long vacancy periods with no rent coming in at all. And if you set the rent too low, you'll find it unnecessarily difficult to meet your holding costs.

CLOSE PROXIMITY TO THE CBD AND AMENITIES

We've already discussed the growing desirability of properties and precincts in established, attractive areas with ready access to the full range of amenities—transport, retail, education, leisure, and so on. When properties are also close to the CBD and demand consistently outstrips supply, they have the makings of a good investment prospect.

ARCHITECTURAL TIMELESSNESS AND/OR CONFORMITY

While location—read: land value—is the number one determinant of capital growth, architectural style also plays an important role. Even if they get the location right, many investors end up buying into a building that is likely to become dated architecturally or is not in keeping with the predominant style of architecture for the area, then wonder why it isn't performing as well as some of its neighbours.

LOGICAL FLOOR PLAN AND STRUCTURAL SOUNDNESS

Ever walked through a property and found yourself wondering why the front door opened into the kitchen, or you had to walk through the bathroom to get to the bedroom? Sometimes, even a property with timeless appeal in the most sought after location is renovated and modified in a way that the majority of buyers and tenants don't find acceptable—undermining demand and therefore capital growth prospects.

Just as bad is the prospect of buying an investment that looks great on the surface but ends up costing you an arm and a leg because of undetected rising damp, termites or poor construction.

Just remember:

Making money out of residential investment property is a *business* venture and requires a rational, detached state of mind. It has everything to do with research, market knowledge and astute negotiation, and *nothing* to do with your emotions or personal tastes!

So where to from here?

It's time to make absolutely sure that your first investment is a veritable humdinger. And there's a very good reason why . . .

PART TWO
Laying the Groundwork

CHAPTER FIVE
Making a Start

WHY YOUR FIRST INVESTMENT PROPERTY IS THE MOST IMPORTANT OF ALL

One of the questions we are most often asked is, 'When should I start?' Invariably our answer is, 'As soon as you possibly can!'

Think about the way most of us view money. We see our working years as the time to build our lives—to travel, buy a home, develop successful careers, perhaps settle down and have kids. To fund these major life goals in addition to our daily living expenses we rely on our wage or salary, often borrowing what we can't pay for with our own resources. Even if we do manage to save a bit here or there, it's usually for relatively short-term things such as furniture or appliances, school fees or holidays. We do contribute to superannuation, but not many of us are confident about the level of capital and income it will ultimately provide.

In our ignorance, we think that super and the pension will pretty much cover our retirement living costs. So we keep on delaying other forms of investment until, before we know it, retirement is right on our doorstep ... and we realise that, in fact, super and the pension may not be enough, after all. *Then* we start scrambling around frantically trying to find investment options that might make the difference between a meagre existence in retirement and a comfortable one.

Now, if you've already reached that point in life, the last thing we want to do is frighten you into thinking that you might have left your run too late. When it comes to property, starting today is definitely better than not starting at all.

Remember your benchmark: top-quality investment property should double in capital value at least every seven to ten years. To achieve this, your property must grow in value at least 7 to 8 per cent on average per annum above the prevailing inflation rate.

And capital growth compounds. This means the growth each year is not just calculated on the original purchase price of the property, but on the purchase price plus growth of previous year(s)—you are reinvesting your profits—the growth rate is enhanced further each year. Just think what an impact this will have on your net worth and your future financial independence. Let's look at some examples of how this works in practice in Table 5.1.

Property A is growing in value at an average of 7 per cent per annum above inflation—the lower end of what we consider to be acceptable capital growth performance. The growth looks relatively unspectacular in the first few years. But look what happens a little further down the track! After five years, the property is worth $384 656. After seven years, it has grown to $457 010—almost double the purchase price. And after ten years, it's worth $591 841.

In other words, if you had bought that property ten years ago you would have more than doubled your money—even without carrying out substantial improvements. And if you held it for the *very* long term, the benefits would increase even further. After 15 years, the

Table 5.1: Compound Growth—the Eighth Wonder of the World!

Purchase price	Property A $250 000	Property B $250 000	Property C $250 000
Deposit (equity)	$25 000	$25 000	$25 000
Percentage growth pa* (incl. 2% avg. inflation)	9%	10%	2%
Value after 1 year	$272 500	$275 000	$255 000
Value after 2 years	$297 025	$302 500	$260 100
Value after 3 years	$323 757	$332 750	$265 302
Value after 5 years	$384 656	$402 628	$276 020
Value after 7 years	$457 010	$487 179	$287 171
Value after 10 years	$591 841	$648 436	$304 749
Value after 15 years	$910 621	$1 044 312	$336 468
Value after 20 years	$1 401 102	$1 681 875**	$371 487

* Assumes no major capital improvements or renovations carried out. Inflation is averaged for the purposes of illustration.
** After 20 years a mere 1% difference in growth between Property A and Property B affords you almost $300 000 extra equity on your initial $250 000 investment.

property's value would have increased to $910 621; and after 20 years, to $1 401 102—almost six times what you paid for it.

Property B, whose value is increasing at 8 per cent above inflation, tells an even better story. In the early years it is not doing much better than Property A. But after five to seven years, the effects of compounding really begin to kick in. After seven years Property B is worth $487 179, almost double what the owner paid for it. After ten years it is worth $648 436—more than two and a half times its original value! The longer the owner holds this property, the greater the compounding benefits become. After 15 years Property B is worth $1 044 312, and after 20 years it has grown to $1 681 875—almost seven times what it originally cost!

You will note we have made no provision here for renovations or improvements to add value to these properties. With these fictional examples and their real-life counterparts, this level of capital growth is based almost entirely on the underlying quality of the assets and their land value. Cosmetic upgrades to maintain appeal to tenants and therefore rental value, such as recarpeting and repainting, are the only means by which the owners actively add value. This small capital input comes with an in-built economy of scale that would impress even the most stringent number-cruncher! All other things being equal, the owners of Property A and Property B may only need to spend a few thousand dollars every few years to keep their properties up to scratch cosmetically—a paltry sum compared with the staggering compound growth that comes from having chosen the right property.

Of course, residential investment properties are not museum pieces—they're exposed to wear and tear from the elements and from the people who live in them. In the real world investors do need to make provision for occasional minor building maintenance. We're not talking about knocking out walls or building extensions here, but things like repairing and/or replacing guttering and fencing. Building maintenance may reduce net rental income for a short period, but it's simply part and parcel of owning property.

Compare this fine scenario with the growth of Property C, which is not a prime investment asset and is barely keeping pace with inflation—the kind of property that, in fact, many financial commentators use to illustrate the *'poor performance of **all** residential investment property.'*

Poor old Property C! Starting from the same purchase price as its counterparts, it's been left in the proverbial dust. After ten years it is worth only $304 749—around 22 per cent more than the owner paid for it. (By comparison, Property A is worth $591 841 at the ten-year mark, and Property B is worth $648 436. Now, as a lump sum and to the unpractised eye, 22 per cent might not appear too bad. But it's only 2.2 per cent on average per year over the ten-year period—little different from the interest paid on most everyday bank accounts. Hardly the optimum way to increase your net worth.

Just as the benefits of compounding increase dramatically the longer you hold a prime investment property, so do the *disadvantages* if you have bought a lemon. At the 20-year mark Property C is worth only $371 487, as compared with Property B which is worth $1 681 875. Property C's owner has missed out on a staggering **$1 310 388 in capital growth**—*all the while incurring the same level of expenses such as interest, municipal rates, insurance and maintenance.*

What's worse, for every year you hold on to an under-performing investment property you lose time—*and time is irreplaceable*. Instead of holding on to the property and hoping things will change, you could be putting your money into a well-chosen asset that does deliver substantial capital growth and does increase your net worth. If you've held the asset for at least three to five years and it hasn't delivered capital growth of the kind we've outlined here, you may need to re-evaluate the situation, bearing in mind the influence of prevailing economic and local property market conditions.

For example, if Australia is experiencing an economic downturn and inflation is running at 2 per cent, the overall residential market is growing at 4 per cent and your property is growing at 7 per cent, then clearly it's weathering the storm pretty well and selling it may not be a productive step. If, however, the overall property market has been growing at, say, 6 per cent for a considerable period but your property has been growing at only 2 to 3 per cent, you may be better off selling and re-investing your funds in a better performing property. We take a detailed look at evaluating the performance of your investment property portfolio in chapter thirteen.

First in, first served

If you're reading this book as a potential first-time investor, the fear of what may lie ahead, or what you *think* lies ahead, can be enough to stop you in your tracks and delay taking the first step. This is absolutely understandable—believe us, we felt the same when we started buying investment property for ourselves, and have witnessed it hundreds of times in the clients we see in the course of our advisory work.

You think, 'Maybe I should wait a few more years, till I feel "ready" for it; till I feel a bit more "in control" of my life; till I'm married/bought a home to live in/had a couple of kids/put a bit more aside for a rainy day.' And it is absolutely appropriate that you invest in property at a stage in life when you feel mentally and financially ready.

But if you *are* ready and you still put off the investment process, you'll do yourself a grave disservice. Because of the exponential nature of compound growth, delaying investing can have significant repercussions on your ability to create sufficient net assets.

Take a look at figures 5.1, 5.2, 5.3 and 5.4 which follow. You'll see how the combination of starting your investment portfolio as soon as practicable, selecting high growth assets and holding on to them for the long term will really give you the financial independence we all desire.

Making a Start

Figure 5.1 The Importance of Starting Early

Procrastination costs a lot of money! How much? In this example the 7 year delay comes at the huge cost of $800 000 on a $200 000 initial purchase to the investor who started at Year 7 on the horizontal axis.

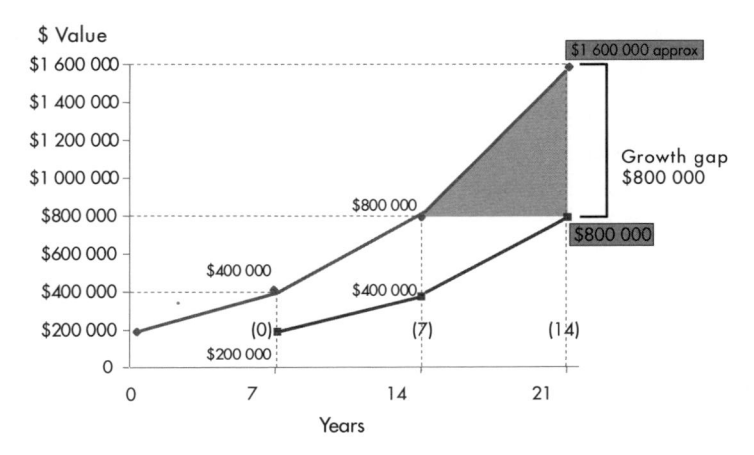

Source: Wakelin Property Advisory

Figure 5.2 The Importance of Compound Growth

Selecting a property for its capital growth potential can create wonderful financial security. In this graph you can see how a correctly selected $200 000 investment property doubles in value every seven years and generates equity of $1.4 million over approximately 21 years.

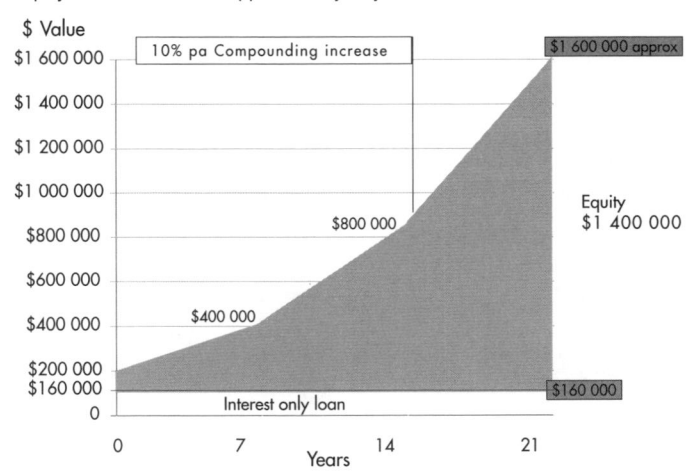

Source: Wakelin Property Advisory

Streets Ahead

Figure 5.3 The Importance of Buying the Right Property

Two properties, same price, same holding costs. But look how the property growing at 10% outperforms the one growing at 5%. The $1 million difference is the result of choosing a scarce resource that will always be in high demand and limited supply.

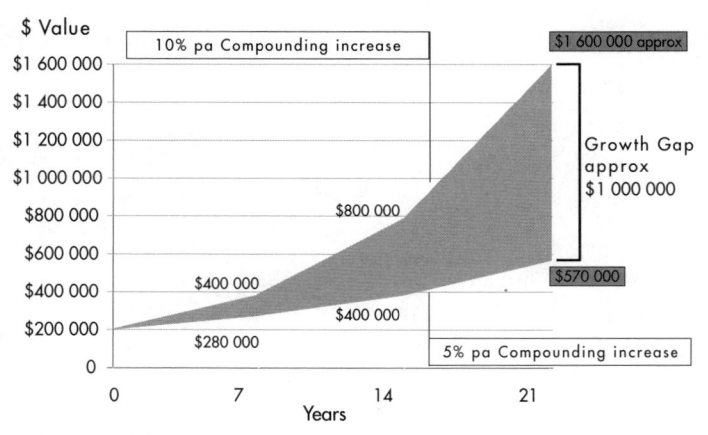

[Chart showing $ Value vs Years (0, 7, 14, 21):
- 10% pa Compounding increase: starts at $200,000, reaches $400,000 at year 7, $800,000 at year 14, $1,600,000 approx at year 21
- 5% pa Compounding increase: $280,000 at year 7, $400,000 at year 14, $570,000 at year 21
- Growth Gap approx $1,000,000]

Source: Wakelin Property Advisory

Figure 5.4 A Case Study

This property was bought in 1980 for $50 000, of which $40 000 (80%) was borrowed. Today, it's worth around $460 000. There have been no major improvements or extensions carried out. Who would have thought it possible in 1980!

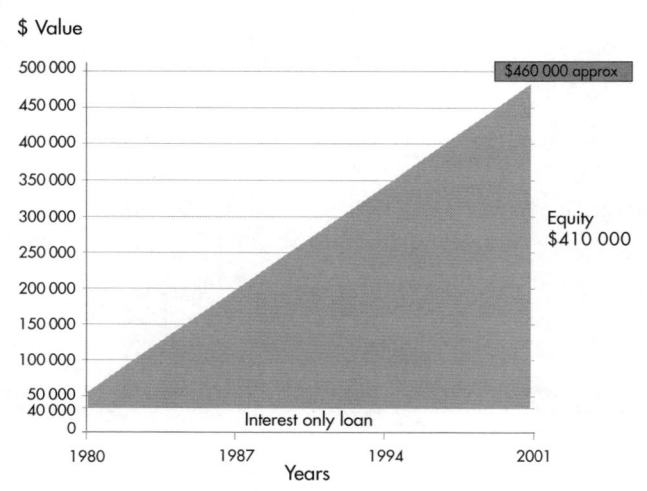

[Chart showing $ Value vs Years (1980, 1987, 1994, 2001):
- Starting value $50,000 in 1980 ($40,000 borrowed)
- $460,000 approx in 2001
- Equity $410,000
- Interest only loan]

Source: Wakelin Property Advisory

The golden rules to be drawn from all this?

- *Start investing in property as soon as practicable.* Even with top-quality investment property, compound growth takes time to kick in, but the benefits after the five- to seven-year mark are exponential.

- *Choose wisely and hold on to a good asset*

    All too often in our capacity as property investment advisers we are contacted by people who have chosen top-performing assets, but, having experienced some impressive capital growth in the early years, they ask us whether that is the best they can do; whether they should realise the profit and/or use it to buy another property that might perform better.

    If the asset is truly an outstanding long-term investment prospect, our answer is an emphatic 'No!' We tell them exactly what we're telling you—that compounding capital growth will increase their net wealth substantially with every passing year—and with minimal effort or cost on their part—underpinning their asset base for years to come. Furthermore, the rental income will help fund holding costs in the early years, eventually replacing their wage or salary in retirement.

    If you do want to purchase a second investment property, the best way forward is not to sell the first one and start over, but to hold it and leverage the accumulated equity instead. Look back at our examples of how much capital can be generated through just one property via compound growth. Just think what two properties will do!

    Holding on to an asset means you also avoid the often-significant expenses associated with selling, such as capital gains tax, agents' commissions, advertising costs and any repairs or improvements needed to make the property more attractive to buyers. Why spend your hard-earned money on these eminently avoidable expenses when you can put it towards reducing debt, purchasing further assets or just enjoying life?

By contrast, if you sell, your cash from the sale proceeds will rapidly diminish along with inflation—or temptation! Since finding a plum investment doesn't happen overnight, you'll probably take some time to re-enter the market. And the longer this takes, the wider the gap between the buy-in price and the amount you have at your disposal—creating a rather vicious cycle.

- *Structure your finances to actively reduce debt*
This means paying off principal as well as interest. The combination of debt reduction and compound capital growth will increase the equity in your assets more quickly than either one alone.

How much do I need to start?

Now that you're revved up, inspired and feeling ready to take the plunge, your next question should be: 'What's the minimum amount I need to pay for a property that will deliver optimum capital growth?'

Because entry-level prices for quality investment properties vary markedly from city to city, we can't give you a magic formula or single buy-in price. The onus is on *you* to do some careful and very specific research on prices for your capital city. Concentrating exclusively on suburbs that have demonstrated that all-important long-term high capital growth, look at recent sale prices for high-quality, *established* one- and two-bedroom units and apartments and/or smaller houses.

case study

Starting early, growing strong

Jenny, a 25-year-old client came to us in 1994, wanting to explore how property investment could assist her in creating financial independence. We helped her source and negotiate the purchase of a two-bedroom 1940s clinker brick unit. The property had a number of distinguishing characteristics that made it a top-shelf investment. One of just four units in the complex, it was optimally positioned on the top floor at the front of the block, with large rooms, high period-style ceilings, a pleasant leafy outlook from each room and undercover off-street parking.

Jenny paid $125 000 to secure the property. Based on sales of very similar units in the immediate vicinity, the property is now worth more than $300,000. With very few capital improvements, besides repainting and recarpeting, the property has more than doubled in value well within the seven to ten year benchmark.

The excellent capital growth from her very first investment means Jenny is in the enviable position of being able to acquire a further asset with relative ease if and when she so desires. If she goes on to property number two, she can use the readily available, tax free equity to fund her borrowings rather than having to delay adding to her portfolio while she saves another deposit from her after tax salary or rental income. Not a bad start!

case study

By 'established', we mean property that has been sold before. New property invariably carries an inflated price tag that reflects the developer's need to make a profit, rather than true market value as determined by supply and demand.

Table 5.2: Some Returns are More Equal than Others: capital growth and rental income on a $200,000 purchase

If you have any doubts about the importance of capital growth when it comes to selecting an investment property these figures will be a real eye-opener. The less emphasis you place on growth in favor of rental income the more you stand to lose both in the value of your assets and the amount of rent you'll naturally generate over time.

	10% Capital Growth	5% Rent	7% Capital Growth	8% Rent	5% Capital Growth	10% Rent
Year 1	$220 000	$11 000	$214 000	$17 120	$210 000	$21 000
Year 5	$322 102	$16 105	$280 510	$22 441	$255 256	$25 526
Year 10	$518 748	$25 937	$393 430	$31 474	$325 780	$32 578
Year 15	$835 450	$41 773	$551 806	$44 144	$415 786	$41 579
Year 20	$1 345 500	$67 275	$773 937	$61 915	$530 660	$53 066

* All rental figures based on annual capital value.

The sale prices of these kinds of established properties are likely to be a fairly accurate reflection of a reasonable entry-level price in your city. However, it's important to realise that these prices will be a guide, not an absolute. Occasionally it may be possible to purchase genuinely good-quality investment property at prices below these levels. However, properties priced too far below these levels almost invariably lack the key attributes required for strong capital growth.

Conversely, it's possible to spend too much, thinking you have to buy a large or elaborate property to achieve substantial capital growth. It is important not to equate price or size with growth potential. As long as you select property that fulfills the selection criteria we have discussed, you can achieve excellent results from modestly priced properties.

CHAPTER SIX
Where to Buy

LOCATION, LOCATION, AND THEN SOME!

We've already established that compound growth will help you build equity and financial independence through residential property investment. Regular rental income will also help you fund the costs of ownership so you can hold the property for the long term, allowing compound growth every opportunity to do its work.

Now, we'll start to show you what long-term capital growth and rental income mean in practical terms, and choosing the right location is a key component.

Your first step is to choose property in capital cities as opposed to regional centres or rural areas. Why? Because, with very few exceptions, these are the only areas with:

- ongoing demand from buyers and tenants—producing consistent growth in land values, which justifies expenditure on improvements, repairs and maintenance; and
- solid, sustainable economic activity—generating long-term employment opportunities and growth.

No doubt many of you know of properties that have sold for astronomical prices down on the peninsula/up the coast/in the hills over the years!

Of course, if you live in or visit one of these areas and you're pretty fond of them, your opinions will probably be tinged with a fair bit of emotion. But as we've already said, it's vital to put your emotions aside when you're buying something purely as an investment.

In many regional and rural areas, there is much more land available than there are people wanting to live there. In these areas, land availability is not restricted by scarcity, but by how quickly essential infrastructure such as roads and power and water, along with amenities such as schools' transport and shops, can be supplied—and how willing purchasers are to sacrifice inner suburban convenience for other perceived benefits such as open space, clean air or a greater feeling of security. Because supply outstrips demand, property values are lower to start with and tend to grow more slowly.

From time to time, strong rises *do* occur in these areas. However, they can generally be attributed to one of two factors:

- *A 'ripple effect' from a strong upturn in urban districts.* After an upturn, property values level out and growth in the urban market normalises to a still healthy but more sustainable level. Growth in outlying areas then tends to stagnate. Because overall demand is higher in metropolitan areas, each upturn gives those markets greater and longer lasting impetus than that experienced by outlying areas— creating an ever-widening gap in capital growth between top-performing urban properties and their regional counterparts.
- *New development.* In a new development, the buy-in price is often substantially higher than the pre-existing land values or housing stock. In these cases, the price difference is not usually a reflection of an area's true investment potential as underpinned by long-standing demand.

We can't tell you how many clients have come to us over the years with tales of woe about poorly performing properties in low-growth areas. The longer you hold on to an investment property in a low-growth area, the more you'll hamper your capacity to build the net worth, and number, of your assets.

So 'where to' in the big city?

Major capital cities make the most suitable investment locations, but it's not just a matter of throwing a dart at a map of one of the 'big eight' and buying a property where it lands! To buy a top-performing asset, you must be far more discerning.

Where to buy, where to avoid, and why

1. CHOOSE PROPERTY IN THE INNER SUBURBS

With very few exceptions, the inner suburbs of capital cities produce the most sustainable patterns of capital growth. Because virtually all the available land is fully developed to its highest and best use as prime residential accommodation, the demand for quality residential property in these areas consistently outstrips the supply. Put another way, more people aspire to live in these areas than there are properties to be bought and land available to build on. This phenomenon maintains the prices at a higher level than middle-ring and outer areas where demand for land and housing does not usually exceed the supply.

Table 6.1 (p. 102) lists the top ten performing suburbs in several capital cities in terms of average annual capital growth for units and houses.

FAQ: We're thinking of buying a holiday house as an investment, though we'll also occupy it ourselves during the school and Christmas holidays. What's your opinion?

With Australians' love of the outdoors and 'getting away from the rat race', it's no wonder many of us contemplate buying a holiday home as an 'investment', thinking we can rent it out to holiday-makers and earn useful income when we're not using it ourselves. Since it's an income-producing asset, we can negatively gear it by claiming a tax deduction if the holding costs are higher than the rental income. This looks like the best of both worlds, at least in theory. Let's look at how it stacks up in practice.

If you buy a holiday home as an investment you'll probably want to occupy it at peak periods such as weekends, school holidays, Christmas and Easter, which is when other holiday-makers usually want to use the property too. If you're occupying the property instead of renting it to tenants, not only will you miss out on the premium rental income available at peak periods, you may also have difficulty convincing the tax department that the property is a genuine income producer—jeopardising the possibility of negative gearing.

Because they have a high vacancy rate, holiday homes can also pose a greater security risk. Thieves find it relatively easy to tell when a property is unoccupied. Furthermore, holiday homes often incur high maintenance costs. Many are located in seaside or mountain areas that take their toll on structural integrity, paintwork, roofing and guttering, and so on. The process of tenants moving in and out can cause more wear and tear than a permanently occupied property, further increasing your maintenance bill. And you will need to provide furniture, linen and kitchenware all year round.

On top of this, a substantial chunk of the rental income you obtain may be eaten away by property management fees. While professional property managers generally charge a modest fee for their services, the high tenant turnover of holiday homes during peak periods creates a substantial amount of work for property managers in finding tenants, drafting leases, organising cleaning, repairs and maintenance, inspecting the property between tenancies, preparing condition reports, and so on. In these circumstances, property managers often charge fees several times the normal rate. Unless you want to travel to the property every few weeks and do all the work yourself, it's an expense that's hard to avoid.

Holiday homes are also more susceptible to changes in the economy. When there is a dramatic change and general investor confidence takes a hammering, holiday homes are high on the list of expendable assets, especially if the owner is in financial difficulty. Combined with the generally lower property values in regional areas, this doesn't augur well for capital growth.

But there are exceptions to the rule. These, almost universally, possess outstanding characteristics such as expansive views that can't be built out or absolute water frontage. If truly exceptional, these properties can show more consistent growth than their less remarkable counterparts. However, they present the same maintenance, rental income and taxation issues. And the cost of such a property may well be higher than is reasonable to tie up in the one asset, given the importance of diversification to spread risk.

If you have the capital and the cash flow to support a holiday home without requiring solid investment performance, then buy and enjoy! However, it's usually best to keep your lifestyle decisions separate from the business of investing in and making money out of growth assets.

Table 6.1: Top ten performing suburbs (based on median values), selected capital cities

City Time period	Houses Suburb (distance from CBD in km)	Avg. % capital growth p.a.	City Time period	Units Suburb (distance from CBD in km)	Avg. % capital growth p.a.
Sydney 1991–2000	Glenwood (35)	13.83	Sydney 1991–2000	Bondi (8)	8.82
	Wattle Grove (30)	11.62		Manly (13)	8.15
	Mount Annan (55)	11.56		Milsons Point (2)	7.65
	Bondi (8)	10.73		Coogee (6)	7.63
	Woolloomooloo (1)	10.54		Bronte (8)	7.62
	Fairlight (12)	10.00		Balgowlah (11)	7.35
	Harbord (15)	9.99		Harbord (15)	7.34
	Bronte (8)	9.98		Bellevue Hill (5)	7.24
	Milsons Point (2)	9.90		Alexandria (4)	7.23
	Quakers Hill (40)	9.90		Mona Vale (28)	7.19
Melbourne 1990–1999	Port Melbourne (4)	9.50	Melbourne 1990–1999	Williamstown North (7)	13.10
	Albert Park (3)	8.80		Richmond (3)	11.60
	Middle Park (4)	8.70		St Kilda West (5)	11.50
	Melbourne CBD	8.30		Maidstone (8)	11.30
	Laverton North (17)	8.20		Fitzroy (3)	11.00
	Richmond (3)	7.80		Albert Park (3)	10.70
	Abbotsford (4)	7.70		Vermont South (23)	9.70
	McKinnon (12)	7.70		Taylors Lakes (19)	9.60
	Sandringham (16)	7.60		Balaclava (8)	9.40
	Yarraville (6)	7.60		Moonee Ponds (7)	8.90
Brisbane 1994–1999	Spring Hill (1)	14.60	Brisbane 1995–2001*	Woolloongabba (1)	140.00
	Bulimba (4)	8.80		Bulimba (5)	125.00
	New Farm (2)	8.70		Fortitude Valley (1)	79.57
	Hawthorne (3)	7.60		South Brisbane (1)	79.56
	Dutton Park (4)	7.00		Highgate Hill (2)	47.14
	Hamilton (5)	6.20		Newstead (3)	44.35
	Robertson (15)	6.20		New Farm (2)	41.94
	Balmoral (4)	6.10		Norman Park (4)	40.54
	Lutwyche (6)	6.10		Greenslopes (6)	31.29
	Grange (7)	5.90		Hawthorne (4)	28.08
Perth 1985–2000	Peppermint Grove (11)	15.10			
	South Fremantle (21)	13.80			
	Cottesloe (11)	13.00			
	Subiaco (4)	13.00			
	Swanbourne (11)	12.70			
	Wembley (7)	12.70			
	Bicton (15)	12.30			
	West Perth (2)	12.20			
	Shenton Park (9)	12.10			
	North Fremantle (19)	11.70			

Source: State real estate institutes/Residex. Brisbane: PRD Realty.
* Brisbane figures for 2001 are preliminary.

The majority of these suburbs are located in close proximity to the CBD, relative to the overall size of the metropolitan area.

But be careful. Where some suburbs have made the list, it is usually because of one-off residential development in a previously unimproved or under-improved (and low capital growth) area. When the area has been fully subdivided and all the properties are sold, its appeal as promoted by the developers often begins to wear off and values subside. So before you consider investing in newly developed areas, track the first and second resales to establish whether the price growth, if any, fully justifies including these areas in your property investment strategy.

In other cases, the apparently excellent performance of outer suburbs is due to cyclical characteristics. You'll notice that in Sydney, for example, four suburbs in the top ten list for houses are in outer areas. This is because Sydney's outer suburban market is still developing and operates quite separately from the inner and middle suburbs. In this particular ten-year period the outer suburbs went through two booms, while the inner and middle suburbs experienced one. This is also a good illustration of the more volatile nature of Sydney's property market, compared with more stable markets such as Melbourne and Brisbane, and therefore the importance of choosing locations with consistent growth over a long period.

So what constitutes an 'inner suburb' in each capital city from a property investment viewpoint? To help you get a feel for this, we've divided maps in the following pages into inner, middle and outer zones, relative to each city's overall size. Bear in mind that in most cities, selected suburbs and precincts outside the inner zones can perform well. Conversely, not all areas within inner zones are excellent performers. However, inner areas tend to show the most consistent, long-term capital growth, so that's where we'll focus our attention.

Remember, these lines of demarcation are a guide—they're not a given—so please do your own research as well.

Note: The following population statistics are taken from the ABS 'Australia Now/Population Distribution as at June 1999' report.

Sydney—population 4.1 million

Inner zone: 2–10 km from CBD.
Middle zone: 10–20 km from CBD.
Outer zone: 20–40 km from CBD.

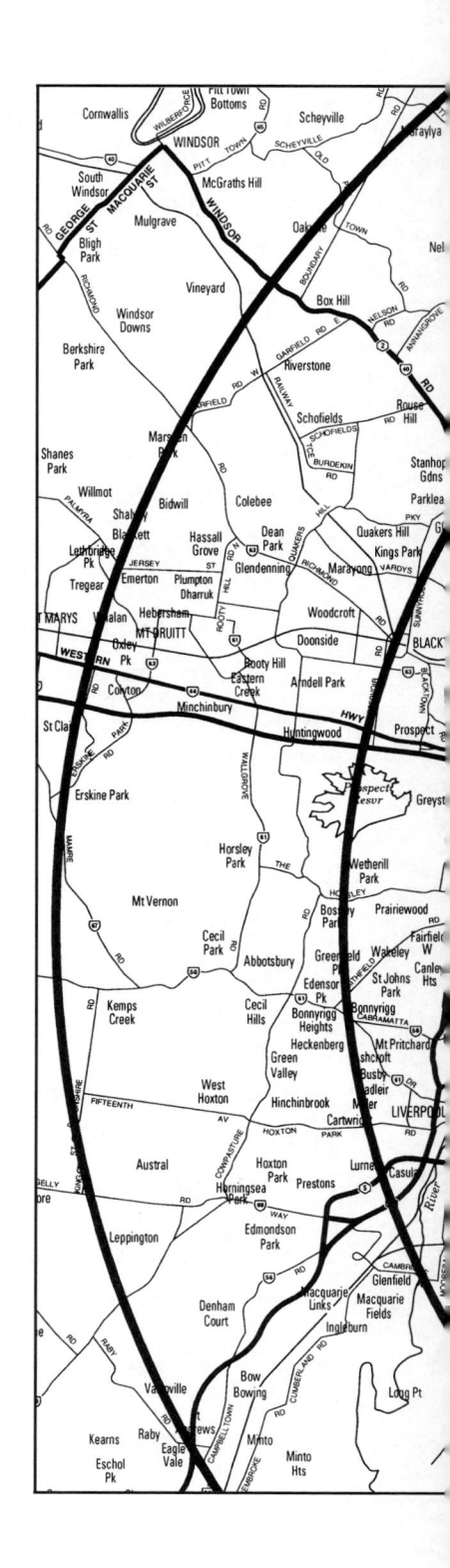

Where to Buy

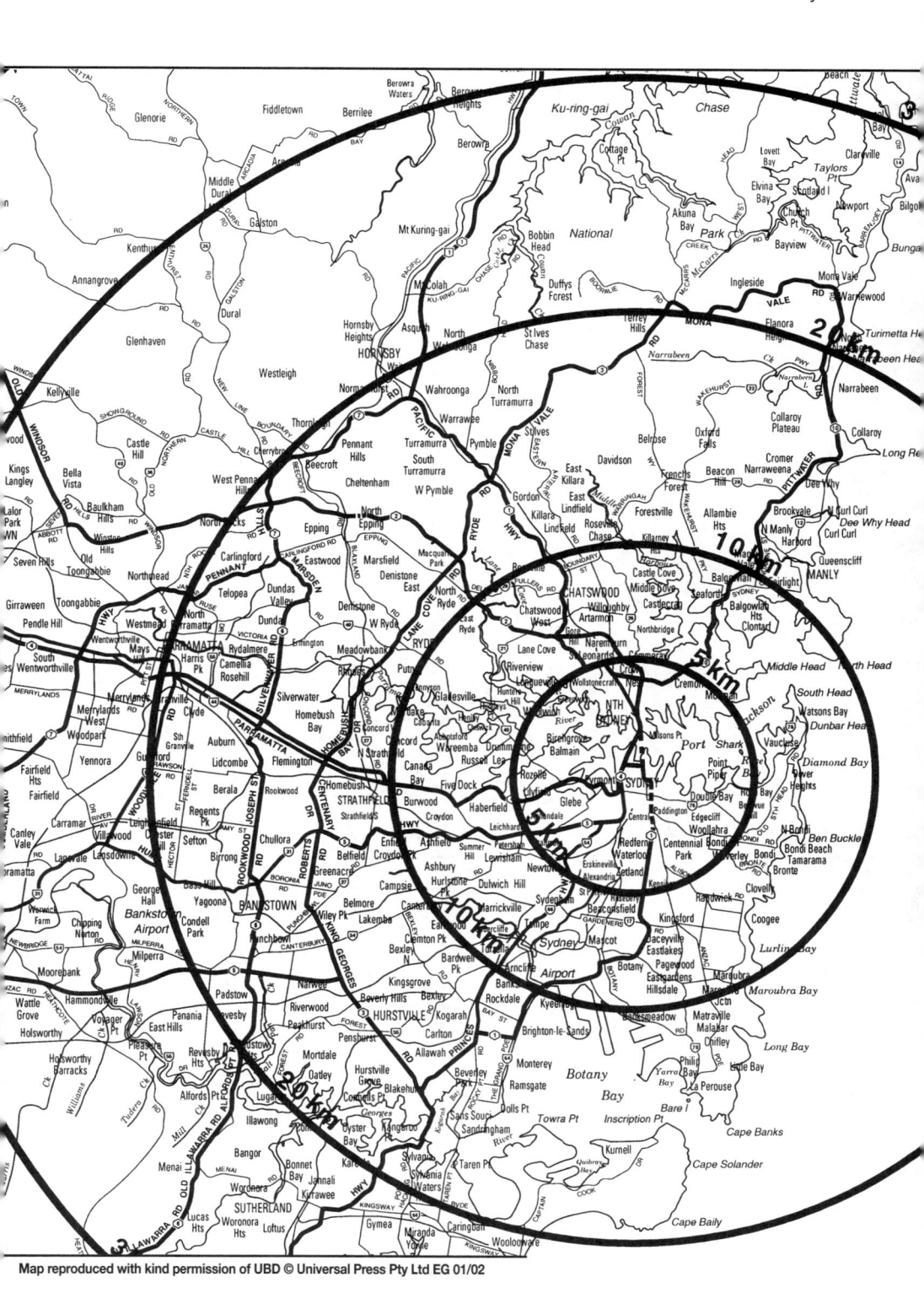

Melbourne—population 3.5 million

Inner zone: 2–10 km from CBD.

Middle zone: 10–20 km from CBD.

Outer zone: 20–40 km from CBD.

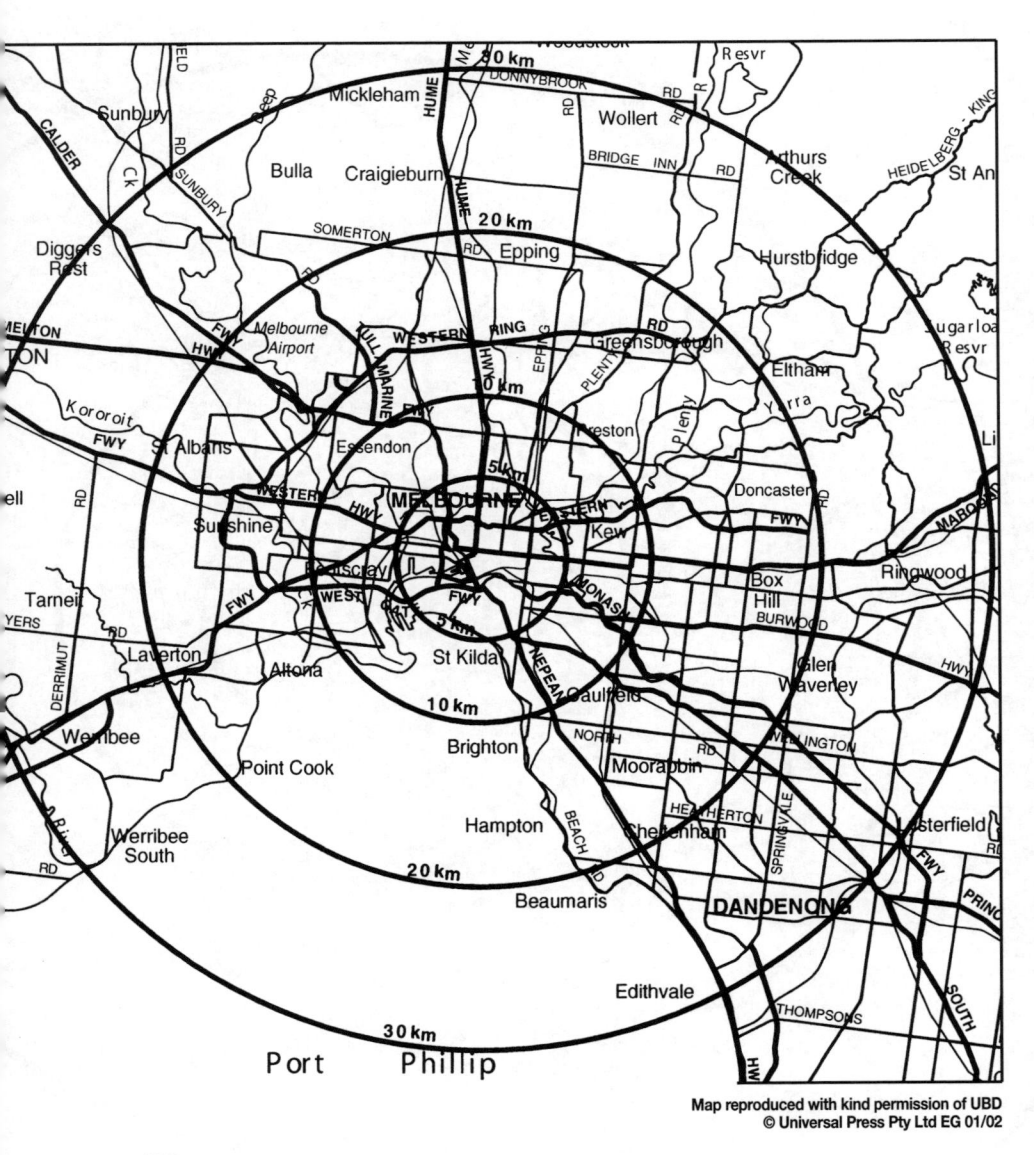

Where to Buy

Brisbane—population 1.6 million

Inner zone: 2–8 km from CBD.

Middle zone: 8–20 km from CBD.

Outer zone: 20–30 km from CBD.

You'll notice that even though Brisbane has a smaller population than Melbourne or Sydney, its middle and outer zones are quite large because it has a relatively low population density.

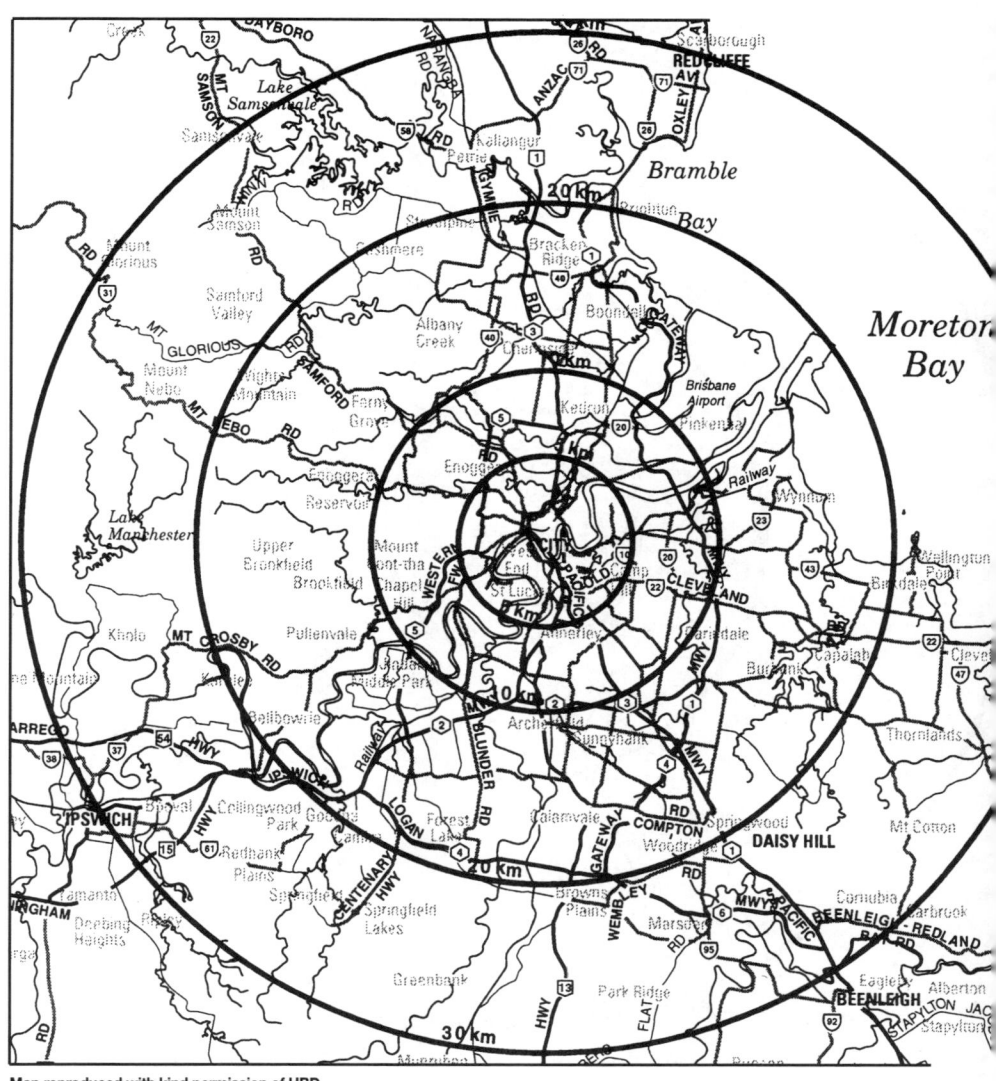

Map reproduced with kind permission of UBD
© Universal Press Pty Ltd EG 01/02

Streets Ahead

Adelaide—population 1.1 million

Inner zone: 2–5 km from CBD.

Middle zone: 5–10 km from CBD.

Outer zone: 10–20 km from CBD.

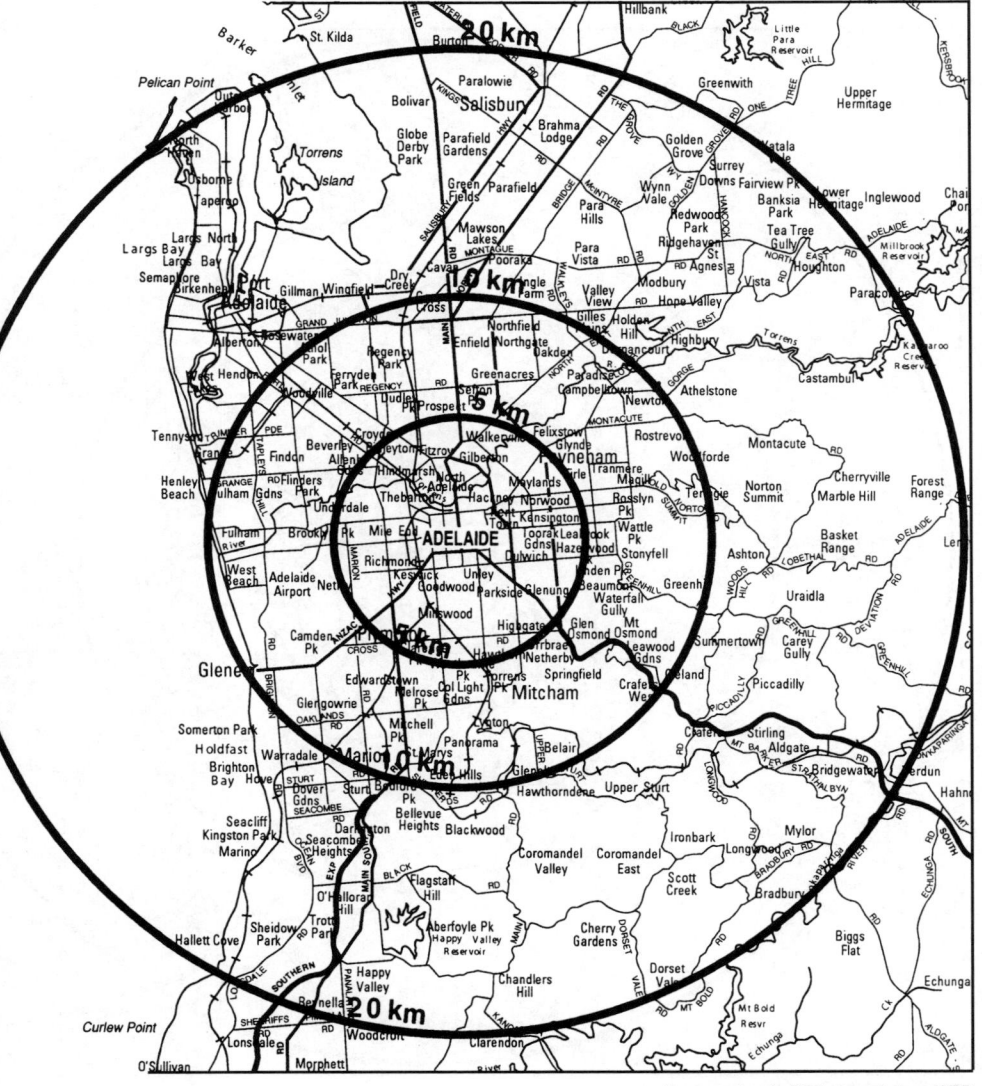

Map reproduced with kind permission of UBD
© Universal Press Pty Ltd EG 01/02

Where to Buy

Perth—population 1.3 million

Inner zone: 2–8 km from CBD.

Middle zone: 8–15 km from CBD.

Outer zone: 15–25 km from CBD.

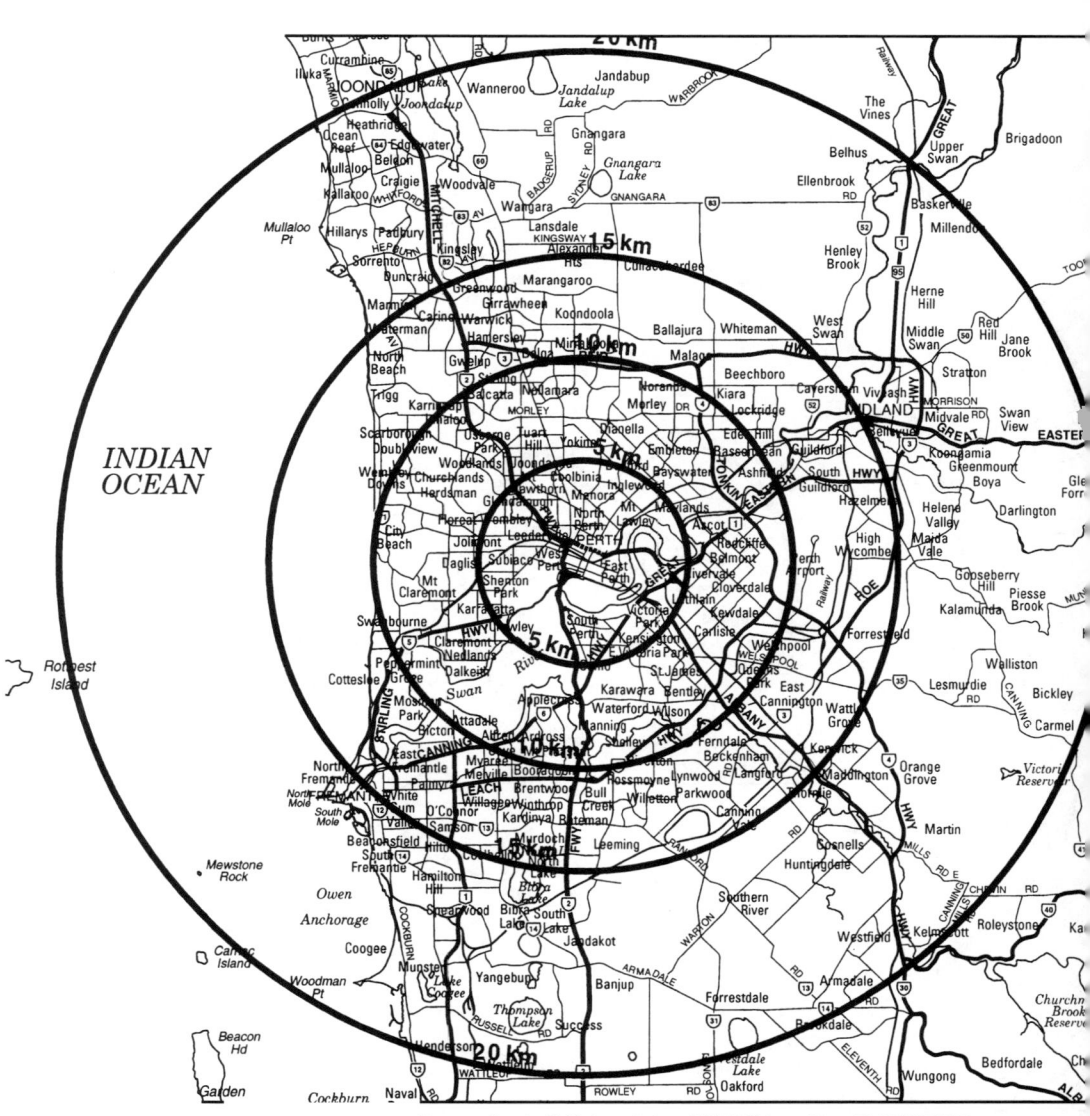

Map reproduced with kind permission of UBD © Universal Press Pty Ltd EG 01/02

Streets Ahead

Darwin—population 90 000

Inner zone: 1–3 km from CBD.

Middle/outer zone: 4–10 km from CBD.

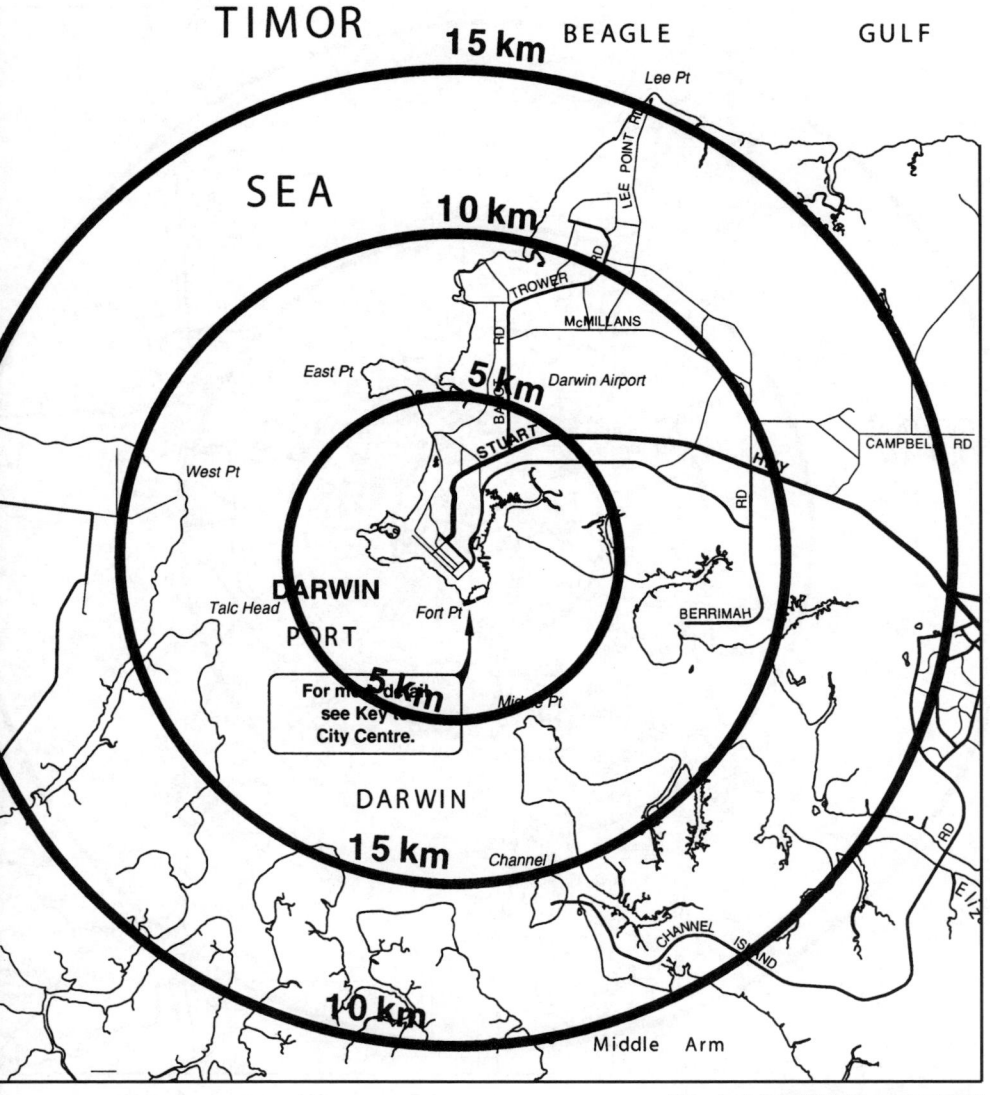

Where to Buy

Hobart—population 200 000

Inner zone: 1–5 km from CBD.

Middle zone: 5–8 km from CBD.

Outer zone: 8–12 km from CBD.

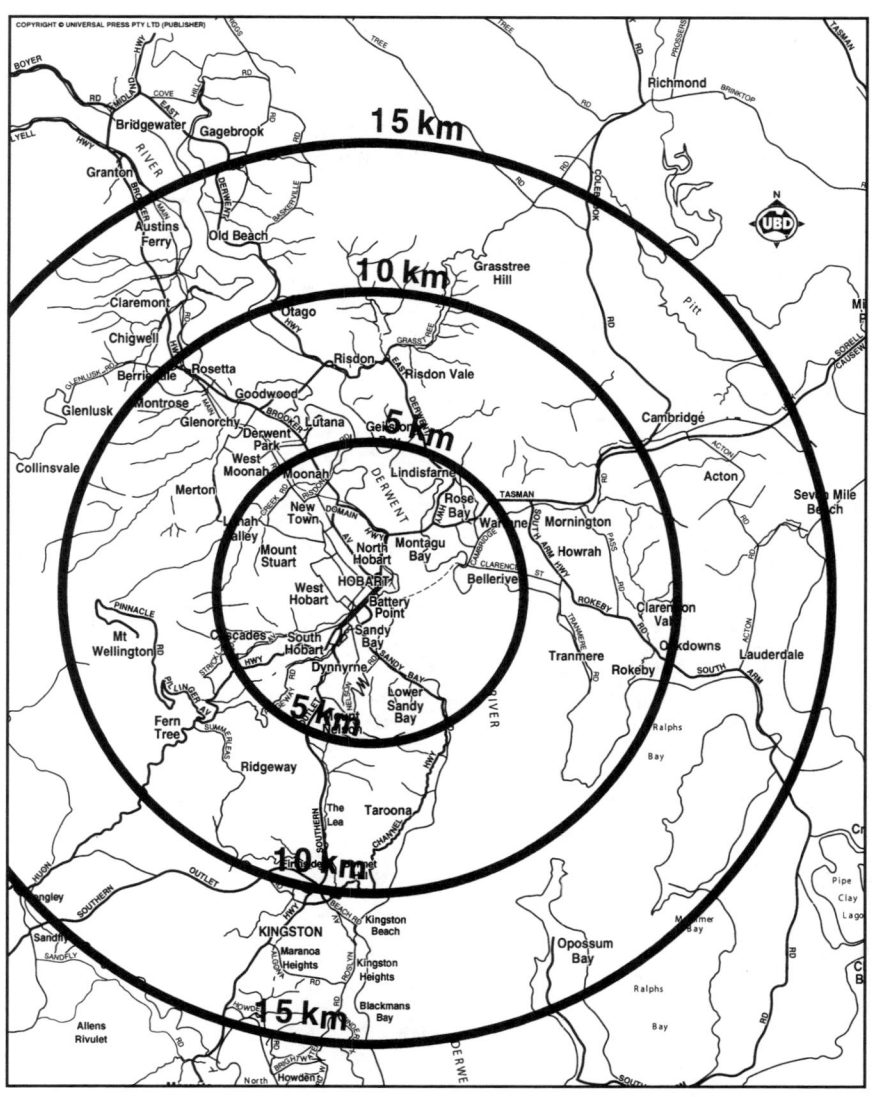

Map reproduced with kind permission of UBD
© Universal Press Pty Ltd EG 01/02

Streets Ahead

Canberra—population 300 000

Inner zone: 1–4 km from Lake Burley Griffin.

Middle zone: 4–10 km from Lake Burley Griffin.

Outer zone: 10–15 km from Lake Burley Griffin.

Because it was planned specifically as our national capital, Canberra is structured differently from other capital cities. It has several 'town centres' around which suburbs are clustered, so its geographical centrepiece is not a CBD as such but is Lake Burley Griffin.

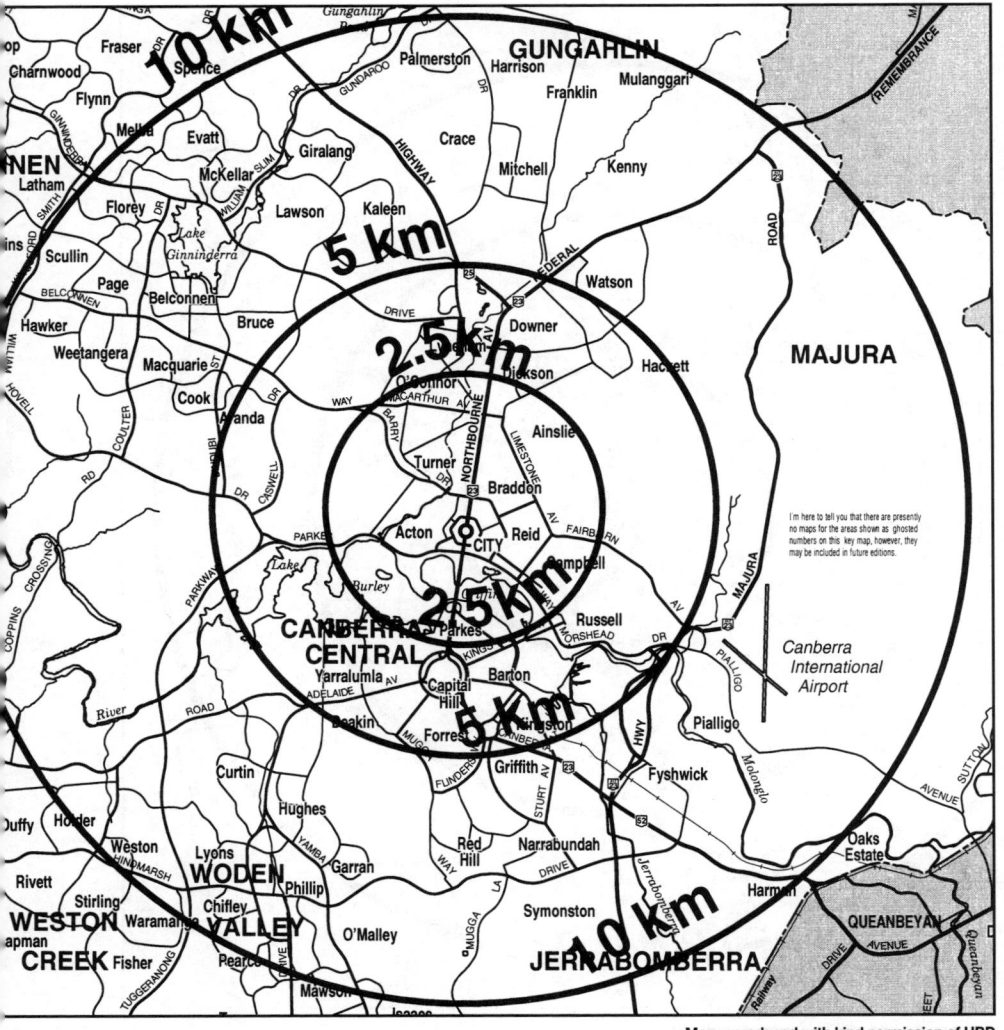

Map reproduced with kind permission of UBD
© Universal Press Pty Ltd EG 01/02

2. IDENTIFY POCKETS WITH LONG-TERM, 'NATURAL' CAPITAL GROWTH

Now that you have zeroed in on the inner suburbs in your chosen capital city, your next step is to uncover specific precincts and streets that have demonstrated, and should continue to demonstrate, consistent, sustained growth in capital value and rental income. Two major tools can help you work this through.

(i) Median values

Newspaper reports often publish median (middle) sales results for cities and suburbs, based on information from State real estate institutes or valuers-general. Because they're collected over a long period of time and encompass a wide range of property, median values can be a useful tool in identifying good growth areas.

As well as the median price itself the statistics often include upper and lower 'quartile' figures, representing the highest 25 per cent and lowest 25 per cent of sales respectively. Together, the three figures can provide a good overall indication of capital growth history and prospects in a given area.

But when it comes to investing in one or two properties in a pool of thousands—all with different characteristics and different market values—relying solely on median values can be a real danger. Here's why.

- *Median values reflect overall property prices in a given area, without distinguishing between new and pre-existing properties.* Because the median value for new properties reflects the developers' profit, median values in these localities may not be an accurate reflection of the area's baseline values.

- *If there is an uncharacteristic cluster of sales in a certain price range the median value will spike or dip accordingly, creating a false impression of the performance of the suburb as a whole.* A good case in point is the proliferation of luxury multi-unit developments that have sprung up in and around the CBD of many capital cities since the mid-1990s. For example, as Table 6.1 shows, Port Melbourne is amongst the best performers in capital growth terms in Melbourne. Located next to Port Phillip Bay, Port Melbourne is about 4 km from the CBD. Traditionally home to modest Victorian weatherboard cottages, the suburb has experienced a tremendous surge in property values in recent years.

In Table 6.2 you will see the jump from $180 000 in 1995 to $265 000 in 1996. That's a one-third increase over 12 months! At face value this seems like stupendous capital growth, so buying any kind of property in Port Melbourne would bring similar results ... right? Wrong.

Table 6.2: Port Melbourne Victoria Median House Values 1989–2000

1989	$172 500
1990	$166 000
1991	$155 000
1992	$162 000
1993	$170 000
1994	$185 000
1995	$180 000
1996	$265 000
1997	$295 000
1998	$340 000
1999	$415 000
2000	$392 500
2001*	$376 000

Source: Valuer-General, Victoria A Guide to Property Values.
*(Preliminary figure)

Median values between 1989 and 1995 increased minimally and, in some years, decreased. So it's clear that the 1996 increase was uncharacteristic of the longer range pattern. What prompted this spike? A large number of new luxury property sales, often at premium price tags of over $350 000.

The concentrated volume of transactions in this price range over such a short time created a median price that, while accurate in itself, did not reflect the capital growth and price movements occurring in pre-existing dwellings. Port Melbourne residents who expected their modest Victorian cottages to sell for sums that reflected the median increase were nonplussed to say the least!

- *Median values do not reveal whether capital growth has been achieved chiefly through extensive renovations or improvements.* For example, if a property is bought for $170 000 today, undergoes a $140 000 renovation and sells in 12 months for $320 000, the *apparently* staggering capital growth is actually minimal, if non-existent, when capital spent, holding costs and professional fees are accounted for.

- *Median values represent relatively short periods of time (usually three months).* Unusual conditions over a reporting period, such as a one-off local building boom or even the normal seasonal variation in the amount or price bracket of property on the market, may give the wrong impression of true long-term growth patterns. Opting for annual figures may help smooth out these factors, but, as the case study of Port Melbourne illustrates, even that's not foolproof!

- *Median values don't reflect current market conditions.* There is often a time lag between the release of median values data and the period it refers to. If market conditions change in the intervening period—and they very often do—the data may not provide reliable price information.

- *They may not cover a sufficient number of properties.* If the median value in a certain location is based on a small number of transactions, it may not be sufficiently representative of wider market conditions.

(ii) Tracking recent sales in specific streets and precincts

If median values only provide a guide to solid long-term growth areas but have their fair share of limitations, where's a beleaguered investor to turn for a bit more certainty? Don't worry, there is an answer ... but, like anything worth doing, it involves a bit of legwork and elbow grease!

Streetwise

To find the very best possible investment, you need to track sales results over two to three months for individual properties of a size, style and location similar to the ones you're interested in and can realistically afford.

Within the context of your budget, identify the sizes and styles of properties that most resemble what you will ultimately buy. For the sake of simplicity, we'll refer to these properties as 'comparables'. While this process is time and labour intensive, it's not as complex as it sounds. Depending on your circumstances you may end up with two or three options in various combinations, for example fully renovated two-bedroom cottages or partially renovated three-bedroom cottages;

one-bedroom units in a high land value area, or two-bedroom units in a slightly more moderate land value area, and so on.

Create a separate category heading for each location and property type, for example 'Two-bedroom units, Bondi'.

Inspect properties, track and record sales results for each category on a weekly basis **for two to three months before you attempt to purchase**. Be sure to find out and note down whether or not a property has undergone substantial capital improvements—as we've discussed, substantial renovations or extensions increase the purchase price but can often mask the property's real underlying growth.

Keep track of media reports on wider economic trends such as changes in interest rates or inflation that might influence supply and demand and therefore property prices.

3. SCOUR THE STREETS!

Now comes the fun part! Once you have gained a firm understanding of values for your desired area and property type, it's vital to get out and about and have a look at the characteristics of the neighbourhood you're considering buying into.

We have seen countless investors select what appears to be a high-growth, high-demand suburb but choose the wrong street or precinct, then wonder why their 'sure-fire' investment has done so poorly.

What constitutes a 'wrong' street or, more importantly, a suitable one, when you're looking to buy an investment? Primarily it comes down to aesthetic appeal and liveability. The more attractive a particular area is, and the higher its level of amenity, the more buyers will want to live there—increasing property values.

So when you're out driving, look for the following:

- *Architecturally consistent streetscapes.* Streets or precincts featuring a predominance of classic architecture with a broad appeal are more likely to experience strong long-term capital growth. It doesn't matter greatly whether the streetscape is of an older style or a more modern one, as long as it is relatively uniform and attractive. For example, concentrate on areas where renovated period homes or refurbished units or contemporary-style townhouses are the dominant property style, rather than places with a jumbled assortment of each.

  Given that local planning laws very often allow for a diversity of property styles in a given neighbourhood, it is hard to find areas that are totally uniform. But if you get to know your area properly, you'll soon be able to tell the uniform streets from the mishmashes.

- *Proximity to local amenities.* The area must also be close to essential and desirable facilities—that is, within walking or a short driving distance. These include schools, public transport, shopping areas, and leisure and entertainment options such as public parks, cafés, restaurants and cinemas.

- *Quiet street with little through-traffic.* As a general rule, residential properties on busy roads don't appreciate in capital value as quickly or consistently as those in side streets, simply because they lack the tranquillity, safety and quality of life that quieter streets can provide. Sure, a main road purchase may save you a significant amount of money on the initial purchase price, but within a short space of time the gap between its ongoing capital growth and that of its quieter neighbours will make your savings look very ordinary indeed—hampering your ability to accumulate equity and add further investments to your portfolio.

Undervalued suburbs—distinguising between a genuine 'sleeping beauty' and a 'lounge lizard'!

Knowing how property values have changed over time, and how they're performing at present, can give you an excellent indication of an area's long-term growth prospects.

However, property is like any other commodity. When a certain segment of the market becomes too expensive for purchasers, as it inevitably does when demand escalates beyond a certain level, they begin looking at more affordable options. In the case of residential property, buyers look at areas slightly further afield, commonly referred to as 'undervalued'. In certain circumstances, values in these suburbs can emerge from a relatively modest base to take their place alongside established prime areas for the long term.

Note that many investors misunderstand the true meaning of 'undervalued'—thinking that any location that is dirt cheap now is going to be worth a fortune in years to come. If that was the case, the entire property market would be performing at a similar level, every investor would be on a sure thing, and we wouldn't be writing this book!

HOW DO I SPOT ONE?

By definition, '**under**valued' means that an area has considerable investment potential that has not yet been recognised by a large number of purchasers. Specifically, the area must have the capital growth potential to outstrip wider market levels in the short to medium term, that is, three to seven years, and sustain this growth for the longer term. What does this mean in practice?

In a genuinely undervalued location, certain factors must be changing within the area itself, the suburbs immediately around it and the wider marketplace.

Undervalued pockets usually emerge during very buoyant parts of the property cycle when values are growing very strongly, finance is relatively affordable and easily obtained, and first home buyers become very active following a tangible incentive to enter the market—like the First Home Owner Grant introduced in July 2000.

Encouraged by this activity, other buyers become more active and the market as a whole experiences a surge in buyer demand. Purchasers who can no longer afford to buy into their preferred areas begin looking in neighbouring streets and suburbs.

For a suburb to qualify as genuinely undervalued, it must possess many of the same features as established prime locations—architectural uniformity and attractive streetscapes consistent with the overall neighbourhood character. It must also have a high level of amenity, or at least the potential to achieve this in a short space of time. Importantly, the existing housing stock must exhibit significant potential to add value.

When precincts have the same characteristics as established prime areas but a lower buy-in price, they often qualify as genuinely undervalued.

Kensington and Flemington in Melbourne are good examples. Located about 3 km from the CBD, with original period cottages and well serviced by schools, shops, major thoroughfares and public transport, Kensington and Flemington were for many years undervalued relative to other inner suburbs. However, in the late 1990s, rapid price growth in neighbouring suburbs encouraged purchasers to enter the area in greater numbers. As a result, Kensington's median house price rose from $128 250 in 1996 to $310 000 in 2001, while Flemington's median house price rose from $136 000 to $335 000 over the same period. (Source: Real Estate Institute of Victoria.)

Streetwise

When you are trying to identify undervalued areas, watch what first home buyers are doing. If they begin moving into and gentrifying a particular area in large numbers once prices in immediately adjoining suburbs or pockets move beyond their reach, you may well have found an undervalued area with excellent investment potential.

Knowing where to buy can save you from making big mistakes, hundreds of thousands of dollars and years of heartache. Now let's add the next step to the equation, by showing you *what* to buy—and what to avoid!

CHAPTER SEVEN
What to Buy

WHY 'ANY OLD PROPERTY' REALLY WON'T DO!

Even if you've identified and targeted the investment locations that are likely to perform best over the long term, buying the right kind of property is crucial. One of the most common mistakes investors can make is to buy into a fabulous location, but choose completely the wrong property.

Very often this mistake is based on the assumption that, because land value is the primary determinant of capital growth, the type of building is unimportant. This is not the case. Even in very high land value areas where a lack of available land and ongoing demand from buyers and tenants virtually ensures that most properties will rise substantially in value over time, the right building can increase a property's value even further. Other investors think the choice of building is unimportant because 'all buildings depreciate in value'. This is not necessarily so. In our experience, certain architectural styles have an enduring appeal and intrinsic capital value that transcend the mere 'bricks and mortar' of which they are comprised.

So what is the right kind of investment property?

Scarcer than hen's teeth ...

The number one criterion that makes an individual property—as distinct from an overall *location*—worth looking at is scarcity value. Property is like any other commodity—the rarer it is, the more people want it and are prepared to pay to secure it, increasing its value. If you find this concept hard to apply to property, think instead about fine art or antiques. Why are they so valuable? It's not just because they *look* good, it's because they are so *rare*.

There are two factors that confer true scarcity value. The first is timeless and broad-ranging architectural appeal. There are relatively few property styles that appeal to a broad range of buyers and tenants for years and years after they were actually built—so demand almost always exceeds supply, producing considerable capital growth..

Broadly speaking, ultra-contemporary buildings or those that are too far outside architectural conventions should be avoided for investment purposes. They might appeal to you as an individual at this point in time but, remember, personal tastes and emotion should not

---

Streetwise

For optimal, ongoing capital growth and rental income, stick with buildings that the majority of the population perceives to be attractive, functional and desirable, both now and in years to come. Don't equate architectural scarcity with a sub-standard level of accommodation! Your aim is to find a property which offers tenants and future buyers contemporary standards of comfort and amenity inside and retains its classic, original architectural character.

play a part when you're buying a property purely for investment purposes.

For example, in most Australian cities styles generally considered to be timeless include, but are not limited to, houses spanning the Victorian, Edwardian, Federation and post-war architectural eras, and 1920s to 1940s units in the moderne style (sometimes called Art Deco). In Brisbane, original 'Queenslanders' with their colonial influences and wide verandahs, which not only reflect the area's history but suit today's casual lifestyle, are also highly sought after.

What about reproductions?

The appeal of classic architecture has seen a proliferation of reproduction period-style houses and units in recent years. From an

> **FAQ: Should I buy a unit or a house?**
>
> You will often hear that houses are better investments than units because they have a lot of land on title. This is not necessarily so. Individual units automatically take on a proportion of the value of the land on which the whole block stands. The size of a property has little to do with its capital growth potential—a property's location and building style are far more important considerations. This is why a one- or two-bedroom unit in a high land value area (e.g. selected inner suburbs of large capital cities) can achieve higher rates of capital growth than a four-bedroom house on a large block of land in the outer suburbs or regional areas.

investment perspective, these buildings do provide tax benefits in the form of depreciation allowances.

However, because you're investing primarily for capital growth not tax purposes, and the authenticity of original buildings contributes significantly to buyer/tenant appeal and capital value, reproductions are best avoided unless they're absolutely faithful, inside and out, to original examples that dominate the local area. Apart from the inclusion of modern-day conveniences, for example, in kitchens and bathrooms, the only real difference should be that they look cleaner and brighter and may be in a better state of repair.

If you're looking at a reproduction that the builder or developer is promoting as 'Victorian-style', for example, familiarise yourself with the architectural characteristics of original properties from this era so you can make a fully informed judgement about whether what is on offer truly measures up. As you become more familiar with period architecture while doing the rounds of the property market, you will develop a keen eye for the faithful latter-day equivalent of the 'Real McCoy' as opposed to a 'near enough is good enough' example.

Streetwise

Just because a building is brand new it is not necessarily more structurally sound than an older one. New buildings can have just as many structural problems as their older counterparts.

And, just as not every reproduction period home is a sound investment prospect, so every authentic period home is not automatically a winner. Even if the property you're looking at is architecturally scarce, it's best avoided if it is poorly located or is not structurally sound relative to its age.

What about properties built in the second half of the twentieth century?

Many of them make excellent investments provided that, just as with period homes, you are *selective*. If you are looking at a house that is similar in size and style to those in the rest of the street, blends well with the overall streetscape and has been well maintained, chances are it is worthy of further investigation. If you are looking at units, concentrate on those in well-kept, low-rise blocks with one to three levels that house a relatively small number of units in the block—say, up to 20. Like houses, the block should blend in well with the surrounding streetscape even though it may have been built in more recent times.

The second key component of scarcity value is limited market supply of the building style in question. Very often, and particularly in the case of period homes, there is a limited supply of timeless property to begin with. When you add in the ongoing demand from buyers and tenants and the reluctance of owners to part with something so valuable, the number of these homes on the market is relatively small—fuelling natural capital growth.

When these properties do come on to the market, the number of interested buyers will always outweigh the actual number of similar properties available for purchase. In these situations, home-buyers and investors alike are often prepared to pay an additional premium to secure them.

The result? Intense competition drives up the ultimate sale price—adding capital value beyond the technical value of the property itself.

MUD STICKS!

Since the early 1990s the inner city areas of many major capitals have experienced an explosion of high-rise, multi-unit developments, colloquially referred to as 'MUDs'. Many have been cleverly marketed as 'superb investments', using tax-driven incentives such as stamp duty savings and building depreciation benefits, along with guaranteed rental returns. At face value these benefits, together with the appeal of buying a brand-new property, appear very attractive indeed.

We strongly advise you to exercise extreme caution when looking at buying into a MUD as an investment. Why?

First, MUDs, by their very nature, often lack the scarcity value necessary for strong, consistent capital growth. In Melbourne and Sydney and Brisbane particularly, thousands of lookalike units in nondescript blocks have already sprung up, with thousands more planned. As more towers go up, so does the likelihood that those built a few years earlier will be considered architecturally obsolete or run of the mill—reducing demand and capital growth.

Given that town planning restrictions in most *suburbs* would preclude high-rise developments and that virtually all the land in inner suburban locations is accounted for, developers are having to build their projects on formerly commercial and industrial land that they can acquire relatively inexpensively in and immediately around central business districts.

Contrary to what the developers may tell you it's probable that, unless or until buyer demand proves consistent in the longer term, the proliferation of inner city high-rise units will lead to an oversupply. Capital growth is likely to remain low, stagnate or even go backwards. And because there are so many units within and across each tower, there will be multiple units for sale and lease at any given time—further decreasing their scarcity value and investment potential.

The high asking price, relative to their true technical value, is the second factor compromising the potential of MUDs as an investment option. Developers **always** attach a premium to the asking price of brand-new property. They take considerable risks in proceeding with projects and in most cases borrow huge amounts of money to do so, it is completely appropriate that they make a fair and reasonable profit.

The problem is that you, the end user, end up paying for their profit, via an over-inflated purchase price. If you are going to live in a unit as a home and you are buying principally for lifestyle reasons, this may not be as much of an issue. But as an **investor**, you are buying for *financial* reasons. You must question the logic of paying tens of thousands of dollars more than a property is really worth, especially when it has no track record of capital growth, to justify the high purchase price. Not to mention the thousands more you'll pay in interest over the years as a result of borrowing more than you need to! Why would you want to line a developer's or lender's pocket when you should be lining your own?

> **Numerous investors Australia-wide have overpaid for new units and resold them two to five years later for less than they paid. And who wants to lose money on an investment?**

The initial premium attached to these units means their true market value is only established upon first and second resale.

If you are considering buying into a MUD, it is essential to investigate the original sale price and resale values of properties in directly comparable blocks to ascertain the long-term capital growth prospects.

'But what about all those tax benefits and rental guarantees?' you ask. 'Surely they are worthwhile?' At face value, yes. What investor wouldn't want stamp duty savings and guaranteed rental income? The trouble is that, just like the developer's profit, tax and rental benefits are often factored into the asking price. You don't get them for free!

Let's look at this issue more closely. Stamp duty is payable on the total transfer value of a property at the time of purchase. When you buy a property off the plan, you only have to pay stamp duty on the land component. The higher the value of the building in relation to the value of the land component, the greater your stamp duty savings. However, **the lower the land value, the lower your likely long-term capital growth potential**—a consideration that should *far* outweigh any short-term tax savings.

> **FAQ: Which is best—new or established property?**
>
> The real question here is not so much 'new or established' but 'scarce or plentiful.' New property tends to accumulate in areas where there is plenty of land available at a reasonable cost for development (e.g. outer suburbs) or scope to build upward (e.g. inner-city). Either way, the net result is an abundance of property for sale and rent and little of the scarcity value needed for strong capital growth.

Streetwise

To achieve the required capital growth the value of the land component, whether or not it forms a part of your direct ownership should account for upwards of 65–70% of the value of the property.

Developers often fund rental guarantees by obtaining part of the rental amount from tenants and subsidising the remainder. And where do they get the money to do that? From the premium you have paid on the purchase price! Furthermore, rental guarantees are finite. If, at the expiration of the guarantee period, the guaranteed rent is substantially higher than the true market rent, as influenced by supply and demand, and you've based your costings on the guaranteed rent, you could well be in hot water. You may be unable to meet your loan repayments and, at worst, be forced to sell, possibly at a loss.

You may also have trouble keeping your tenants once they realise their rent was subsidised by a rental guarantee and it is about to rise. This is particularly likely once the gloss wears off the apartment and it starts to look a little tired. They will either ask you to reduce the rent or look for a newer, shinier apartment to justify the extra rent. Either way, you lose out.

Investing in MUDs carries several other difficulties. Many of these complexes have elevators, gymnasiums and other elaborate extras. These facilities cost a lot to maintain, resulting in high body corporate fees. Ask yourself if these ongoing costs would be better spent on reducing debt or saving towards a further investment.

The MUD sector is beset by numerous examples of buildings with poor construction and orientation, creating insufficient acoustic privacy, especially between adjoining units, and unremarkable, even undesirable, views. This can affect your tenants' quality of life and result in a high tenancy turnover, additional wear and tear and long or frequent vacancy periods.

So are any inner city units worth investing in?

Yes—there are always exceptions. There are buildings that are pre-existing landmarks with unique characteristics, both in location and architectural terms. They have:

- a location offering total convenience *and* a relatively quiet lifestyle;
- uninterrupted views that cannot be built out;
- a wide and useable balcony;
- good acoustic privacy;
- an exceptional standard of fittings and finishes;
- provision for individually allocated car parking; and
- minimal competition from other high-rise towers in the immediate vicinity.

Buildings or individual units that fulfil all these criteria are relatively hard to find. As you'd expect, they also tend to be in the middle to upper price brackets. Once you get to this price level, think hard about the wisdom of tying up so much capital in a single investment. Are you making the best use of your money?

What about new properties that aren't MUDs?

Provided a new property is well located and reasonably priced, with all the other attributes that confer scarcity value, capital growth and rental income potential, the physical age of the property per se is not a detriment to its investment viability. You just need to consider carefully whether long-term benefits, including strong capital growth, will outlive the short-term tax savings and rental guarantees, and the marketing hype that goes with them.

Units vs houses—the great inferiority complex

One of the most common property investment myths is that units or apartments make an inferior investment because they have only a small parcel of land on title, or none at all. **This is simply *not* the case!**

Many investors don't realise that because the whole block sits on a parcel of land, each unit has a notional share of the block's land value. So, while any land on a unit's individual title such as a small yard or courtyard can certainly increase its value, it is not essential.

In fact, in the case of established units, the lion's share of the value can be attributed to the notional land component, particularly in inner suburban areas where land values are high. Think about it. Even in units that occupy the middle to upper price ranges, the likelihood that the internal walls, windows, floor coverings, fixtures and fittings are worth as much as the sale price is pretty small. So, unless the unit is new and you are paying the developer's premium, most of the price can be attributed to the land component.

Many investors who buy units do so because they have a relatively modest budget, and/or because they don't want to worry about maintenance. Provided you are selective, this is a perfectly viable and effective investment choice. In fact, given the rate at which property values grow in some of our major capital cities, buying a moderately priced unit is often the only way an individual private investor can make a start in the property market.

Before the advent of strata titling, many blocks of units were owned on one title, making it very difficult for investors with modest purchasing power to enter the prime residential market. Only when these blocks were subdivided for individual ownership did units become a realistic option for these investors. While not all these units turned out to be prime investments in themselves, they very often provided an ideal springboard for first-time investors, who went on to acquire and control multi-million dollar property portfolios. In fact, despite rising prices, today's investors may well find it easier to enter the residential property market than investors in years gone by.

Yet many people who would ordinarily consider buying a first-class unit are made to feel as though they are making a second-rate investment, purely because it's smaller than a house and lacks land on title.

Streetwise

Don't be misled! You will obtain far better investment results by buying a small unit in a prime location rather than a large house in an outlying area.

If you want to buy in an area where property values are high, for example Sydney or Melbourne's inner suburbs, and a one-bedroom unit is all you can afford, that's fine. Choose your investment property for its scarcity value and high underlying demand.

Interestingly, this misinformation often comes from those with a vested interest in selling house and land packages!

HOW DO I SELECT THE RIGHT UNIT?

Choose an appealing street in a suburb with superior, proven long-term capital growth. The street you choose should be of a reasonably consistent architectural style and representative of the most sought-after parts of the suburb.

Choose a block with an attractive presentation and architectural style that is similar to or compatible with the street's overall style. The greater the architectural similarity between your block and the rest of the housing in the street the better. However, if you're looking at an attractive, well-maintained 1950s to 1990s block in an area with a predominance of period-style houses from the 1880s to the 1940s, it may still be worth further investigation, especially if it blends in with the streetscape.

Buy in blocks with a limited number of units. The fewer residents there are in a block, the quieter and more desirable buyers and tenants perceive it to be. This is why small, select developments of up to 20 units often perform better in capital growth and rental terms than larger ones.

Maintenance

Now you know how to identify properties with true scarcity value, the next issue you need to consider is maintenance and improvements. Contrary to popular belief, quality investment property does not require frequent or major upgrades—either cosmetic or structural—to underpin the rental and capital value. Sheer demand for accommodation in the area, along with the scarcity of the building style, should do the work for you.

Even if a property satisfies the scarcity factor and appears to be a good investment at face value, the novelty will soon wear off if you are continually dipping into your rental or other income to fund major maintenance or improvements.

You may be wondering about tenants' expectations when it comes to standards of accommodation. Do they expect granite bench tops and state-of-the-art appliances? Will your rental income suffer if your property is not finished to this high standard?

Many tenants do expect a good standard of accommodation and this is perfectly appropriate, given that no one wants to live in substandard conditions. And, since their rental income is helping fund your investment, it makes sense to maximise rent levels by offering tenants an attractive, functional environment.

But if you take this logic too far, you may be setting yourself up for unnecessary problems. Expensive ultra-modern fittings and fixtures often require frequent and considerable maintenance. Ironically, the more cutting edge they are, the more quickly they'll date and need upgrading or replacing. This means you will have to charge a premium rent to help recoup the extra costs. In turn, this can narrow the pool of potential tenants, increasing the likelihood of vacancies.

There is a way you can provide a good standard of accommodation for tenants and obtain a solid, sustainable rental return. Always choose property that is, or can be, inexpensively improved to a good, clean and eminently livable—as distinct from luxurious—standard. This means it should have:

- functional, built-in heating or cooling;
- fresh paintwork;
- clean, functional and relatively modern-looking kitchen and bathroom;
- clean carpet, polished floorboards or floor tiles; and
- if at all possible, built-in wardrobes and adequate storage—remember, not all tenants are fresh out of home and they may have as many possessions as you do.

Far from choosing or creating an overly elaborate rental property, other investors go to the opposite extreme and buy property in need of fundamental structural improvements such as restumping, rewiring or curing rising damp. They reason that if they opt for a run-down property, they're likely to save a bundle on the purchase price because no one else will want the headache that goes hand in hand with a major renovation. They then spend thousands of dollars doing it up, thinking this will increase the capital value over and above the actual cost of the improvements. And they're usually disappointed.

While a modest level of work must be carried out on any property from time to time as maintenance, structural improvements are largely invisible and do not increase the capital value of property. Would *you* get all excited over, and pay a premium for, new stumps or wiring, a cured damp course or termite problem?

There is no doubt that structural works are essential to the long-term integrity of the building and to the comfort, health and safety of the occupants. However if, as an investor, the property you are considering requires restumping, rewiring or the curing of rising damp, you need to ask yourself whether the tens of thousands of dollars it will cost you to attend to these problems is money well spent. Because these 'invisible' improvements do not translate to added capital value and diminish the return on the investment, it's best to disregard the property in question altogether and locate an alternative property that is structurally sound, for its age or on which this structural work has already been done by previous owners.

With very few exceptions, it's primarily visible cosmetic and functional improvements such as repainting, recarpeting, adding storage facilities, and re-tiling that influence the property's appeal to buyers and tenants and therefore add to its capital value.

The finer points of property selection

PARKING

Even though public transport is readily available in many prime residential investment areas, the fact is that Australia is a car-loving nation and many of us still prefer to drive to get around. As we buy more and more cars the inner suburbs of major capital cities—built in the days when cars were scarce—are becoming increasingly congested.

If you are buying a period home in an established area, off-street parking is desirable though not essential. Most of these homes and streets pre-date the time when cars became readily available and affordable for the majority of the population, so parking on the street has always been considered reasonably acceptable. If you find a home of this kind and it has off-street parking, or sufficient land to create it, so much the better.

The 'adding value' life cycle of an investment property

Since quality investment property should be held for the long term, the following is a guide to the improvements that may be needed at various stages to maintain capital and rental value.

Year one

Generally speaking, avoid spending money on a property in the first year of ownership. However, from time to time, a property with exceptional scarcity value in a high-quality location may justify some initial expenditure. This could be appropriate if the 'as purchased' condition of the property will have a detrimental effect on its rental value, and if the intended long-term hold will fully justify the cost of initial moderate cosmetic improvements. If that's the case, don't be overly concerned about spending a few thousand dollars in the first year.

Years two to four

From time to time you'll need to undertake maintenance and minor improvements. The best time to do this is in between tenancies, when the property is vacant. These improvements will typically include:

- repainting to reflect prevailing fashions (nothing too bold; it won't have broad market appeal);
- re-carpeting or swapping soiled carpet for polished floorboards;
- adding inexpensive heating or cooling;
- replacing lino or worn tiles in wet areas;

- ensuring fences are in good repair;
- improving and maintaining basic security to comply with relevant legislation;
- providing extra storage space;
- replacing an old sink or resurfacing the bath; and
- other basic improvements that are comparatively inexpensive in relation to the capital growth being achieved through the forces of supply and demand.

Years five to eight

At around Year 5 you may like to consider a moderate upgrade of the kitchen and bathroom if they haven't been updated in the last ten to 15 years. This could include retiling, replacing the cupboard fronts and bench tops and adding some extra built-in storage if there isn't enough. As time goes on, capital values will increase and easily justify this level of improvement. Avoid big extensions, marble, granite, state-of-the-art décor, fancy dishwashers or insinkerators! Confine your improvements to mid-range works within the existing shell.

Beyond year eight

Assuming you hold the property long term, you'll repeat some of these steps from time to time—usually those described in Years 2 to 4.

At some point all buildings require a degree of maintenance. Around the 8- to 10-year mark, it's a good idea to have a professional builder assess what, if any, structural works are required, when they should be carried out and how much they are likely to cost in order to maintain the value of the building.

If you are looking at a contemporary house or a unit, then off-street parking is more important, because these properties post-date the arrival of the motor car and buyers and tenants more often expect it as a standard inclusion. In these cases, the presence of off-street parking (especially if it's on title) can add tens of thousands of dollars to the capital value.

FLOOR PLANS

When assessing a property for investment purposes, the layout of rooms should be conventional and logical rather than too individual or quirky. The property must appeal to the vast majority of the rental market and, for that matter, the owner-occupier market, just in case you ever need to sell.

So the more conventional it is, the greater the pool of prospective tenants and buyers will be.

ORIENTATION

Houses

The orientation, or direction in which a house faces, exerts an influence on its appeal and therefore its capital and rental value. A north–south orientation is the most desirable, since it maximises natural light year round without subjecting the occupants to harsh western sun in the summer months. Optimal orientation is especially important in the southern states where it can make cold, dark winters more bearable. Having said this, don't automatically dismiss a property with an east–west orientation if it meets other important selection criteria.

case study

Keeping it 'all in the family'!

Longstanding clients Tom, an executive manager, and Michelle, a teacher, have been investing in property for the last ten years. They bought their home in 1990 and, after some serious debt reduction, they embarked on their first investment property purchase two years later.

In 1992, Tom and Michelle bought their first investment property, a two bedroom 1940s unit with a lock-up garage for which they paid $130 000. By 1995 the unit was worth $180 000 and Tom and Michelle decided that the excellent capital growth on their home and the investment property justified the purchase of a second investment. This time they secured a two-bedroom Victorian terrace house for $220 000. The growing value of their first two investments plus further debt reduction on their home facilitated the purchase of their third investment in 1998, a freestanding two-bedroom Edwardian house for $301 000.

In the meantime their son David finished his accounting degree and found a job, but opted to stay at home rather than flat with friends. As a budding accountant and keen observer of his parents' investment activities, David was not going to be outdone! He wanted in on the act too, but didn't have the cash reserves or equity in another asset he needed to make a start.

Having experienced the benefits of sound investing for themselves, Tom and Michelle were all too aware of how time on your side can be an investor's greatest ally, and were keen to give David a head start. They decided to make some of the equity in the family home available to help

▶

David buy his very first investment. David settled on a 1950s one-bedroom unit with off-street parking for $120 000 in 1997.

Between the three of them Tom, Michelle and David now control a substantial investment portfolio that they are likely to add to from time to time.

Have a look at just how well their investments have performed so far:

Tom and Michelle

1940s unit bought in 1992 for $130 000 now worth $380 000—capital growth of $250 000.

1890s Victorian Terrace bought in 1995 for $220 000 now worth $390 000—capital growth of $170 000.

1900s Edwardian House bought in 1998 for $301 000 now worth $450 000—capital growth of $149 000.

Total equity in their investment properties built over 10 years: $569 000.

David

1950s unit bought in 1997 for $120 000 now worth $220 000—capital growth of $100 000.

Tom, Michelle and David's story is a classic example of how parents can help to educate their children on the importance of creating financial security early in life. Whilst not all parents will have the financial resources to release equity for their children's use, it's primarily the example Tom and Michelle set for David by encouraging him to observe the family's investment strategy that kindled his desire and interest in investing—and that is one of the greatest legacies we can leave our children!

case study

Units

When it comes to units, correct orientation that maximises natural light and provides a pleasant outlook is critically important, because most of them don't offer the same capacity for outdoor living as houses.

Wherever possible, choose units that are optimally positioned in the block—for example, on the first floor or at the front of the building—although, depending on the individual building, there are many other equally acceptable positions. Try to avoid units that are immediately adjacent to parking spaces or utility areas such as shared laundries and rubbish bin corrals. They may be cheaper, but that's because they are less desirable to buyers and tenants. And remember: property that is cheap today will probably be cheap tomorrow—this is not the reason you're investing.

Is vacant land a good investment?

Time and again we hear tales of woe from investors who bought a block of land intending to build their dream home on it one day, and to hold it in the meantime to maximise capital growth.

While some blocks of vacant land may be well located for capital growth purposes—for example, in sought-after inner suburban pockets or prime beachfront areas—they do not produce an income. This prevents you from claiming holding costs as tax deductions. For this reason, we don't recommend vacant land as a property investment strategy.

If you still have your heart set on buying vacant land and building on it in the long term—here we go again, emotions and lifestyle considerations creeping into the midst of a financial decision!—remember that what you want now may not be what you want in ten or 15 years' time. Life's twists and turns can steer us in unexpected directions, prompting a change of heart.

Too many eggs, not enough baskets—the importance of diversification

When it comes to property, you really can have too much of a good thing! While it is vital to choose investment property in a prime location and with a timeless architectural style, it is equally important that you resist the urge to stick rigidly to one location or property type just because you become familiar with it.

Most major cities have a variety of property styles and not all properties grow in value at the same rate or at the same time in the wider property cycle. Just like any other form of investment, it is important to spread your risk by diversifying your property holdings. Choose the very best from a variety of styles, price ranges and locations to help ensure that your investments benefit from seasonal and cyclical variations in capital growth and rental supply/demand, and withstand the impact of external influences such as inflation, interest rates, tax reform, economic volatility and changes to surrounding infrastructure.

This way, your property portfolio will be the safety net that underpins and cushions you through economic ups and downs—not the highwire you fall off!

> **FAQ: Is vacant land a good investment?**
>
> In most cases, no. Most vacant land is located in outer suburban or rural areas, where there is insufficient demand relative to supply to

generate strong capital growth. Furthermore, vacant land does not generate rental income or attract income-related tax concessions—making it harder to meet holding costs, such as municipal rates and loan repayments.

A far better option would be to purchase a top-quality house or unit in a prime location, just as we have recommended for other investors. This way, you can reap the benefits of capital growth, rental income and tax savings, *then* make a lifestyle decision when your timeline is more realistic.

CHAPTER EIGHT
Organising Finance

LOOKING AFTER *YOUR* BOTTOM LINE

How many of you remember the days when getting a loan was a matter of donning your best gear, visiting the local bank manager to prove your credentials and hoping for the best? If the loan was approved it would most likely be a standard principal and interest loan, with the one variable interest rate, taken out over a 25- or 30-year period. You would then pay off the minimum amount each month, eagerly awaiting each statement to see whether the debt was decreasing. If interest rates went up, you dug deeper into your pockets and paid more. If they went down, you thanked your lucky stars and used the extra money to buy a treat for the kids, maybe go on a holiday or repaint the house. Years later you made that momentous visit to the bank to make the final payment and collect your cleared title—debt free at last!

This scenario began to change considerably when the government progressively deregulated the banking industry in the mid-1980s. The number and nature of players in the mortgage market increased significantly, with everyone from fund managers and credit unions to insurance companies and mortgage originators getting in on the act, understandably keen to establish their brand and build a share of a hitherto restricted market. And somewhere in among all this the banks, Australia's traditional lenders, had to hold their own.

No longer could lenders—and the major banks in particular—enjoy an almost god-like status in the eyes of consumers! To maximise their prospects of reasonable market share in this newly competitive arena, they had to become much more creative and flexible in the products and benefits they offered. Down came interest charges as each lender sought to obtain an edge over the others. Out came strange and exotic creatures called tailored loan packages, with all manner of value-added features such as four-way splits—principal/interest/fixed/variable—offset accounts and redraw facilities, ostensibly designed to suit the needs of individual borrowers and save them time and money.

Today, consumers are encouraged to apply for loans in all kinds of ways—over the phone, with roving lenders in the comfort of their own home, even over the Internet. Borrowers are rewarded for taking out particular loans through honeymoon periods with discounted interest rates, gifts, incentives and points programs. To promote all these options there is an equally dizzying array of glossy brochures, interactive websites and feel-good media advertising.

When confronted with such a complex web of providers, products and services, small wonder so many consumers find applying for a loan one of the most labour-intensive and confusing aspects of purchasing investment property. In fact, the complexity of today's lending market is such that many people ask someone else to do the searching for them. Rather than approaching lending institutions directly, they appoint a mortgage originator or broker to source products and companies on their behalf and recommend the most suitable package for their needs.

This brave new world of flexibility and choice has benefits *and* pitfalls for property investors. On the one hand, interest rates for loans have declined markedly as lenders cut their margins in the face of increased competition. The fact that this coincides with a period in which Australia's official interest rates have also been low is a further bonus for investors. Interest rates for investment property loans, charged at a premium rate before deregulation, are now identical to those for home loans. The advent of value-added extras such as flexible repayments and offset facilities has enabled investors to reduce the amount of interest they pay and channel the savings into paying off the principal, thereby building equity more quickly for future use. And because loyalty to a particular lender is far less important than it used to be, investors can review their loans periodically and shop around for alternatives if they are not happy.

On the other hand, choosing the wrong type of loan—structure, interest rate, fees, penalties—could see you channelling more funds than necessary into paying for the privilege of having the loan, and less into building up equity or undertaking necessary maintenance and improvement, not to mention being saddled with a range of extras you're paying for but do not really need.

Thorough research and a healthy dose of pragmatism are essential when choosing a finance provider and loan package. We are not mortgage specialists and can't tell you which lender you should choose or the kind of loan that will work best for your individual needs. We can, however, help point you in the right direction and build your overall knowledge. We will look at the basic steps, issues and principles involved in finding and structuring loans, specifically as they relate to investment property.

Getting Started

Depending on your personal and financial circumstances, you can raise the finance to purchase an investment property in one of two ways.

1. If you don't have substantial equity in another asset you can borrow up to 90 per cent of the value of the investment property, depending on your financial circumstances and the lender's policies. Note that you'll need to pay mortgage insurance if you're borrowing over 80 per cent of the property's value.

This means you will need to raise cash to fund the deposit and mortgage insurance, as well as the following purchasing costs:

- loan application fee;
- stamp duty on the land transfer and mortgage;
- conveyancing;
- registration of transfer;
- title registration;
- adjustments to any council and water rates paid for in advance by the vendor; and
- body corporate fees (if you're buying a unit).

2. If you already own, or are paying off, a home you live in, you can leverage off the accumulated equity, known as 'borrowing against your home'. This equity comes from three sources: the initial deposit amount; any principal you've paid back; and any capital growth the home has achieved.

Using the equity in your home has two key benefits.

Firstly, you may be able to borrow up to 100 per cent of the value of the investment property, plus costs—again, depending on your financial circumstances and the lender's policies. You may still need to pay mortgage insurance at this level.

The second benefit is that you don't need to own your home outright or sell it to access equity to purchase the investment. This means you can acquire growth and income-producing assets much more quickly.

Because most Australians who purchase investment property already have a home, they use leverage, which can be something of a mysterious concept to the uninitiated. Basically, leverage enables you to effectively 're-borrow' part of the equity in your home to help purchase an investment property. These borrowings become a small part of a loan that you pay back at the applicable rate, along with any other funds you've borrowed to purchase the investment property.

Many Australians shy away from leveraging against their home because they dislike the idea of tapping into what they consider to be their main source of security—particularly if they have spent years ploughing in all that equity in the first place through active debt reduction!

If this is how you think, consider the following.

- Even if you use the equity in your home, the investment property remains the primary source of collateral because lenders will generally fund around 90 to 95 per cent of value secured against the investment property itself. This means that you will not, in

reality, be 'putting up your home'. You will only need to access enough equity in your home to make up the difference between what you can borrow on the investment property and the purchase price plus costs and mortgage insurance.
- Even though you will once again have a large mortgage, a wisely chosen investment property will provide enough compounding capital growth to outstrip the cost of servicing the debt. As an investor it's vital to focus on what you will own, not what you currently owe.

It may help here to distinguish between productive and non-productive debt. *Productive debt* is debt you incur to purchase assets that will grow in capital value and help contribute to your financial security, such as property or shares. The income from rent or dividends helps you meet the loan repayments.

Non-productive debt is debt you incur to buy 'consumable' items that don't increase in value or provide an income, such as cars, holidays and clothes. It usually incurs higher interest rates than productive debt because the finance is obtained through credit cards or unsecured personal loans. This can create a cycle that's hard to break—eroding your financial security.

By understanding the difference between productive and non-productive debt, you will be able to look more objectively at the idea of using the equity in your home to purchase investment property.

Remember why you're investing—it's to make money through capital growth. All the debt does is help you get there.

Knowing your limit

You may wonder why we have placed this chapter ahead of the one on actually searching for a property.

Unless you are buying a property that is subject to a short cooling-off period—giving you the option of pulling out of the contract—buying subject to finance may be inappropriate. This is especially the case when it comes to auctions, when the sale is unconditional. Cooling-off periods only apply to private sales, and even then only in some states and for some properties. Check with your local real estate institute or your solicitor about whether, and to what extent, cooling-off periods apply in your state or territory.

Buying subject to finance is also based on a common, but often incorrect, myth: If you have a deposit and a relatively secure job, you will be able to borrow as much as you like. This is not the case. A reasonable deposit, usually 10 per cent of the purchase price, is generally required for a binding exchange of contracts. However, it's your income, equity and any other debts that ultimately establish how

---

Streetwise

Most importantly from a property investment perspective, buying subject to finance approval diminishes your bargaining power. If the vendor is not assured of your ability to go through with the purchase, they may be less inclined to negotiate on their proposed sale price and conditions. This is not a position you want to be in as an investor, when buying at the right price is almost as important as buying the right kind of asset.

---

much you can borrow and, in turn, the type of asset you will end up buying.

For these reasons, it is advisable to apply for pre-approved finance. As the name implies, you approach lenders and apply for a loan before embarking on the search and selection process. Provided you satisfy their screening process, the lender will offer pre-approval to a maximum notional amount. You can then focus your search on those locations and properties you can realistically afford. Once you have found a property at or below this limit and signed the contract, the lender then draws up the loan documentation based on the actual valuation.

Apart from reducing your risk, pre-approval helps you come to grips early on with what you can and can't afford—if you've been thinking of purchasing a three-bedroom property in a certain area but find your budget is more suited to a unit, far better you know this now than after you sign a contract.

Pre-approval also helps you to refine your search criteria so you don't waste time finding and searching for unsuitable properties. If you're buying at auction, bid with an exact upper limit in mind and withdraw if the bidding goes over that limit. This will minimise your chances of committing to a loan you can't afford.

FINDING A LENDER

Of course, to gain pre-approval you need to find a lender. So how do you find a good one? One way is to ask your family, friends and trusted colleagues which lenders they use, and what their experiences have been.

You could also contact a number of organisations across the spectrum of lenders—major national banks; smaller state-based banks; credit unions; banking divisions of fund management and insurance companies; and local and national mortgage brokers or originators. This will give you a good representative sample of business and customer service philosophies—after all, if you're going to borrow many thousands of dollars from an organisation, it's important to feel comfortable with them. If they are a lesser known company or one not traditionally associated with lending, ask about their bona fides: how long they've been operating, how they are structured and who their directors are.

Rather than asking for information on their pre-existing loan packages and trying to see if or where you fit in, ask the lender what they can offer you as a property investor. Putting the onus on *them* to prove that they are worthy of your business will place you in a position of power. Remember, their profits come from the interest on your loan, so they need you just as much as you need them.

HOW MUCH CAN YOU BORROW?

Once you have found a suitable lender and want to apply for pre-approval, you will need to assemble a raft of information on your personal and financial background to prove to them that you are a good risk and help them calculate how much you can borrow.

They will want to see evidence of identification; employment; wage or salary; debts, for example car loan, credit card, home loan; assets, for example home, car, superannuation, shares, managed funds; savings record; insurances and living expenses. As you are applying to borrow for an investment property, your likely rental income will also be

Organising Finance

considered. In most cases this will increase the amount you can notionally borrow.

But the conditions don't stop here. To protect themselves against the possibility of your defaulting on the loan, lenders also calculate your notional living expenses, taking into account your household structure. For example, a family of two adults and three children might reasonably be expected to have higher living expenses than a couple or a single person. This method has replaced the 30 per cent rule whereby lenders capped borrowings at 30 per cent of a purchaser's gross income, regardless of their household/family structure and living expenses.

To work out your notional living expenses, lenders add your after-tax wage or salary to your expected rental income, net of holding costs. They then factor in an allowance for living expenses, as determined by your household structure.

Your total living expenses and loan repayments must be less than your total net income, including the net rent from your investment property.

Lenders also factor in prevailing interest rates—that is, cash rates set by the Reserve Bank, and commercial rates set by your lender. They also factor in a contingency for future interest rate rises. Because interest on property loans is usually calculated daily, even a 0.5 per cent rise in interest rates can mean a significant rise in your repayments and therefore a decrease in what you can afford to borrow.

Once they have worked out what you can notionally borrow, lenders install two more self-protection mechanisms. First, most will limit your borrowings to 80 per cent of a property's assessed value. However, they will often lend up to 90 per cent of the valuation provided you take out mortgage insurance. Even though you have to pay the premium, mortgage insurance protects the lender in the event that you default on the loan. However, from the lender's perspective you are not paying for their risk, you are sharing it. If the worst happens and you default on your repayments, the costs associated with selling the asset to recover the principal—such as repairs, improvements, agents' and advertising fees—far outweigh the cost of mortgage insurance. Check with your lender about the rate of mortgage insurance that applies to your particular circumstances.

Choosing a loan package

Once you have chosen a lender and have pre-approved finance, your next task will be to navigate your way through the plethora of loan packages available to select the one that is right for you. As we have mentioned, loans these days vary enormously from the basic 25-year, principal and variable interest model through to the 'Rolls Royce' models with four-way principal/interest/fixed/variable splits, offset accounts, redraw and credit card facilities. The more sophisticated models may be right for you, or they may not. Only a detailed investigation of each one will help you make up your mind.

From a property investment perspective, several financing issues can impact on the viability of your investment.

1. PRINCIPAL OR INTEREST? A NEW ANGLE ON AN AGE-OLD DILEMMA

When you take out a property loan you are not just borrowing the cost of the property itself—the principal—but paying extra for the

The early years—funding the shortfall

One challenge many investors face during the early years of owning a property is that, when the mortgage is still large, the rental income may not be enough to cover loan repayments and running costs. Rather than increasing the rent by a considerable percentage and risk pricing yourself out of the market, you have a number of options.

- Buy a property at around the entry level for your capital city to minimise your mortgage size.

- Reduce the principal owing whenever you can, even if it's only by $100 or $200 at a time, to reduce your total interest bill.

- Make your repayments fortnightly or weekly instead of monthly; this also reduces your interest bill.

- Set up a dedicated bank account for each property to receive rental income and disburse loan repayments and other expenses. Work out the difference between your net rental income (usually 75 per cent of gross after running costs) and your loan repayments. Top up your account periodically with enough funds to cover that shortfall.

- Vary your income tax instalments by lodging a Section 221D form with the tax office, which will provide additional cash flow to help meet the shortfall. It also means that you receive the benefits of negative gearing in small parcels at regular intervals, rather than one large tax deduction at the end of each financial year.

privilege of being able to borrow—the interest. Most lenders offer a range of ways in which you repay the two components. You can repay a combination of principal and interest throughout the loan period, or just the interest. With the latter option, you repay the principal in a lump sum on selling the asset. Each option has definite, and different, effects on the viability of your investment.

The tax textbooks—and quite a few professionals who work from them—will always advise in favour of interest-only loans. From a pure taxation point of view they are quite correct, because interest, not principal, is tax deductible.

However, this theory also relies on the assumption that inflation will boost your property's value sufficiently over time so that, when you eventually sell, you'll recoup enough capital to pay out the principal portion of the loan in full. And therein lies the rub! *In times of high inflation, almost any property, anywhere, will go up in value.* The trouble, as we discussed in chapter three, is that inflation-driven growth does not necessarily represent the true market-driven value of the asset. Apparent capital growth in high inflation periods may very well stop once inflation falls, as it inevitably does. This is especially the case if you haven't chosen the right kind of asset in the first place.

If the asset's growth stagnates or drops once inflation levels fall, you could be faced with two nasty problems:

- Because you haven't paid off any principal, the only equity in the property you will have is your original deposit plus any remaining capital growth. And if you don't have much equity, you won't have sufficient leverage to facilitate further acquisitions. We've heard of 'get rich slow', but this is ridiculous!

- You won't have anything to show for the higher repayments you've had to meet during the high interest rate period that goes hand in hand with high inflation. All that money will have been wasted on a non-performing asset.

Paying off principal as well as interest will minimise these possibilities and deliver the benefits of property investment much more quickly than interest payments alone. If you have chosen the asset wisely and it continues to grow in value, albeit at a slower rate, when inflation drops, the resulting tax problem probably isn't going to bother you very much. If you have chosen the asset poorly, it falls significantly in value and you are forced to sell, at least you have made some inroads into the principal component—reducing the potential for negative equity.

2. FIXED VS VARIABLE—WHICH IS BEST?

While purchasers spend hours agonising about this issue, it may surprise you to learn that neither a fixed nor a variable interest rate is inherently 'better' when it comes to the impact on your investment. Each has its advantages and disadvantages, depending on movements in official interest rates—and one thing's for sure, interest rates *will* move during the life of your loan.

In a *rising* interest rate environment, *fixed rates* can save you unnecessary expenditure and create greater certainty by locking in lower interest repayments for a long period of time. If the lender allows it, you can channel the savings into paying off more of the principal component. Bear in mind, however, that some fixed rate loans cap the amount of additional repayments you can make or prevent you from making them altogether, which can be somewhat of a disincentive if you are trying to build up equity quickly. So if you are considering a fixed rate loan, try to opt for one that allows additional principal repayments with few strings attached.

If you choose a fixed rate and official interest rates go down, you'll be stuck paying more interest than necessary for the remainder of the fixed interest period. Lenders may also charge a hefty fee for early termination of the fixed period.

Variable rates link your loan closely to changes in the official cash rate set by the Reserve Bank. If official rates go down you can enjoy some breathing space in the form of lower repayments or, preferably, keep your repayments at the same level and channel more into the principal component. But if rates rise you'll be first in line for an *involuntary* repayment increase.

This is why, in recent years, lenders have offered borrowers a combination of fixed and variable interest, with the ability to nominate what proportion of the loan will be devoted to each type of interest. You can usually adjust these proportions in accordance with changing market conditions. Regardless of which option you choose, it's important not to become too hung up over every interest rate movement—why worry about your loan when you could be thinking about your growing equity?

Ultimately, choosing the type or types of interest for your loan comes down to research and your personal circumstances. The most important thing is to set your initial borrowings at a sensible level to help keep your repayments sustainable and your sleep sound at night.

3. ADDITIONAL LOAN FEATURES—DO THEY MAKE MUCH DIFFERENCE?

After you have sorted out the two key loan structuring issues, you then have to make sense of all the extras on offer. Many of these facilities are offered with the ostensible purpose of making it easier for you to manage your loan on a day-to-day basis and save money over the long term into the bargain. So you will need to look at what is on offer from two perspectives—what suits your individual needs and preferences, and what will help support the viability of your investment. We can't help you with the first one, but here are our thoughts on the second.

Mortgage offset facilities

We're sure you've read all those glossy brochures that extol the virtues of special loans that come with a credit card and substantial savings on your interest bill! And yes, they may be worth considering provided you know how the offset facility works, you don't abuse the privilege, and it's not costing you a fortune in fees.

In case you don't know, mortgage offset facilities work like this: when the lender draws down the loan, they link it to a nominated bank account. Your salary or wage is paid into that account and you pay all your day-to-day expenses with a credit card, which you pay off in full each month. This works by taking advantage of the card's interest-free period. The idea is that your money stays in the account until you transfer it to your credit card on the due date, offsetting the amount of principal owing on your mortgage and therefore reducing the interest you pay. For example, if you have a mortgage of $150 000 and a 100 per cent mortgage offset on an account in which you have $3000, you only pay interest on $147 000.

From a property investment viewpoint, offset facilities can be an excellent way of helping your property pay its way more quickly. Every dollar you save on interest gives you the opportunity to put more money towards repaying the principal component—building up your equity and increasing your net worth.

But beware of the potential pitfalls. The trade-off for saving interest on your loan is that you don't earn any interest on the account itself, not that most standard accounts earn much interest anyway. Offset facilities also usually attract a maintenance fee which, while modest in itself, adds to the cost of servicing the loan. Furthermore, not all these facilities offer the full 100 per cent offset; check with the lender before you commit. Finally, if you don't pay off the credit card debt in full each month you will be faced with a big interest bill at credit card rates (ouch!), as well as the interest on the property loan itself. But if you think you can maintain the discipline, offset facilities may be a good way to go.

Redraw facility for surplus loan repayments

Making more than the minimum repayment can be an excellent way to build up equity in your property and discharge your loan sooner, provided your lender or accountant is supportive. However, many lenders offer a 'redraw' facility that allows you to withdraw these additional repayments for lifestyle or financial purposes. Minimum and maximum withdrawal thresholds usually apply.

While it is comforting to know you can access the equity in your property if you really need to, think twice before using redraw facilities for non-income-producing purposes such as a car, a holiday or a boat. This negates the reason for making additional repayments in the first place, and lengthens the time it takes to build up equity. Furthermore, the interest you'll pay on the redrawn money for these consumer items will not be tax deductible.

And remember, redraw facilities, like offset facilities, usually attract a fee each time you use them. Most lenders also place a lower or upper limit on how much you can redraw. Speak to your accountant or financial adviser about other ways to compile a store of easily accessible funds for lifestyle purposes.

Lines of credit

Lines of credit operate like an extended redraw facility. Subject to the lender's criteria, you can draw up to 80 per cent of a property's valuation less any outstanding debt. You repay as little or as much principal as you like; only the interest, fees and charges are mandatory.

Many lenders promote these loans as a boon for people who encounter relatively large expenses at certain times in their lives, such as when educating children. These kinds of loans can be useful when you need a deposit for your next investment, or to add to your share portfolio. However, just like redraw facilities, the more you dip into the equity in the property the longer it will take to build up substantial net worth.

Honeymoon rates

Many loans come with a seemingly irresistible sweetener—a discounted interest rate for the first year, colloquially known as a honeymoon rate. This can be especially attractive if you are investing for the first time because the repayments are less prohibitive.

By all means, take advantage of honeymoon rates. But be sure you can afford the standard interest rates that will kick in once the honeymoon is over!

Weekly or fortnightly repayments

These options were among the earliest to hit our shores when the finance industry was deregulated. They work in two ways.

1. Making loan repayments weekly or fortnightly helps you discharge the debt more quickly than the traditional monthly repayments. For example, there are 12 months in a year, but 26 fortnights, so if you pay fortnightly, you are paying the equivalent of 13 months, but in one year.
2. More significantly, daily interest calculations mean you receive the benefits of more frequent repayments almost immediately.

Together, the two have a compounding effect over time. If you keep up the original level of repayments, even as the principal is reduced, you will save interest and reduce the loan term.

Reviewing your loan—keeping your mortgage working for you

So, you've chosen a loan and begun chipping away at that seemingly irreducible balance. While you should not lose any sleep over the way your loan is structured, it is important to remember that your loan must keep working for you just as well in years to come as it does at the outset. Your lifestyle and financial needs change over time, so the loan that suits you today may not be the one that works best tomorrow.

It is vital to review all aspects of your loan periodically to ensure you can keep increasing the equity in your property as quickly as possible. Look at your loan statement. How much interest have you paid? 'Too much', you say, but don't sweat it! What inroads have you made into that all-important principal? If you have extras such as an offset facility, have they been easy to manage and what benefits have they actually delivered?

At the same time, take a close look at your lending institution. How do they treat you as a customer? Do they answer your queries promptly and courteously? Can they resolve difficulties or disputes quickly and to your satisfaction? Are they genuinely willing to work with you to help you reach your goals? Are there other lenders who could do a better job or offer a better product?

Remember, your lender may have done you the 'favour' of lending you the money to buy the property, but *you are* paying the interest, fees and charges that deliver their profit. Shop around and tell them what you have found. They might just come to the party rather quickly if they think you are about to take your business elsewhere!

PART THREE
Leaving No Stone Unturned

CHAPTER NINE
The Nuts and Bolts of Getting Your House in Order

BUILDING INSPECTIONS, CONVEYANCING, INSURANCE AND OTHER LESSER EVILS

Finding the right property and organising suitable finance can take up so much of your time and effort that it is tempting to think all you have to do now is bid at auction or negotiate and the property is as good as yours. Sorry to say, there is a bit more legwork to do before you get to that stage. Before you even think about entering into a purchase, it is important to source and contact three key professionals:

- a building inspector or architect, who will inspect the property and assess its structural integrity;
- a solicitor or conveyancer, who will advise on complex legal procedures and documentation; and
- an insurer, who will organise coverage for you and your property against unforeseen events.

Organisations who represent these professionals can provide referrals to qualified providers; check our Useful Contacts list at the back of the book.

Because inspections, conveyancing and insurance don't take much time to organise and are relatively inexpensive, many people think they are not important. They leave them till the last minute or, worse still, forget about them entirely. Do this at your peril! If you go ahead and buy a property that is structurally unsound, does not comply with planning regulations or is not covered against life's unpleasant surprises, it could be you, not the vendor, mopping up the mess.

Apart from the real estate agent—who is accountable to the vendor, not to you—and a building inspector or architect, you may well be the only person who sees the property before you purchase it.

It is important to realise that, while it is the job of inspectors, solicitors and insurers to advise you within their areas of expertise, *they are not ultimately responsible for ensuring that all is OK before you purchase. The onus rests on you!*

So, while the solicitor and insurer are working in your interests, it is wise to brief them as thoroughly as possible about the property so they can advise you from a position of strength. When you view the property, note down relevant structural features such as extensions and renovations, outbuildings (carport/garage/shed), verandahs or pergolas, driveways, chimneys, fencing and any common property such as a right of way, courtyard or nature strip. Find out whether unseen improvements such as rewiring, replumbing and restumping have been carried out. Check whether there are adequate locks on external windows and doors.

You can also give your solicitor a copy of the property brochure and floor plan, but they seldom show every feature of a property so should not be relied upon absolutely.

Building Inspections—a little foresight goes a long way

For as long as we can remember, television current affairs and lifestyle shows have been replete with horror stories about the woes of purchasers who proudly buy a property that 'looked fine to them'—only to discover rotting floorboards, dodgy roofs or termites that gleefully chomp their way through walls and floors.

The bad news is that these things could happen to you, and the resulting repair bills could cost you tens of thousands of dollars and set your asset creation plans back somewhere in the Stone Age! The good news is that they are easily avoided—by spending just a few hundred dollars on a pre-purchase structural inspection.

INSPECTION CHECKLIST

When it comes to property, seeing is only partially believing. A properly trained and qualified architect or building inspector has the key advantage of being able to find all kinds of defects that are not apparent to the layperson. A thorough structural inspection will reveal any defects and make recommendations as to what needs to be done about them. The written or verbal report should cover, but may not be limited to:

- roofing and gutters;
- wiring;
- stumps and sub-floor area;
- evidence of damp;

- evidence of pest infestation;
- plumbing and drainage;
- ventilation;
- brickwork and weatherboards;
- windows, doors and frames;
- internal joinery, e.g. in kitchen and bathroom;
- fencing;
- outbuildings; and
- impact of trees and root systems on structural integrity.

It is important to realise that building inspectors and architects are not responsible for ascertaining whether the property complies with municipal and state planning regulations—this is your responsibility. Ask your solicitor for advice.

We can't stress enough the importance of obtaining a pre-purchase structural inspection. As many as 15 to 20 per cent of properties require substantial remedial work—a figure too high to leave to chance. Remember, if you sign the contract of sale in blissful ignorance of any structural flaws, the vendor's problems will become *your* problems. Don't bury your head in the sand!

Streetwise

If the inspection report for your property uncovers serious structural problems that will cost many thousands to repair, you will need to carefully consider whether or not the purchase is viable.

This will depend to some extent on the property's other investment-related attributes. For example, if the roof needs major repairs but the property is otherwise sound and satisfies key investment criteria such as location and building style, it may be worth going ahead and asking the vendor to complete the work before settlement, or negotiating a lower purchase price and organising the repairs yourself after settlement.

However, other structural defects such as extensive damp, rotting or insect-infested stumps can be far more difficult and costly to fix. In these cases, it is probably best to quit while you are ahead and resume your search. As we discussed in chapter seven, not only will extensive repairs cost you time and money, but it is unlikely you will recoup the expenditure through increased capital value because the improvements are structural, not cosmetic.

Conveyancing—cutting through the red tape

When you buy a property you are effectively taking over the 'title', becoming its registered proprietor. This means you have the right to modify any aspect of the property's structure or appearance—within the constraints of municipal or body corporate regulations and any heritage overlays that might be in place to safeguard the character of the locality.

However, the road to this kind of freedom comes at the end of a long chain of events. The term 'conveyancing' refers to the transfer of the title from one owner to the next. In some states you have the choice of a solicitor or specialist conveyancer. However, for the purposes of simplicity in this chapter, we will use the term 'solicitor'.

Some investors choose to do their own conveyancing, thinking they will save money by not engaging a professional to undertake a relatively 'simple' process.

The trouble is that it's **not** a simple process! This is partly because of the number of parties who need to become involved—you, the vendor, your lenders, local/state authorities and, if it's a strata title unit, the body corporate, to name a few. And the complexities of property law in each state and territory make for pretty heavy going for the untrained—with no professional indemnity insurance to cushion the blow if something goes wrong.

If you are thinking of doing your own conveyancing purely to save on the cost of engaging a qualified solicitor, you might want to think again. Most professionals charge a relatively modest fee, considering what is at stake.

Other investors want to do their own conveyancing because of the extra control it affords them. Either way, as a layperson, you may be leaving yourself open to a legal minefield if you miss something important. Take our advice and engage a professional. Not only will you get service from someone who is professionally trained, you will also keep emotion out of the equation and create a business-like distance

---

Streetwise

With conveyancing, as with most other stages of the property investment process, the 'buyer beware' principle applies right from the outset. All auctions, and many private sales, are unconditional. Once you have signed the contract of sale there is no going back. So it is vital to find a qualified solicitor and have them check the contract and any related documentation before you actually purchase, rather than after the event when it's too late.

between you and the vendor. And, of course, you are now familiar with the potential perils of mixing business and emotion!

MAKING IT ALL LEGAL

Now that you have engaged an appropriate professional, you probably want to know what they will actually do when you buy the property.

The conveyancing process works somewhat differently in each state and territory, so we can't give you a complete explanation of what you will encounter. As a general guide, however, your conveyance will probably include some or all of the following steps.

1. The vendor's solicitor prepares a contract note or contract of sale expressing an intention to transfer the title from the vendor to you for an agreed amount and on a specified date. This date is known as 'settlement' and, while it is often set for 30 or 60 days after the date you sign the contract, it can be any period of time to which you and the vendor agree. You may be able to negotiate with the vendor if their proposed settlement period does not suit your requirements.

   The contract can also be amended to note special conditions stipulated by you or the vendor. For example, if you have bought a property and want to undertake cosmetic improvements to maximise its appeal to prospective tenants, you may be able to request the inclusion of a clause giving you permission to access the property before settlement, provided it is vacant.

   In some states, the vendor is also required to prepare a document, sometimes known as the vendor's statement, with information on the status of the property. As a guide, this can include:

- a copy of the title;
- a copy of the plan of subdivision;
- 'covenants' precluding certain types of usage;
- 'easements' or shared boundaries/driveways between properties;
- approval status of buildings and works;
- current municipal zoning status and any potential for reassignment;
- proposed infrastructure changes, for example, roads, freeways, carparks; and
- outgoings such as municipal rates, water, sewerage and, if relevant, body corporate fees.

2. Your solicitor will look over the contract of sale and the vendor's statement if applicable to ensure all required disclosures have been made and there is nothing that will affect your intended use of the property or ability to fulfil your legal and commercial obligations to the vendor. It is also a good idea to ask them to check the lender's loan offer document and loan contract, to ensure you understand your rights and obligations.

3. Your solicitor will request a certificate of title through the state or territory land titles office to ensure that the vendor is, in fact, the current registered proprietor, and to check whether there are any caveats—interests held over the property from a third party. In most cases the only caveat will be from the vendor's lender, known as the mortgagee, unless the vendor owns the property outright. The certificate of title will also include a plan of the property showing boundary measurements and identifying what is common and what is private property.

4. You will be asked to sign, but not date, a land transfer document, which will be finalised on settlement day and lodged along with the stamp duty payable on the value of the land transfer.
5. If you have bought a unit, your solicitor will request a body corporate certificate detailing current and proposed activities in relation to buildings and common property, including any special levies which may be struck to pay for maintenance or repairs where costs cannot be met from standard body corporate fees.
6. Your lender will ask for a range of documents to draw up the mortgage papers, including the contract of sale, vendor's statement if applicable, title search, land transfer document, insurance certificate and associated statements from municipal bodies and utilities. Your solicitor can supply these on your behalf.
7. Your lender will then forward the mortgage documents to your solicitor for your signature. These documents verify that you are the mortgagor (debtor) of the property, and ask you to confirm that you understand and agree to abide by the conditions of the loan contract and associated documents. They also include a list of the parties to whom various portions of your loan will be disbursed, such as the mortgage insurance provider, state revenue office, land titles office and lender's solicitor.
8. Part of the settlement process involves making sure that municipal and utility payments are up to date. Your solicitor will liaise with the vendor's solicitor about this, and you may have to write some additional cheques to meet your side of the bargain.
9. It is highly advisable to inspect the property again just before settlement, to check that it is in the same condition, with the same fittings and fixtures, as it was when you signed the contract. Speak

with your solicitor immediately if you notice any discrepancies beyond fair wear and tear.
10. Assuming everything is OK, your solicitor will attend settlement on your behalf as scheduled. The bank's solicitors will collect the title and land transfer document. They will then arrange payment of stamp duty and register the transfer at the land titles office. Your solicitor should contact you when settlement has gone through.

At this point, you are entitled to yell loudly and jump for joy. A bottle of your favourite drop wouldn't go astray either!

Insurance—expect the best but prepare for the worst

Under-insuring is one of the most common—yet easily avoidable—oversights of property ownership. Most investors realise they need building and/or contents insurance to recoup any structural losses due to unforeseen events such as fire or burglary. However, few people think about protecting the other potentially vulnerable aspects of their investment. What, for example, would you do if someone was injured or killed on your property? Or if your tenant left the premises with rent owing? What if you had an accident and could no longer use your wage or salary to meet the difference between the rental income and holding costs?

These are all possible scenarios, they do happen—and the consequences can be devastating. When insurance is available to cover them and it doesn't have to cost an arm or a leg, you would have to be mad not to protect yourself. How do you go about it?

> ## case study
> ### *You want how much?*
>
> Like building inspections, getting your solicitor to check the contract of sale can often bring to light problems that even the most astute purchaser could not readily identify . . .
>
> Louise was a keen first-time investor for whom we identified an inner suburban unit. At face value, the property was a prime investment—a small development, located in an attractive, established residential street with high land value, close to a popular retail and entertainment precinct. We knew the unit and location would be attractive to purchasers and tenants alike for years to come, underpinning its capital and rental value.
>
> While checking the contractual documentation, Louise's solicitor uncovered something that stopped us in our tracks. The body corporate certificate for the block of units revealed plans for almost $100,000 worth of repairs and improvements! This amount was additional to the usual quarterly body corporate fees.
>
> So, as one of a fairly small group of owners, Lousie would have had to find thousands of dollars to pay her share of the proposed improvements—reducing the amount she could put into the unit as a deposit, or increasing the amount she had to borrow. Either way, it was not a sensible start to an investment portfolio. Needless to say, in spite of the property's otherwise excellent investment prospects, we advised Louise not to proceed with the purchase.
>
> ### case study

First of all it is crucial to understand that you have a legally insurable interest in a property from the moment you sign the contract of sale. In other words, while you are not officially recognised as the owner of the property until settlement, you have an interest in ensuring that the contract can be acted on. Furthermore, in some contracts, a vendor may stipulate that the property is at **your** risk from the time the contract is signed. This is why you should take out comprehensive insurance from the moment you sign the contract of sale. This will protect your interests before settlement if the *vendor* isn't adequately insured.

Interestingly, residential property insurance is only compulsory in Australia if you have a mortgage over the property, when a third party, that is, your lender, has a vested interest. This seems a ridiculous situation, when basic insurance is mandatory for far less valuable assets—for example, third party insurance for your car, regardless of whether or not you owe money on it. Governments should legislate to ensure all owners take out and maintain an adequate building/contents insurance policy whether or not they have paid off their property loan.

If you're bidding at auction, ask your insurer to prepare a cover note in advance, ready to come into effect from the auction day when you're the successful bidder (how's that for optimism!). If you're buying via private sale, organise the cover note as soon as you enter into negotiations to come into effect from the day you sign the contract.

Let's look at the various types of insurance you'll need to consider.

BUILDING AND/OR CONTENTS INSURANCE

Most building and contents insurance policies cover your repair or replacement costs for loss or damage in the event of natural (and unnatural!) things like fire, storm and theft. While most policies cover a comprehensive range of possible occurrences, there are usually exclusions. Check with your insurer about exactly what their proposed policy covers, to ensure it suits your individual circumstances. Never under-insure! There is little point in taking out a policy unless it accurately reflects the value of your property and contents. Your insurer will tell you how to estimate this figure.

If you have bought a house, you will need to insure the building and its contents. If you have bought a unit, you will probably only need to insure its contents. The building component—along with other common property such as stairwells, landings, pathways, shared laundries and courtyards—is usually included in the body corporate's insurance policy.

Note, however, that items such as floor coverings and window furnishings are not covered under building or body corporate insurance policies. You should include their replacement value in your contents policy.

The cost of building/contents insurance varies depending on who is providing it, their assessment of your property's relative security risk and a range of other factors, so it pays to shop around. Remember, too, that while insuring a unit for contents only may appear cheaper than insuring a house for combined building and contents, the costs may be more evenly matched than you think. This is because a portion

---

Streetwise

Regardless of the types and extent of insurance you choose, it is wise to shop around for the policies and premiums that best suit your needs. And remember that, just like property, the cost of an insurance policy does not always reflect its quality or long-term effectiveness.

of your body corporate fees will go into maintaining the shared building insurance policy.

PUBLIC LIABILITY INSURANCE

This covers you in the very unlikely, but serious, event that someone other than yourself who is legally on the premises, for example, your tenant, a friend of the tenant or a tradesperson, is injured or killed on the property. While purchasers will routinely take out comprehensive insurance, including public liability insurance when buying a house, when it comes to units, many mistakenly believe their body corporate or strata manager automatically insures their unit and don't bother.

Whilst the legislation will vary between states and territories, generally speaking strata managers and body coroporates insure the building's structure and the common property. However it is usually up to each individual owner to comprehensively insure their own unit. This should include taking out contents and public liability insurance. Public liability insurance is often included in building and contents policies. Always check with your own body corporate manager or strata manager for the conditions that apply to your particular situation.

LANDLORD PROTECTION INSURANCE

Many investors make the mistake of thinking that a standard home and contents policy will cover them for events such as rental default or accidental or malicious damage caused by tenants—in other words, setbacks that are unique to *investors*, as distinct from homebuyers. This is not usually the case. To obtain this kind of cover, you will need to take out a separate landlord protection policy. Like home and contents policies, this type of insurance costs very little when compared with the potential loss it covers you against. So please, organise this cover to take effect from the day you sign the contract, and don't let it lapse!

AND THEN THERE'S ...

In the previous chapter we mentioned mortgage protection insurance, which protects the lender in the event that you default on the loan repayments. This is one of the few kinds of insurance in which you pay the premium but someone else gets the benefits!

But there is something you can do to even the score! We strongly suggest you consider taking out *income protection insurance*, which is designed to replace your income in the event that you are unable to work through illness or injury. Most policies provide cover of up to 75 per cent of your gross income, enabling you to keep meeting most of your financial commitments including your mortgage. Some providers also offer *trauma cover*, which covers you for more specific injuries or illnesses. Check which type of insurance is right for you.

Finally, if buying the property puts you in significant debt or you have a partner and/or dependent children, it's also worth considering *life insurance*. This means your family has the funds to discharge any remaining debt when you no longer can. After all, you are buying an investment property to help secure your future, not create unnecessary risk and stress.

CHAPTER TEN

Tax and Residential Property

FIGHTING THE DEMONS WITHOUT CREATING A NIGHTMARE!

When it comes to tax, property investors fall into one of two camps. Many think, 'Whoopee, tax deductions—lemme at 'em!' They then run out and buy the first property offering big tax incentives without looking properly into its long-term potential for capital growth and rental income.

Other investors take the 'If I ignore it, will it go away?' approach. 'Tax? You're kidding! ... I'd rather sort my sock drawer every day for a year than think about that!'

Humour aside, neither of these is a very helpful approach. In case you haven't already absorbed this message, tax should *never* be the primary reason you invest in residential property. But, as it can exert a significant impact on your property's investment viability, neither is it a good idea to pull down the shutters and trust that ignorance equals bliss.

This chapter will give you an overview of some of the major issues concerning taxation and investment property. However, because we are not taxation specialists, you should consult your tax adviser or accountant for guidance in relation to your individual situation.

Paying your way

OK, let's do the 'good news, bad news' thing, with the 'bad news' first so you have something to look forward to. When you invest in property for individual gain, you have to share some of the gain with the broader community in the form of tax. That is how governments raise money for basic infrastructure such as roads, schools, parks and other facilities that serve the public and, in turn, make your investment property more desirable.

When you own an investment property, you may be liable for any or all of the following taxes:

- goods and services tax (GST);
- capital gains tax (CGT);
- income tax;
- stamp duty; or
- land tax.

Let's look at each in turn and how they impact on your investment.

GST—SHEEP IN WOLF'S CLOTHING?

Unless you have been marooned on a desert island, the federal government's Goods and Services Tax (GST) will have been an integral part of your daily life since July 2000. But the GST's impact on residential property is relatively complex, and many investors are still confused. Here's a brief rundown.

You will not pay GST on the purchase price of *established* property, but you will pay GST on the purchase price of *new* property. If GST is payable it is calculated on the total purchase price of the property, including the land and buildings.

Regardless of whether your property is new or established, you will also pay GST on a range of other costs associated with its purchase, ownership and sale. These include, but may not be limited to:

- property advisory services;
- building inspections;
- conveyancing;
- insurance premiums;
- repairs, maintenance and improvements (materials and labour);
- property management and associated fees;
- estate agents' commissions and auction fees; and
- advertising.

Your accountant or tax adviser will be able to give you a clear idea of how GST affects your particular property.

Unlike most businesses, individual property investors are unable to claim GST outlays back from the government. Nor can you recoup the costs from your tenant in the form of a 10 per cent increase in rent amounts. This creates an interesting dilemma that we discuss in more detail in chapter twelve, when we cover property management issues.

Whilst it is crucial to be aware of how the GST affects your particular situation, it is also important to understand how it has affected the wider property market.

Predictably, in the months leading up to the introduction of the GST, the new property sector boomed, with investors and home-buyers alike rushing to complete building works before 1 July 2000. As tradesmen became busier, they were harder to find and hire and they increased their costs accordingly—the old supply and demand rule at work again! This increased the purchase price of new property, so that in the end there probably was not much difference between the pre-GST and post-GST price.

Nonetheless, the popular perception was that new property would be prohibitively more expensive after the GST came in—so many people who would have ordinarily bought or built new property turned to the established sector to avoid the new tax. Along with increased demand came higher prices. This exacerbated the differences between the new and established sectors and had the building industry crying out for additional measures to boost home building activity. In March 2001, the Federal Government temporarily increased the First Home Owner Grant for first home buyers purchasing new property. While the Grant is only available to first-time owner-occupiers, there are far more first home buyers than investors, so the Grant has had a significant impact on overall market activity and values.

The extra grant amount did indeed increase activity in the new housing sector for a short period, with a subsequent easing of demand in the established sector. Ironically, this brought the relative demand for property in both sectors back to their pre-GST balance. In short, despite all the initial hubbub, the introduction of the GST proved only a temporary hiccup in the property cycle's longer term ebb and flow.

As an investor, the main thing you need to remember is that, provided you select the right property, the additional costs of goods and services you incur as a result of GST will be more than compensated for by an exceptional rate of long-term capital growth.

CAPITAL GAINS TAX—NOT PROPERTY INVESTMENT ARMAGEDDON!

Since 20 September 1985, any investor who realises a capital gain from an investment property must pay capital gains tax. CGT is payable on the net capital gain, (profit) not the total value of the property. But it's payable at your marginal income tax rate, so if you've chosen a prime property your CGT liability could theoretically be very high indeed.

Fortunately, the reality isn't that dark. You only pay CGT if you actually 'realise' the gain—if you sell the property. Furthermore, if you sold the property after 21 September 1999 and held it for at least 12 months, only half the capital gain is taxed. If you bought the property before 20 September 1985 it will be CGT-exempt.

If you don't sell, all those gains are yours to keep and use for leverage to purchase other assets. This is one of the great untold truths of property investment, and one that the anti-property pundits don't always want to share!

To compensate for a loss of public revenue due to CGT reductions, the government removed indexation relief from 21 September 1999. This meant investors could no longer use the effects of inflation to reduce the amount of capital gain, and therefore the amount of CGT they had to pay. Some property commentators have raised concerns that the removal of indexation will increase investors' CGT burden. If inflation rises for a sustained period, with an associated capital gain, extra CGT could indeed be payable as a result of the removal of indexation. But if you buy a quality asset and hold it for the long term, this risk is only theoretical, anyway. Be aware that from time to time, all governments will tinker with the taxation laws affecting property investors. Make sure you check with your accountant on a regular basis.

INCOME TAX

As a property investor, any income you make from the investment—rent—will be subject to income tax at your marginal rate, just like income from wages or salary. Some rent-related income you make, like full or partial bond payments retained to pay for damage caused by a tenant, may also be subject to income tax. Check with your accountant or tax adviser.

STAMP DUTY

State and territory governments levy this tax based on the total 'transfer value' or purchase price of a property. In some states and territories, stamp duty may also be payable on the value of the mortgage itself, but at a lower rate.

As you can see in Table 10.1, stamp duty rates vary greatly between jurisdictions, partly because of state-based differences in property values. In states where residential property values are relatively modest, most individual investors will not be paying the kind of rates you see here.

Table 10.1: Stamp Duty on the Transfer of a $250 000 Investment Property

NSW	$7244
VIC	$10 660
QLD	$7225
WA	$7680
SA	$8830
TAS	$7550
NT	$9313
ACT	$7265

But in locations where values have climbed steeply and $250 000 buys a fairly modest property, for example, the inner suburbs of Melbourne and Sydney, investors are significantly disadvantaged by stamp duty regimes that haven't kept pace.

Furthermore, stamp duty can't be claimed as a tax deduction because the tax department regards it as a capital cost, like the actual purchase price of the property.

Unless or until the legislation changes, be prepared to factor the appropriate sum into your overall purchasing costs and bear the imposition as best you can.

On the bright side, if you have a first-class asset the capital growth should outstrip the initial stamp duty impost within a relatively short space of time—yet another reason to make absolutely sure you don't buy a lemon!

LAND TAX

Apart from stamp duty, which is a one-off acquisition cost, state and territory governments (with the exception of the Northern Territory) also levy an annual tax on the unimproved value of the land on which an investment property sits (see Table 10.2, p. 191).

Land tax rates vary from state to state, with some governments applying a threshold, or minimum value, before any land tax is payable. However, if you hold multiple investment properties whose land components, individually, are worth less than the threshold, you will still be liable for land tax based on the combined land value of the properties.

Table 10.2: Annual Land Tax on Unimproved Land Value of $200 000 based on a single holding for a private individual

NSW*	$nil
Vic	$200
Qld	$nil
WA	$420
SA	$525
Tas	$2013
ACT	$2250
NT**	nil

* A higher threshold applies.
** The Northern Territory does not levy land tax.

Unlike stamp duty, land tax is tax-deductible at your marginal rate, because it is a recurring cost associated with holding the asset (as long as the asset is actually producing income).

And now for the good news!

Now that we've discussed the tax you have to pay on residential property, let's look at the tax benefits you can claim! When you buy an income-producing property you can obtain the following benefits, all of which can be offset against your rental and other income:

- negative gearing relief;
- depreciation of fixtures, fittings and, in certain cases, construction costs of the building itself; and
- tax deductions on expenses associated with holding the property and borrowing to buy it.

ALL GEARED UP

Given that few of us have sufficient funds to purchase a property outright, 'gearing'—borrowing money to fund investments—is a fact of life. Depending on the amount of equity you have in your property, gearing can take three different forms:

- *positive gearing*, where the rental income exceeds the interest on your loan repayments and holding expenses;
- *neutral gearing*, where the rental income equals the interest on your loan repayments and holding expenses; or
- *negative gearing*, where the rental income falls short of the interest on your loan repayments and holding expenses.

In the early years when you are unlikely to have much equity in your property, particularly if it is the first, your borrowings will be high, so interest will form a substantial proportion of your repayments. At this stage your property will probably be negatively geared. The tax office will allow you to offset the difference between your rental income and the interest on your loan repayments and holding costs against your other taxable income, so you end up paying less tax.

You have the option of taking your negative gearing benefits in small parcels throughout the financial year by reducing your PAYG income tax withholdings or in one large parcel at the end of each financial year. This flexibility is a boon for first-time investors, because it helps control your cash flow.

'But what if they abolish negative gearing?' Each and every year the same question rears its ugly head. Perhaps a bit of history will help put things in perspective. Those of you old enough to remember back to the 1980s may recall the Hawke government's quarantining of negative gearing provisions, where investors could only claim gearing benefits upon selling the asset. Faced with a high interest rate environment, and unable to claim the shortfall between their net rental income and holding costs, investors began deserting residential property in droves. Rents skyrocketed and tenants could no longer afford to rent their homes. The government was faced with two options: supply accommodation for all the displaced tenants at a huge cost to the taxpayer; or encourage private investors to re-enter the market.

Not surprisingly, the government reinstated negative gearing provisions in 1987. We believe it's a pretty safe bet that, given the social, economic and political ramifications, it is unlikely that future governments will repeat the exercise!

DEPRECIATION

Land generally appreciates in value, while buildings, fittings and fixtures generally depreciate. In recognition of this, the tax department allows investors to claim depreciation on certain kinds of construction expenditure and on a range of items including, but not limited to, floor and window coverings, heaters, air-conditioners and stoves. In fact, the list of depreciable items, as well as the list of non-depreciable items, is as long as your arm. Furthermore, the allowable depreciation rates vary from item to item, as do the number of years over which you can claim depreciation. So give yourself a break—don't try to muddle through it. Ask your accountant or tax adviser for advice on what is relevant to your situation.

TAX DEDUCTIONS ON HOLDING COSTS

The tax department allows investors to claim a wide range of expenses incurred in holding investment properties. These can include, but are not necessarily limited to:

- repairs;
- maintenance;
- property management fees;
- interest on the loan (not the principal);
- bank charges;
- body corporate fees where applicable;
- municipal rates;
- insurance;
- postage;
- telephone calls; and
- travel to and from the property.

SETTING THE RECORD STRAIGHT ...

Because the type and number of expenses you can incur in purchasing and holding a rental property are so diverse and the taxation concessions vary just as much, the accountants we talked to in putting together this chapter had two pleas.

- Establish a separate loan account for each of your investment properties, so the interest payments are clearly identifiable as investment related rather than private expenses.
- Keep written records of all financial transactions relating to your investment property in a safe place and in some semblance of order. You don't want to get to 30 June and find you have lost half the evidence for items you intended to claim!

Ultimately, legally minimising your tax liability will help improve your cash flow and help you to hold on to your investment property for the long term, until that wonderful day when it becomes self-funding. But, yes, we'll say it again—your decision to buy *any* investment property should be based primarily on its potential to deliver the desired levels of growth and income, not on the prevailing tax climate.

FAQ: Should I buy an investment property for tax reasons?

No! While all income-producing properties offer the capacity to claim certain holding and capital expenses as tax deductions, this alone does not make them good investments. Capital growth potential, as influenced by the level of ongoing market demand relative to supply, must always be your primary consideration when purchasing investment property.

CHAPTER ELEVEN
Mastering the Skills of Searching and Negotiation

POUNDING THE PAVEMENT FOR PROFIT

Well, you probably thought we would never get this far! All the groundwork you have laid in previous chapters is about to bear fruit.

- You now have a clearly defined set of suburbs to target.
- You have amassed your own mini-database of high-quality comparable properties that meet investment criteria and are representative of what can be bought within your price range in your preferred areas.
- Your lender and/or financial adviser have helped you determine how much you can afford to spend and how best to manage the debt.
- You've studied median values for the target areas, you know how to use and interpret them and you understand their limitations.

The real work, satisfaction and fun of sourcing and selecting property is about to begin!

Here you will strike one of the most common problems associated with the search process. Once you have looked at ten to 20 properties over a few days or a weekend and tried to take in all the relevant information, they all start to look pretty much the same.

So to help make the process a little easier for you, we've devised a four-stage assessment system.

STAGE 1: THE FIRST VIEWING

Expect to see a maximum of seven to ten properties per day. If you live in an area where auctions and public viewings—often called 'open for inspections'—are the norm, plan your day around the advertised inspection times. If most properties in your city are viewed via private appointments made with the selling agent, make sure you leave enough time to get from one to the next. Get a search kit together. Include a loose leaf file with labelled tabs for each suburb you are searching in, notepaper, pencil, eraser, stapler, hole puncher and a top-quality, up-to-date street directory. For many properties, agents produce colour brochures or include a listing of properties for sale on their website. The website listing usually comprises one or two photos and basic information such as the floor plan, land size and number of bedrooms. Gather the most comprehensive information together and take it with you as you walk through each property with the agent. You should make detailed notes during each inspection.

Prepare an assessment sheet for each property you view so that you can take notes and assess it as you walk through. Don't make the mistake of leaving the note-taking until later that day or in between inspections—it's guaranteed you won't remember the critical details of even one or two properties, let alone ten! The sample property assessment sheet depicted in Table 11.1 (p. 199) will get you started. The sample sheet also gives you some guidance on the kinds of comments and notes you should make about each property you inspect. Staple it to the brochure, advertisement or web page printout and file it under the appropriate section of your file when completed.

Having recorded this information for each property, rank them on a scale of one to ten. Reject those that score below seven. You will probably find that at least half the properties you initially inspect don't make the grade.

STAGE 2: REFINING YOUR LIST

Inspect the properties you have marked 'yes' and 'possibly' for a second time within a few days of the first inspection, then rank them again. This will probably eliminate half the remainder.

STAGE 3: GETTING SERIOUS!

It is likely you will be left with less than a quarter of the properties you started with. Now comes the time for a more intensive level of assessment—and yes, another table.

Table 11.2 (p. 200) includes provision for a detailed breakdown of every major investment criterion. At first it may seem a little over the top to be speaking in terms of a percentage breakdown, but when you are faced with the potential to gain (or lose!) hundreds of thousands of dollars in capital growth, you need as much detail as possible to make an informed decision.

Inspect the remaining properties and rate them using the table. Keep assessing the properties against comparable sales, too. In doing so you may well find that you eliminate a few more properties on the basis of likely selling price in relation to the maximum amount you can spend. This is important because even when a property rates well from an investment selection perspective, you will be wasting your time if all the directly comparable sales evidence clearly suggests that its value is, say, $300 000 while your spending limit is $250 000.

Table 11.1: Property Assessment Sheet—Stages One and Two

			Stage One	Stage Two
1	**Property address**	.... *rating out of ten*		
2	**Neighbourhood character and amenity**	e.g. consistent streetscape of 1980s houses; close proximity to primary/secondary schools, retail outlets, parks		
3	**Architectural style**	e.g. Federation, moderne (sometimes called 'Art Deco'), 1950s–1970s		
4	**Dwelling size and type (i.e. house/unit)**	e.g. 1-bedroom unit, 2-bedroom house; single fronted, double fronted		
5	**Land size**	(relevant for houses, or units and townhouses with a land component on title, e.g. courtyard)		
6	**Floor plan**	Make a few basic notations as you walk through the property, e.g. 'House; central hallway running the length of the property; 2 bedrooms off hallway; central bathroom; kitchen & family room at rear opening to courtyard.' Or: '1st floor flat; entrance leading to kitchen & living room on right; bedroom and bathroom on left; living room opens to balcony.'		
7	**Off-street parking**	Yes/No		
8	**Lock-up garage**	Yes/No		
9	**Level of renovation**	e.g. fully renovated, needs cosmetic spruce-up, needs major surgery		
10	**Comparable property recently sold**	Record relevant details of comparable sales (using 1–4 and 6–8 above). Include the agent's quoted price as well as the actual sale price if the two differ substantially.		
	Additional notes	Note down anything else of relevance to help you remember the details of the property for later reference.		
	CONCLUSION	YES/ POSSIBLY/ NO		

Source: Wakelin Property Advisory. This Table is a general guide and weightings may vary slightly from region to region.

Table 11.2: Stage Three Assessment Table

Address	Benchmark weighting (%)	Actual weighting (%)
Location	50	
Desirability of area		
Proximity to key amenities— schools, shops, public transport		
Supply/demand		
Off-street parking		
Population and employment growth		
Quiet and privacy		
Building	20	
Architectural style		
Floor plan		
Aspect		
Quality of fittings		
Maintenance requirement		
Natural light		
Security		
Marketability to tenants and buyers	15	
Perceived ongoing demand		
Tenant	10	
Calibre of likely tenant		
Projected market rent		
Zoning/legal	5	
Form of titles (e.g. freehold, strata)		
Potential to add value via cosmetic improvements and/or additional accommodation		
Town planning compliance		
Covenants and restrictions		
Total	**100**	

Ranking scheme
90–100%   Excellent
80–89%   Good
70–79%   Acceptable
Less than 70%   Not recommended

Source: Wakelin Property Advisory. *This table is a general guide and weightings may vary slightly from region to region.*

STAGE 4: ALMOST THERE

By now, if you have not eliminated all the properties you initially inspected you will probably be left with two or three properties at most. At this point there should be little doubt in your mind that, subject to a structural inspection and your solicitor's assessment of the documentation, each of these properties is likely to be worthy of inclusion in your property portfolio. If you have serious doubts, go back to the drawing board and inspect the property again, or cross it off the list.

Negotiation—how to buy quality property without paying through the nose!

Congratulations! You have done your homework thoroughly and are ready to begin the purchasing process.

Remember Meg Ryan's obsession with food in the film *When Harry Met Sally*? In its most basic form, negotiating is a case of 'I want it the way I want it' and knowing *how* to get it. Let us assure you that luck, which so many would-be investors believe is a prerequisite for successful negotiation, has very little to do with it.

> **Information and experience are the keys to effective negotiation.**

By now you know that *information* within a property investment context involves understanding local real estate values, building styles that confer scarcity value and the economic influences on property cycles.

Experience is the other essential cog in the wheel. Why do so many investors who read voraciously and go to every property investment seminar under the sun *still* make fundamental mistakes? Because they are approaching the selection and negotiation of a tangible asset in an ever-shifting marketplace with an academic mindset—with little practical, real-life research.

When negotiating, the primary risk of an overly academic approach is overpaying. Even if you buy a top-quality asset in a prime location, paying tens of thousands more than fair market value will significantly reduce the potential for strong capital growth in excess of the purchase price during the early years of the investment. In fact, instead of having capital growth do the work for you, you will be heavily reliant on your own active debt reduction to increase your equity in the property while lining the bank's pocket in the process.

Of course, astute negotiation requires more than a sound knowledge of markets and property values. To maximise the likelihood of a successful and cost-effective outcome, it is essential to know the ins and outs of the various methods used to transact property and how to make the most of each.

Private sale

Private sales are based on a set asking price from which the buyer and seller negotiate to a mutually acceptable level. Buying by private sale will spare you the nerves and agony of attending an auction and facing an auctioneer and a crowd of people.

Streetwise

Don't make the mistake of thinking that private sales are plain sailing in comparison! A private sale will put you under equal pressure—it is just a different kind of pressure, and you will need just as much knowledge as you would if you were attending an auction.

For a start, unlike auctions, you will never come into contact with another buyer, genuine or otherwise, during the negotiation process. You will be totally reliant on the selling agent's word if they tell you they have an offer on a property at a particular level and invite you to better it.

So what can you expect to experience if you buy privately?

The vendor and estate agent will usually market the property via a combination of media advertising, the agent's website, brochures or catalogues and a 'For Sale' board posted outside the property. This promotion is usually accompanied by the predetermined asking price.

The agent and vendor know that every buyer will try to beat the price down because their aim is to snare the bargain of the century—or at least to feel like they have! In light of this, the asking price will probably be set above recent comparable sales results for properties of a similar size and style within the immediate vicinity.

Typically, interested buyers inspect a property by appointment with the selling agent, who highlights the property's features and benefits and ascertains the buyers' needs and level of interest. The agent reports back to the vendor, discussing their original price expectations relative to individual buyer feedback and wider market sentiment.

Once a buyer has expressed genuine interest in the property, the agent will usually 'qualify' them. This means establishing whether they are genuinely motivated to buy and have the financial resources to do so. Typically, the agent will also ask whether they have already sold an existing property or intend to put one on the market in the very short term. If the intention to sell is there but has not yet been acted upon, the agent may vie for the ultimate prize—to list the buyer's current property for sale and sell them their next one.

Once genuine interest and capacity to pay is established, a process of negotiation between the parties ensues. The agent acts as intermediary, until a mutually agreeable price level is struck. At this point, contracts are signed and exchanged.

PURCHASE AND SETTLEMENT TERMS

The negotiation process also entails establishing how long the settlement period will be and whether the execution of the contract will be subject to any special conditions. Settlement periods can vary from a matter of days to several months or even longer.

In some instances, the buyer's ability to meet a vendor's special needs, such as an extra long or very short settlement, can be used as a bargaining tool. If, for example, the vendor has bought another property, needs the proceeds of the current sale to settle the new purchase and does not want to resort to expensive bridging finance, they may be willing to consider a slightly lower price in exchange for a matching settlement.

As a smart investor it is in your best interests to ask the agent as much as you can about the vendor's circumstances and ideal settlement, just in case there is some manoeuvring to be done. Chances are you will uncover something that will give you a degree of bargaining power.

OFF-MARKET TRANSACTIONS

In some cases it is possible to purchase a property that has not been marketed publicly.

Some vendors prefer the off-market method because it maximises their privacy and facilitates a relatively quick sale. In most instances the vendor instructs the agent to submit the property to existing pre-qualified buyers registered on their buyer database. The purchase is then negotiated as per a normal private sale.

Sometimes an interested buyer will approach an owner directly without involvement from an agent. In this case, once a mutually agreeable price is struck the transfer of ownership is simply conducted by each party's solicitor.

Auctions—when all the world's a stage!

Auctions are prevalent in some major cities, particularly in inner suburban areas where a consistently limited supply of property ensures strong buyer competition. Prospective buyers must declare their intention and financial capacity openly to secure their property of choice.

A large part of the appeal of auctions comes from the emotion generated when purchasers compete openly to secure their prize. If you want to see the auction system at its most theatrical, inner suburban Melbourne is the place to be. It's widely acknowledged as the world's auction capital!

The auction day is usually preceded by a three- to four-week promotional period that usually includes media and web advertising and public inspections.

Unlike a private sale, a property sold by public auction is not advertised with a set asking price. Instead, the seller sets an unpublished reserve price in conjunction with the selling agent. Prospective purchasers are usually given a (very!) conservative price estimate by the estate agent when they inspect the property. These strategies are designed to generate abundant interest and intense competition among buyers to produce a successful outcome for the seller.

Recent years have seen considerable public dissent over auction quoting ranges, especially in Melbourne and Sydney. In many instances buyers have been quoted price estimates that have been well short of the actual sale price—sometimes by tens of thousands of dollars. A number of agents have finally begun to advertise more reliable auction quoting ranges in an effort to bring transparency and credibility to the process.

As an investor and purchaser, the message here is that when you are looking for accurate price information, you can't rely solely on pre-auction estimates provided by estate agents. The most reliable source is actual sale results. As you gather more and more sales data you will build up an increasingly clear picture of values, property styles and capital growth performance in your preferred areas.

'LADIES AND GENTLEMEN ...'

The auction may take place either at the property itself, or off-site in an auction room. Generally speaking, the auctioneer will read the conditions of sale and summarise the contract to the assembled crowd, then

---

Buying at auction—a recipe for disaster!
Ingredients (in no particular order)

700 g persuasion, persistence and superb sales techniques from the selling agent

1 kg desperation and insecurity (yours, that is!)

2 kg pressure from family or spouse ('We just have to buy this property—I'm so sick of looking!')

5 kg 'auction street theatre' (including rhetoric and scare tactics from the auctioneer—'... For the third and final call, are you all finished, all done?')

5 kg nervous dysfunction (sweaty palms, hyperventilating—not least because you're about to sign a very large cheque)

5 g factual market information

Method

Combine all ingredients in a large iron cauldron and stir vigorously.

Now stand back ...

---

make some brief remarks about the property's location, style, benefits and features before inviting members of the crowd to open the bidding.

Predictably, an excruciating period of silence ensues during which members of the crowd look around expectantly to see who, if anyone, will be plucky enough to make the first bid. If it looks as though no genuine bidder is going to make the first move, the auctioneer or someone else chosen by the agent or vendor, usually referred to as a vendor bidder, will get the ball rolling.

Once it is in progress, the bidding sequence continues until the vendor's reserve is reached or the bidding stalls. At this point, the auctioneer may pause to confer in private with the vendor. If the reserve has been reached, the auctioneer will usually declare the property 'on the market' which means the property is now available for *unreserved* sale to the highest bidder. If the reserve has not been reached, the property is resubmitted to the crowd for further bidding. If none is forthcoming, the property is 'passed in' to the highest bidder for private negotiation in the vicinity of the vendor's reserve price. A sale is usually effected within a few hours but can occasionally take longer, depending on the nature of the negotiations and the price expectations of both parties.

Buying at auction—the seven deadly sins!

For a bit of fun but with a deadly earnest message, we have concocted a list of auction commotion, dastardly deeds, persistent blunders and how to avoid them when buying property under auction conditions.

All jokes aside and through no fault of their own, auctions place purchasers in a situation designed to relieve them of as much of their hard-earned dollars as possible. Hence the need to be aware of the major pitfalls and, more importantly, how to overcome them.

SIN NO. 1: NOT BEING VALUE SAVVY

This mistake is undoubtedly the most common—and the worst. A lack of market knowledge means you have no reliable benchmark with which to compare your desired purchase.

Remember: always do your research by tracking sales results of directly comparable properties in the immediate vicinity of the one you want to buy. If you have all this information to hand before you even set foot near an auction, you can save thousands of dollars.

Spitting the 'dummy'?

Despite widespread public concerns, vendor bidding (sometimes called 'dummy' bidding) is still legal in all States and Territories, although the practice is under review in some states and regulations governing its use vary. Members of State real estate institutes subscribe to a national code of conduct agreeing that vendor bids can only be utilised until the reserve price is reached. However, some states allow only one vendor bid per auction, while others allow as many as are required to generate participation and encourage bidding to reach the reserve.

Given that few States require the vendor to declare when they are making a bid, most genuine purchasers find it almost impossible to know who is bidding on behalf of the vendor and who isn't. Only when you spend half your life attending auctions (like we do!) can you develop a keen, though not foolproof, instinct for identifying vendor bidders and even recognising the same faces and patterns of behaviour week in, week out!

Unfortunately, if you are like most people and buy property relatively infrequently, it's a case of accepting that unless legislation is enacted to effectively outlaw it, vendor bidding is a fact of life. The best way to get around it is to tender a bid only when the property is declared to be 'on the market'—auction speak for 'about to be sold to the highest bidder if there's no further advance in the bidding'. Auctioneers usually make it very clear when the reserve has been reached.

SIN NO. 2: IMPULSE BUYING

Have you ever known someone who turned up to bid at auction without ever having set foot inside the property beforehand? Buying on the spur of the moment is a surprisingly common mistake and the perfect way to become intimately acquainted with Murphy's Law! You know the one: 'Anything that can go wrong will go wrong.' Seriously, though, buying property without carrying out all your due diligence is very high risk. Avoid this at all costs.

SIN NO. 3: BUYING BEFORE AUCTION

This isn't always a mistake in itself. However, unless the vendor is under considerable pressure to sell, it will take an offer that simply can't be refused (read exorbitant!) to withdraw the property from the market before auction.

Before considering this approach, try to ascertain the vendor's attitude to the negotiations. Are they anxious? Conciliatory? Desperate? What is their motivation for selling at this particular point in time? Are they moving interstate? Upgrading their home? Realising a profit? How many other buyers have expressed genuine interest in the property, and at what price level?

If you do make an offer prior to auction, your offer will be referred to the vendor. If the vendor is receptive, this process could go back and forth several times and can test the steeliest of nerves. If the vendor accepts your offer, other interested parties will usually be given a chance to tender their highest and best offer. Almost universally, however, the unsuccessful purchasers end up unhappy with the process, not to mention the result.

SIN NO. 4: LETTING EMOTIONS GET THE BETTER OF YOU

Buyers rarely succeed in purchasing the ideal investment on their first attempt. More often than not, it is patience and persistence that win the day. To minimise emotional fallout, it is essential to adopt the right mindset from the very beginning. Never adopt a 'do or die' approach to securing a property. Be prepared to buy or lose it based on prevailing values and your price limit. Do your research, give it your best shot, and if you reach your limit stop and move on to the next property. The right investment will come up sooner or later.

SIN NO. 5: ASSUMING THE PROPERTY IS ALWAYS 'PASSED IN' TO A GENUINE BIDDER

Be aware that a property may be 'passed in' to a 'vendor bidder' when a genuine buyer has attended the auction but failed to bid, or has not submitted the highest bid. If the auctioneer begins protracted discussions with you and other genuine buyers soon after a property has been passed in it may be a signal that the highest bidder was not genuine.

Under these circumstances, you may opt to offer less than the pass-in price. But be warned, you will need to be fairly certain if you intend to make your suspicions known. If you are unsure and the agents approach you saying the negotiations have broken down, simply resubmit your last bid as a starting point.

SIN NO. 6: THE ATTACK OF THE 'KILLER BID'

While opening the bidding at an auction is a perfectly legitimate way of declaring your interest, submitting your first bid at a very high level is a recipe for wasting your hard-earned (or borrowed!) money.

In fact, far from being successful, it is almost guaranteed that you have paid a huge premium, declared your capacity without having first ascertained the capacity of the other buyers, and revealed your ignorance of market values. Hardly the actions of a sensible investor. How would you feel, for example, knowing you have spent $380 000

case study

So who's the dummy now?

We vividly recall being at an auction where there were apparently two bidders vying for the property. One was an obviously genuine bidder whose limit, it turned out, was well below the true market value of the property. The second was a vendor bidder—we knew that because he had become a familiar sight on the auction circuit. He would always bid in a predictable pattern and drop out at precisely the same stage of each auction, regardless of the circumstances. We elected not to bid at all and observed the auction's progress.

Predictably, the property was passed in to the person we suspected was acting for the vendor. Our suspicions were confirmed when the agents made a beeline for us and the other buyer and asked both parties to come inside just in case the current buyer elected not to proceed. The other genuine bidder declined, saying he reached his limit within his first few bids. We elected to remain outside and told the agent that we had to leave in ten minutes to go to another auction.

Sure enough, the vendor bidder didn't take the matter any further and we were invited to tender an offer. We offered $5000 less than the pass-in price and bought the property for $15 000 under the vendor's reserve.

case study

even if you could afford to when the vendor's reserve was $300 000 and the underbidder's limit was $320 000! Was that extra $60 000 wisely spent? Believe us, this is not an extreme example—we see this scenario unfolding week after week. Don't become its next victim!

SIN NO. 7: NEVER QUESTIONING AUCTION PROTOCOL

If you have had a few auction disappointments and are reaching the 'why-bother-it's-all-too-hard stage', consider this—you, the purchaser, have control of the auction situation, because you have the money the vendor wants. Go ahead and do what Meg Ryan did! Ask for what *you* want the way *you* want it; before and during the auction or negotiations.

For example, there is absolutely no reason why you can't tender bids that are less than the auctioneer's nominated increments, especially in the later stages of an auction. Don't be afraid to offer $1000 or $500 bids even if the auctioneer is calling for $2500 rises—the worst thing they can say is 'no'. And even if they do, it is a pretty safe bet that they will come around to your point of view if there are very few other bidders.

You can also negotiate the proposed terms of purchase before the auction. If a settlement is advertised as 30 or 60 days, go ahead and ask for 90 or 120 if it suits you better. You can even ask to vary the normal 10 per cent deposit to 5 per cent, or split the 10 per cent into two equal instalments.

AUCTION DEMEANOUR ... WHEN THE 'POKER' FACE COMES INTO ITS OWN!

From years of experience, we can tell you that all the market knowledge in the world won't amount to much if you don't know how to conduct yourself at an auction. While many bidders are not assertive enough in an auction situation, in recent times we have seen an increasing number of professional bidders or 'buyer advocates' who adopt an overly aggressive attitude at auctions. Some bid in substantially higher increments than necessary, so their client ends up paying the vendor tens of thousands of dollars too much for the property. Others attempt to intimidate the auctioneer and other purchasers, potentially reducing their ability to negotiate favourably on the standard terms of purchase.

Streetwise

The reality is that purchasers who are knowledgeable and polite, yet firm, in their approach to negotiations get the best results and gain the respect of the other parties. And this is a lot easier than you think!

Here are our top tips for auction conduct to give you an edge.

- Stand where you can see the entire crowd and the auctioneer.
- When bidding or observing the auction, practise being expressionless and virtually immobile. The less you move your face and body, the harder other bidders and the auctioneer will find you to read. You will have plenty of time to show your emotions after you have bought the property!
- Bid when you are fairly certain the property is on the market.
- If you elect to tender bids at increments less than those being nominated, bid verbally rather than by nodding or signalling, otherwise the auctioneer will assume your bid is in accordance with the nominated amount.
- If you do bid below the nominated increment and the auctioneer refuses your bid on that basis, do not, we repeat, *do not* abuse the auctioneer. The old adage about catching more flies with honey is never truer than in the middle of an auction!

Table 11.3: Auctions vs Private Sales—Pluses and Pitfalls at a Glance

Method of sale	Auctions	Private sales
Advantages for purchasers	• Negotiations take place in an open public forum • Price is determined by prevailing market conditions • Vendor is usually highly motivated to sell • No waiting around—a clear-cut result is achieved very quickly	• Less pressure to make on-the-spot decisions • Easier to negotiate unusual or non-standard settlement requirements • Purchase may be conditional in some cases, e.g. subject to finance, the sale of your existing property, or cooling off provisions
Disadvantages for purchasers	• Purchase is unconditional • Vendor bidding may create a false impression of interest and competition • Less opportunity to negotiate outside of standard terms • Need to make quick yet unemotional decisions • Need for considerable market familiarity in the locality • Pressure to compete publicly against other buyers	• Not knowing whether there are other genuine buyers and what they are willing to pay • Waiting for the response to an offer can be time consuming and emotionally draining

- Mutual respect, cooperation and a business-like approach are the keys to getting what you want—not just at this point, but throughout the auction and negotiation process.

If you are purchasing in an area where private sales, not auctions, are the norm, you will still be able to apply many of these strategies to your negotiations.

If you have followed our negotiation guidelines and purchased a quality investment property at the right price, well done!

PART FOUR
Keeping the Good Times Rolling

CHAPTER TWELVE
Managing Your Investment Property

FORFEITING THE ILLUSION OF CONTROL

You have finally bought a ripper of an investment property—right style, right location, right price. Now's your chance to sit back, enjoy the fruits of all that hard work and watch the property grow in value month by month, year by year. After all, compared with searching for, selecting, evaluating and negotiating your property, tenanting and maintaining it is pretty much a walk in the park, right? You just get a tenant and collect the rent!

Not quite. There are the small matters of:

- sourcing and screening potential tenants to find those who are most likely to pay the rent on time, every time and maintain your property in good clean order;
- drawing up a lease that legally protects and benefits you and your tenant;
- setting and collecting an appropriate rent;
- organising and paying for repairs, insurances and rates;
- dealing with complaints and disputes in a productive and lawful manner; and
- staying abreast of continuously changing tenancy legislation to achieve all of the above.

Hardly a job for the uninitiated! Yet so many investors—either ignorant of the reality, or over-confident of their ability to handle it—truly believe that managing a property is a straightforward exercise that can easily be slotted into everyday life. Let's put this myth to rest here and now.

Managing an investment property is an onerous, complex, time-consuming undertaking. When it is done poorly, the potential for trouble is considerable—which is why it is often the weakest link in the property investment chain.

Property managers

Unless you have plenty of time on your hands, a comprehensive knowledge of tenancy legislation and don't mind being called about burst water pipes or blocked toilets at all hours of the day and night, don't go down the DIY route. Make your life easier—and protect your investment—by appointing an experienced, professional property manager.

(We can assure you that we practise what we preach—our personal property portfolio is managed by professionals, so we can get on with our lives!)

Unlike most individual investors, professional property managers offer three major advantages.

1. Broad-reaching practical knowledge borne of experience in managing hundreds of properties on a daily basis.
2. Comprehensive knowledge of residential tenancy legislation.

3. Access to tools such as the National Tenancy Database, which is available only to professional property managers. This database contains a wealth of information on the rental records of potential tenants—including broken leases, damage to property, rental default and matters taken to courts or tribunals. Tools like these can be a useful way of screening out potential tenants, over and above the usual direct inquiries. Just like any other aspect of property investment, it always pays to look below the surface. Even the most respectable-looking tenants can sometimes turn out to have less than rosy rental histories!

And just as importantly, property managers have no personal or emotional attachment to your property—making them an ideal independent umpire, particularly in the event of difficulties or disputes. Remember that managing an investment property is akin to managing a business. If you go to an accountant for business advice you are going to get the best from someone who is knowledgeable and objective, with no personal or emotional stake in the outcome. Similarly, by engaging a professional property manager, you will not only receive expert advice, but maintain that all-important arm's length perspective—minimising the likelihood of decisions that may not be in your, or your tenant's, best interests.

Still need convincing about the benefits of professional property managers? Perhaps the following story will get you thinking differently.

> In Victoria, residential tenancy legislation requires investors to install locks on all external doors and windows. One investor, who had chosen to manage their own property, had received repeated requests from their tenant to install these locks but had not done anything about it.

After the work was finally organised, the property was broken into just two days before the appointed installation and the tenant was murdered.

A true and tragic story.

That's one heck of an emotional and financial fallout over a simple request for legislative compliance and an outlay of a few hundred dollars. And if you think it will never happen to you, you can bet this investor didn't either. If the owner had engaged a professional property manager who not only had full knowledge of tenancy legislation but ensured compliance works had been carried out, this need never have happened.

But even having read this sad tale, no doubt some of you will still question the need for property managers. 'They charge an arm and a leg!' we hear you cry. 'And even if I could afford a property manager, how could I find a good one? I mean, they could be doing absolutely nothing to look after my property, but as long as the rent rolled in I wouldn't know any different!'

Let's look at each of these objections in turn.

PROPERTY MANAGEMENT FEES—ECONOMY OF SCALE

Property managers, like any other professionals, do not work for free. A good investment property is like any other valuable commodity: If it is worth buying in the first place, it is worth spending a little extra to protect and enhance its value.

Property management fees vary, but are generally in the range of 6 to 9 per cent of the gross rental income. This modest sum usually covers core services such as rent collection, routine inspections and coordination of simple maintenance requests. Occasional services such as advertising and letting may be charged as separate items.

Do not be put off if your property manager's fees are at the higher end of this scale. It is far better to pay a little extra, provided they are prepared to take a pro-active role in the management of the property.

What's more, like many other expenses associated with holding an investment property, the tax department takes a positive view of property management fees. They are fully tax deductible at your marginal rate—reducing the effective cost of the service.

In fact, far from *costing* you money, a good property manager will *save* it for you by protecting your interests—selecting and advising you on suitable rent levels, lease terms and conditions, property maintenance and repairs, and compliance with legal obligations to your tenant.

FINDING A GOOD PROPERTY MANAGER—AND HOW TO MAKE THEM ACCOUNTABLE

So, having established that engaging a property manager should be an integral part of your property investment strategy, let's address the second burning issue—how do you find a good one, and make sure they are doing the right thing by you and your property?

The best place to start when you look for a property manager is your family, friends and colleagues. If any of them invest in property, ask them who they use, what their fees are and whether or not they are happy with the level of service. Does the property manager collect the rent and deposit it in their account promptly, take swift action to recover late payments, inspect the property regularly and report back with any recommendations on maintenance or repairs? Do they respond quickly and fully to requests from clients and tenants? Do they handle any disputes in a timely and appropriate manner? Do they review the rent level and lease conditions periodically to reflect changes in the rental market and the needs of their client and tenant?

Whether or not someone has referred you to a property manager, it pays to cross-check their bona fides with at least one independent source. Remember that one person's property management heaven can be another's property management hell! The property manager who was appropriate for one investor and one location may not be appropriate for another. This is why you should do the following.

Contact your State or Territory real estate institute (see Appendix B for details) for a list of member property managers nearby—that is, within a few kilometres of your investment property. You might travel across town to your favourite hairdresser or faithful accountant but, unlike your investment property, your hair travels with you and so do your taxes! When it comes to property management, you need someone with detailed local knowledge—market cycles, vacancy rates and rent levels. If they are a Real Estate Institute (REI) member, you are afforded additional protection. In addition to their obligations to you, the client, REI members must abide by a strict code of professional standards and behaviour. They can therefore be held accountable for their actions through the institute's disciplinary committees and processes, over and above any other remedies available to you through general consumer and business practice legislation.

Ask about the REI member's qualifications. In some states property managers have special REI accreditation, showing that they have completed formal training in a comprehensive range of property management issues and responsibilities. Some states also require property managers to be licensed estate agents. This enhances their knowledge and ability to advise you.

Once you have a list of potential property managers, it is essential to ask them a range of questions before you make a decision. Go and visit them at their office if at all possible, rather than just speaking to them over the phone. First impressions do count here. If the office is tidy and professional looking and the staff greet you courteously, it is often an indication that their property management service will be professional too. But, as beauty is so often only skin deep, ask them the following questions:

- How long have you been a property manager?
- What are your professional qualifications? When was the last time you undertook professional development training, and when do you next plan to upgrade your skills?
- How long have you worked in the local area? How long has your company been established here?
- How long have you worked with this company? Where did you work previously, and for what period of time?
- What are your reporting arrangements? Quite apart from contacting you as a matter of priority when urgent repairs are needed or a tenant is vacating, a good property manager should inspect the property regularly—at least every six months, or in accordance with tenancy legislation. They should also give you regular—three-to-six monthly—reports on the overall progress of the tenancy, including whether the tenant is looking after the property, whether any repairs or maintenance are needed, and, towards

the end of a tenancy, whether the rent level or lease terms and conditions should be reviewed to keep pace with market conditions or your changing circumstances. If there are any vacancy periods between tenancies, ask how often they will check on the security of the property and keep you informed of their endeavours to secure a new tenant.

- Do you own a property? While this is not an essential criterion for choosing the right property manager, it is our experience that when a property manager owns their own property they will have stronger personal appreciation of what is at stake and will take a more active interest in looking after your investment.
- What is your line of accountability? If you experience any problems with your property manager, you need to know to whom they are responsible so you can pursue the matter further if needed. Remember, however, that you have appointed them as your agent, with the authority to do what is lawfully necessary to fulfil your responsibilities under residential tenancies and associated legislation. This means that, while you have every right to expect efficiency, attention to detail and well-considered advice, you still bear ultimate responsibility for the property management process.
- Does the company offer written standards by which you can measure their quality of service? While written standards are not essential, they can indicate the company's commitment to your satisfaction.
- Can I speak with some of your current clients? Speaking with two or three of the property manager's current clients will help give you a more objective view of the company, its staff and its services.

WHAT SHOULD A GOOD PROPERTY MANAGER DO?

The work of a property manager throughout the life of any tenancy falls into four broad categories.

Pre-leasing

After you have signed a property management authority, the property manager should inspect your property thoroughly. They will assess its likely rental value, generate a condition report or similar document, note any special features that will appeal to tenants and recommend any necessary improvements or repairs. To maximise the property's appeal to tenants, they should also ensure it is cleaned to a reasonable standard. In some states this is *mandatory* under tenancy legislation.

When estimating the likely rental income, a good property manager will consider several factors:

- *Rental demand for that particular size, style and location of property* Remember that the factors underpinning rental demand differ from the factors affecting buyer demand. The most popular properties among tenants are attractive yet low maintenance—no elaborate gardens, pools or tennis courts—with neutral décor, built-in wardrobes and basic heating or cooling, depending on the climate. They are also in close proximity to—that is, no more than a few minutes from—public transport, shopping, leisure and educational facilities. And, because many tenants live in small households, properties with one to three bedrooms tend to lease more readily than larger, more elaborate ones—maximising your rental income and occupancy rates.

- *Current market conditions* The rental market, just like the buying and selling market, is subject to cyclical ebbs and flows. When rental demand is high, for example, when buyers are delaying purchasing their first home, rental vacancies drop—placing a rental premium on the properties that are still available. Conversely, when rental demand is low, vacancy rates increase—releasing price pressure and reducing or stabilising rent levels.

If you set a rent level too high for current market conditions, you may not be able to lease your property quickly—and the longer your property remains vacant, the more you will have to dip into your own funds to help cover outgoings such as interest, rates and insurance. Your insurance may well be higher, too—insurers like to know that properties are occupied, as it lessens the likelihood of break-ins. Some will not insure a property that is vacant for longer than a specified period.

Conversely, if you set the rent level too low, you will miss out on valuable income that could help you reduce your loan more quickly and build that all important equity.

To ensure your rental income remains relatively stable in the face of changing market conditions—and market conditions will change many times over the lifespan of your investment—a good property manager will set a rent level that makes the best of prevailing market conditions without alienating tenants. Remember that there are costs associated with re-letting a property. There are letting, advertising, cleaning and repair costs. If you have found a good tenant, you should be doing everything to encourage them to stay.

Streetwise

It is far better to have a stable long-term tenant in your property at a reasonable rental level than to have a succession of disruptive short-term tenancies because you won't compromise by $10 or $15 a week on the rental amount.

Tenant selection

Once the property is ready for leasing, the property manager should begin sourcing potential tenants. They may do this through a variety of avenues, including window advertisements, rental lists, their website and existing databases of potential tenants. They may also choose to advertise in local and metropolitan daily newspapers. When inquiries come in, the property manager will arrange for prospective tenants to inspect the property either by giving them the key in exchange for a refundable deposit, by accompanying them at a pre-arranged time or by inviting them to attend a scheduled 'open for inspection' time.

If the tenant likes the property and decides to apply, the property manager will give them an application form with a series of detailed questions including current and previous addresses, contact details for previous landlords or property managers, current and past employment and income. They will also request identification and the contact details of reputable, objective referees—not a relative or best friend!—who can vouch for the tenant's reliability.

The property manager will then assess the applications, cross-checking them with objective information from sources such as the National Tenancy database and referees. The property manager must examine each application solely on its merits. Under anti-discrimination legislation, they cannot make recommendations to you about the suitability of potential tenants based on personal characteristics such as age, race, marital status, gender or disability.

Having assessed and verified the applications, the property manager will recommend the tenant they believe is the most suitable for your property.

Remember the arm's length rule: You don't need to meet and screen the tenant—that is what you are paying the property manager for!

Assuming you accept their recommendation, the property manager will offer the tenant a lease and prepare written documentation. Property managers who are members of State or Territory real estate institutes will generally use an institute-approved lease.

Remember that a lease is a contract between you and the tenant, not your property manager and the tenant, and as such sets out mutual rights and obligations, with the overriding objective of ensuring fair dealings between each party. It is not an opportunity for you to put on the thumbscrews and track your tenant's every move, nor for your tenant to mistreat your property or ask for every luxury under the sun!

Standard leases set out the basic terms and conditions applying to your relationship with the tenant, as well as covering the majority of issues you can expect to arise during the life of a tenancy agreement, including:

- type and length of tenancy;
- rental amount, frequency and due dates for payment;
- the amount of bond or security deposit;
- obligations regarding the property's use, condition and cleanliness;
- prohibitions on specific activities that may be unlawful or damage the property;
- depending on the state or territory, provisions for recourse to a tenancies tribunal in the event of damage or disputes;
- frequency of rent reviews; and
- requirements for notice when either party wishes to end the tenancy.

Many property managers also exercise the option to include special conditions that enhance your rights and/or obligations under the lease, such as a requirement that the tenant have the carpets professionally cleaned on vacating the property.

At the time of signing the lease, your property manager will ask the tenant to pay a bond or security deposit, generally equivalent to a month's rent. In most states and territories, property managers submit the bond to a residential tenancies bond authority or similar government authority, which holds the money in trust for the duration of the lease. The bond is fully refundable on vacating the property, provided the tenant has met all their obligations under the lease.

In some states and territories tenants must also sign a condition report which, as the name implies, records the condition of each part of the property, including walls, ceiling, floor coverings, appliances, tapware, lighting, window dressings and so on. The tenant records any discrepancies between the property manager's assessment of the property's condition and their own, and returns a copy of the report to the property manager. At the end of the tenancy the condition report can provide a useful reference point in the unlikely event that the tenant has damaged the property beyond normal wear and tear.

Increasingly, written condition reports are being supplemented by photographic evidence of the property's state of repair. This makes it easy for you and your property manager to distinguish between normal wear and tear and more serious damage.

Smoothing the way

After the tenancy has commenced, the property manager's role becomes that of a caretaker and adviser, ensuring that everything runs smoothly. They must collect the rent by the due date or take appropriate action if it is late, then distribute it to you in a timely manner. They must assess requests for repairs and maintenance, contact you promptly with recommendations, organise quotes and supervise the work to ensure it is completed satisfactorily. They must also inspect the property at or above the minimum required frequency, to ascertain whether the tenant is taking care of the property and abiding by the tenancy agreement. They should report back to you after each inspection, recommending appropriate action if needed.

Towards the end of the tenancy, or when allowed for under the lease, the property manager should also review the current rent level to ensure it remains competitive in light of changes in market conditions without pricing you, or your tenants, out of the rental market. Remember that your tenant can complain if they think the proposed rent increase is unreasonable—or vote with their feet by vacating the premises. The property manager should also review the terms and

FAQ: I'd like to manage my own investment property to save money and keep an eye on the tenants. What do you think?

Unless you have substantial knowledge of tenancy legislation and considerable time on your hands, we recommend you pay a professional property manager to do the job for you. Property management fees are modest and tax deductible. Furthermore, the relationship between an investor and tenant is a business one, and should be conducted at arm's length. Hand the job over to a professional and make them accountable to you.

conditions of the lease to make sure they are still appropriate for your needs and those of your tenant.

Getting defensive

As your authorised representative, your property manager is also your first line of defence should any dispute arise during the tenancy. In some states and territories investors and tenants have recourse to a residential tenancies or small claims tribunal, an independent civil body that handles the general range of disputes which can arise out of residential tenancy leases, such as damage, repairs and rent increases or default.

In most instances, disputes can be settled between your property manager and tenant without recourse to a tribunal. In fact this is preferable, as it saves time, money and the stress of tribunal appearances. However, should a dispute proceed to tribunal stage, your property manager can prepare the necessary paperwork and appear on your behalf. If the tenant has complained and the tribunal finds in their favour, your property manager can implement any required reparation. If you have complained and the tribunal finds in your favour, the property manager can make representations on your behalf to ensure the tenant complies with the ruling, including recovering any unpaid rent or obtaining recompense for damage bills, generally via a deduction from the tenant's bond. Of course, since your property manager cannot take the law into their own hands, they can't force compliance. If the tenant fails to comply with a tribunal order, the property manager should pursue the matter through the appropriate channels. In rare cases, you may need to obtain separate legal representation.

If, at the conclusion of the tenancy, you and the tenant wish to renew the agreement, the property manager prepares the necessary paperwork and things carry on as usual. If you or the tenant wish to end the relationship the property manager sees to it that the tenant fulfils their obligation under the lease before vacating, conducts a final inspection and organises the return of bond, before starting the cycle again by advertising for new tenants.

With so many responsibilities, it is easy to see why engaging a professional property manager is essential to the ongoing viability of your investment—and why it's vital to keep them accountable.

The GST and Your Property Management—Bottom Line

Holding and maintaining an investment property involves supplying goods and services to your tenants and receiving them from property managers, tradespeople and others who help maintain the viability of your investment. This means you will have to pay GST. In chapter ten we examined the GST's overall impact on residential investment property. The GST as it relates to property management is particularly complex and has been a source of confusion for many investors, so we thought it worthwhile to devote a small section to it here.

INPUTS AND OUTPUTS

Residential property investors pay GST on most of the goods and services associated with holding an investment property. These include:

- property management and associated fees;
- materials and labour for repairs and maintenance;
- body corporate fees if the property is a strata title unit; and
- insurance.

Council rates, water and sewerage services are GST free.

As covered in chapter ten, most businesspeople can separate their GST expenditure from the actual cost of the expense incurred and claim it back in full at the end of the reporting period. However, residential property investors are input taxed, that is, while you must pay GST on most goods and services associated with holding your property, you can't claim it back separately.

All you can do is claim the GST-inclusive cost of your property-related products or services as a normal tax deduction. However, because deductions are only allowable at your marginal rate, you will only receive a proportion of your original GST expenditure.

How, then, do you recoup the shortfall? 'Easy,' you say, 'I'll just pass it on to my tenant by increasing the rent proportionately.' Afraid not!

Residential rents are GST-free. You can't simply ask tenants to pay GST on top of their normal rental payments, or add your GST shortfall to the base rent amount, either at the end of a lease when a rent review would normally be due or at any time during the lease. Tenants can complain to the Australian Consumer and Competition Commission (ACCC) if they believe you are trying to pass your GST costs on to them. The ACCC can impose hefty penalties if they find you are in breach of GST guidelines and legislation.

The best way to recoup any GST-related shortfall is to maximise your rental income by purchasing in precincts where rental demand is consistently strong.

A final reminder—if you are in any doubt about GST and property management issues (or even if you're not!), always check on how the GST affects your particular circumstances with your accountant or tax adviser.

CHAPTER THIRTEEN
Evaluating the Success of Your Investment

WHAT TO DO WITH WHAT YOU'VE GOT

A worthwhile investment property must fully justify inclusion in your portfolio—not just at the time of purchase, but for many years afterwards. To ensure your property earns its keep, enabling you to build substantial equity and purchase further investments, it is vital to put it through an annual 'health check'. Your body needs regular physicals to check that it is running in good order; and your car needs servicing to keep it on the road. Residential investment property is exactly the same.

So many people buy an investment property and then, based on its capital performance after just a few months, make premature and sweeping judgements about its long-term potential. Don't make this mistake. Remember what we said earlier—the property market, at the national, metropolitan, suburban and even street level, always ebbs and flows.

This is why, when you are buying to hold for the long term—at least seven to ten years, and preferably much longer—capital growth or loss over an interval any shorter than two years or so is of minor significance. Even then, exceptional national and local factors such as high inflation or the sale of a nearby redevelopment at a premium price can create glitches and make your property appear worth more or less than its true technical value.

It is crucial to keep such external influences in perspective because you, as an individual investor, have little control over them. There is nothing to stop you from raising your concerns over interest rates, inflation and so on with the relevant authorities—if enough people do it, governments are sometimes forced to listen! But generally, for the sake of your sanity and the ongoing viability of your investment, you are better off directing your energies towards matters over which you *can* exercise some control. We will focus on these in this chapter.

Remember, too, that while capital growth should be your prime consideration, other factors like rental income, taxation benefits and the structure of your loan also have a significant impact on your property's investment viability.

Tracking your property's performance— seven simple steps

So how do you realistically assess your property's progress, let alone interpret the results and decide what to do with them? Let's work through it, step by step.

STEP 1: ASCERTAIN CURRENT CAPITAL VALUE

In chapter six we discussed the importance of gauging local market values by tracking sales results of directly comparable properties, that is, those of a similar location, style, land size, number of bedrooms and level of cosmetic appeal to the ones you wanted to buy. The same applies when you have bought a property and want to evaluate its progress in capital growth terms. Make sure you obtain sales results for at least three to five comparables to iron out any anomalies caused by unusual factors such as an overly enthusiastic purchaser who paid more than necessary for one of the properties.

STEP 2: ASSESS CAPITAL GROWTH ACHIEVED

Once you know how much your property is worth on today's market, you will be able to calculate the dollar or percentage increase—or, if you have chosen the wrong property, decrease!—on the original purchase price. For example, if you bought a property for $200 000 and your research shows it is now worth around $240 000, you have achieved capital growth of $40 000, or 20 per cent.

Another method of calculating your success as a property investor is to establish its rate of return on equity—in other words, the percentage by which your equity has increased beyond the amount you initially put into the property.

For example, if you have purchased a $200 000 property and paid a 10 per cent deposit (this is your equity at the time of purchase), or $20 000, and the property grows 10 per cent in the first year, your return on equity would be $20 000, or 100 per cent. Like the overall capital growth, this compounds in subsequent years. It is a fairly complex concept, but perhaps the illustration in Table 13.1 will help.

Note that this table is designed purely to illustrate the *basic principle* of rate of return on equity through capital growth. It does not include

Table 13.1: Return on Equity

John and Jane Smith's investment property: Purchase price $200 000; deposit $20 000
Average compound growth @ 10% pa

Year	Capital value	Return on initial equity	
Year 1	$220 000	$20 000	100%
Year 2	$242 000	$42 000	210%
Year 3	$266 200	$66 200	331%
Year 4	$292 820	$92 820	464%
Year 5	**$322 102**	**$122 102**	**611%**
Year 7	$389 743	$189 743	949%
Year 10	**$518 748**	**$318 748**	**1594%**
Year 15	$835 449	$635 449	3177%
Year 20	**$1 345 499**	**$1 145 499**	**5727%**

factors that can alter the rate of return in a real-life situation, such as natural capital growth fluctuations, changes to rental income, personal income tax rates, interest rates, and other out of pocket expenses, or repaying principal (active debt reduction) over and above capital growth (passive equity building). However, what counts here is that you understand the principle of rate of return—and the level of ongoing capital growth your property is achieving relative to the top-performing suburbs in your capital city. If you want to get a very precise assessment of your own property's return on equity, speak to your accountant.

The Smiths' property doubled its capital value between years seven and ten. And the return on their initial $20 000 investment doubled in just two years—simply because they chose an asset with high capital growth potential.

If your property has achieved this kind of growth, well done—you are well on the way to achieving financial independence through property investment.

case study

Capital growth: a very awesome foursome!

Example One In 1997 we purchased a two-storey, three-bedroom 1940s maisonette on behalf of Robert, an investor client. With a purchase price of $331 000, the property was structurally sound, clean and attractive to tenants.

Three years later, without any improvements, the property was worth $560 000. It achieved capital growth of $229 000, purely because of its quality location and architecturally timeless appeal.

Example Two Robyn, an investor client, purchased a two-bedroom, solid brick, original period cottage in 1996. The property had already undergone cosmetic renovation at the time of purchase so Robyn was able to lease it without incurring additional expense. In 2000 the property received a fresh coat of paint to maintain its attractiveness to tenants. From a purchase price of $181 000, the property grew to $470 000 by 2001, based on directly comparable sales nearby.

Example Three In 1996 Leslie and Lisa bought a two-bedroom, 1930s unit in a small, select development. The unit was optimally positioned at the front of the block with a north-south aspect and water views. It also had a lock-up garage on the title. From a purchase price of $176 000, this unit grew to a value of $360 000 in 2001—an astonishing $184 000 in capital growth! Our clients, Leslie and Lisa are very pleased indeed and have since purchased their second investment.

Example Four When the recession was biting hard, we purchased a one-bedroom 1960s unit for Jonathan for $115 000. The unit had off-street parking and two courtyards on title. During the period of ownership, Johnathan has recarpeted the property once and repainted it twice. By 2001, this property had grown in value to $250 000. Again, our assessment of the capital growth was based on the sale of two identical units in the same block.

STEP 3: ASSESS OTHER ASSETS AND NON-RENTAL INCOME

If you have acquired any extra cash, shares or other assets during the review period, note them down. Your present non-rental income, for example, from wages, salary, other investments or allowances, is also important. This information can help provide a clear picture of your overall resources should you wish to branch out and purchase a further investment, whether it is another property or something from a different asset class.

STEP 4: REVIEW YOUR LOAN STRUCTURE

Speak with your lender or mortgage broker to ascertain whether your loan structure is still working effectively for you. For example, if you are paying off principal as well as interest, the pace at which you can reduce the debt will depend on the type and rate of interest. If your loan is fixed, does it still provide a beneficial alternative to a variable rate loan? If your loan is variable, or part variable, its interest rate will be influenced by the Reserve Bank's cash rate, over which you have little control. What about extras such as offset accounts? Are you gaining enough benefit from them to justify the associated fees and charges?

Streetwise

Remember, given the highly competitive nature of today's lending environment, most lenders are accustomed to operating on slender margins. You should ensure they give you the most competitive package possible, not just when you take out the initial mortgage, but throughout the life of the loan.

STEP 5: REASSESS YOUR PROPERTY MANAGER

We said in chapter twelve that it's important to engage a professional to manage your property on your behalf, ensuring you benefit from their expertise while at the same time remaining at arm's length from the day-to-day operational issues. Having said this, when you place the ongoing management of your property in someone else's hands, it is important to review their performance.

Look at your property's current rent level—is it comparable with other properties of similar style, size and level of amenity in the street and/or nearby areas? What is the current level of demand for your style of property—can the rent be increased to reflect high demand? Should it remain the same or decrease slightly if demand is not so strong? Is your property manager doing a thorough job in advising you on and reviewing the appropriate rent level?

Are any cosmetic improvements or repairs required to maintain or enhance your property's rent level and appeal to tenants? Your property manager should be able to advise you on what constitutes a reasonable level of improvement, without overcapitalising, and liaise with service providers and tradespeople to obtain competitive quotes and complete the required works on your behalf.

How well does the property manager attend to day-to-day operational issues? Look back at chapter twelve for a checklist of what you should expect from them.

If your property manager is not performing in one or more of these areas, speak to them about how they can improve their service and retain your business. If they continue to perform poorly, it may be time to look elsewhere. Changing property management companies is a relatively straightforward process, and the end results will be well worth the time involved.

STEP 6: REVIEW YOUR INSURANCES

In chapter nine we discussed the importance of taking out the relevant insurances to cushion you in the event of unforeseen circumstances such as damage to your property or loss of personal income through illness or injury.

Your annual property portfolio review is an ideal time to revisit the level of insurance you have and make any necessary adjustments. For example, if the value of your property has risen considerably, it is advisable to upgrade your landlord protection insurance as well as your building insurance (if it is a house). You may also need to review your contents insurance in light of changes in replacement value. If your wage or salary-based income has changed, reassess your level of income protection insurance coverage along with any other personal insurances that are linked to income.

STEP 7: REVIEW YOUR TAX BENEFITS

We have laboured the point that tax benefits should never be the primary reason to buy an investment property—and the same applies throughout the period you hold it. If, however, you are not getting the optimum allowable tax benefits, while spending money from your after-tax personal income to cover any gap between holding costs and rental income, you will be making things harder for yourself than necessary. Check with your accountant that you are taking full advantage of gearing provisions and that you are claiming appropriately for depreciable items and holding costs.

So what to do now?

Once you have reviewed all seven areas, the first logical step is to attend to any matters that need rectification and are within your immediate control, for example, by changing property managers, upgrading your insurances, refinancing and carrying out maintenance if required.

Then it is time to return to Steps One and Two. Look again at your assessment of the property's current capital value and any change since the date of purchase. It is important to remember that for the first three to four years these figures will give a general indication of how the property is performing relative to local and national trends in the property market and the wider economy. So at this stage, it is probably premature to make judgements as to the property's true investment potential. Reviews of capital value during this period should be *informative* rather than *directive*.

After the first few years, as external effects play themselves out, it will become easier to judge whether or not your property deserves its place in your portfolio and what, if any, major changes need to be made.

Once you reach this point you will probably be confronted with all manner of complex suggestions to help you measure whether or not your investment property is worth keeping. Many of these, it must be said, require something close to the mind of Einstein and the patience of Job to calculate! But fear not—we are about to make the process a whole lot easier.

We have said before that prime investment property should double in value at least every seven to ten years. For a property to double in value after seven years, it must grow at 10 per cent per annum. If it is to double in value after ten years, it must grow at 7 per cent per annum.

In times of high inflation, it is likely that a higher proportion of this 7 to 10 per cent will come from inflation-driven growth, as distinct from demand-driven growth.

But, because you are buying to hold for the long term, you will also be holding the property in times of low inflation. In a low-inflation environment, such as we've experienced in the 1990s and early 2000s, you can't rely on inflation to drive capital growth. True growth, as driven by high market demand, will be the major contributor.

This is why, to double in value every seven to ten years, your property must achieve average annual capital growth of 7 to 8 per cent above the prevailing inflation rate—whatever that may be.

Let's look at table 13.2 which shows a baseline growth of 7% exclusive of inflation and two equally prime investment properties, all purchased for $200 000. Property A was purchased in a high inflation environment of 6 per cent per annum. Property B was purchased in a low inflation environment of 2 per cent. And let's assume for argument's sake that both Property A and Property B are growing in capital value at an average annual rate of 7 per cent above the prevailing inflation rate.

Table 13.2: Property Performance Benchmark

Benchmark property Purchase price $200 000		Property A Purchase price $200 000		Property B Purchase price $200 000	
Overall capital growth 7% (no inflation)		Overall capital growth 13% pa (including inflation @ 6% pa)		Overall capital growth 9% pa (including inflation @ 2% pa)	
Year 1	$214 000	Year 1	$226 000	Year 1	$218 000
Year 2	$228 980	Year 2	$255 380	Year 2	$237 620
Year 3	$245 009	Year 3	$288 579	Year 3	$259 006
Year 4	$262 159	Year 4	$326 095	Year 4	$282 316
Year 5	$280 510	Year 5	$368 487	Year 5	$307 725
Year 6	$300 146	**Year 6**	**$416 390**	Year 6	$335 420
Year 7	$321 156	Year 7	$470 521	Year 7	$365 608
Year 8	$343 637	Year 8	$531 689	**Year 8**	**$398 513**
Year 9	$367 692	Year 9	$600 808	Year 9	$434 379
Year 10	$393 430	Year 10	$678 913	Year 10	$473 473

In a high inflation environment Property A doubles its value at year six, slightly before our recommended benchmark. Property B, in a *low* inflation environment, takes a bit longer, doubling around year eight. But it has still achieved this well within the seven- to ten-year time-frame—and the owner has the security of knowing that true, demand-driven—that is sustainable—growth is the primary reason. It may be worthwhile revisiting the sections on property and inflation on pages 31 and 45 to ensure you keep the inflation issue in its correct perspective when you are evaluating your investment property performance.

Does your property measure up?

If you have assessed your property in accordance with this benchmark and it is coming up roses, congratulations! You now have two options:

(a) hold on to the property and reduce the debt further, while watching the equity accumulate; or (b) leverage off the accumulated equity to purchase a second investment, whether it be a property or otherwise.

Whether you choose option (a) or (b) will depend largely on your personal and financial circumstances. Throughout this book we have said that procrastination is your arch enemy. You should not delay purchasing top-quality investment property because the buy-in price of quality residential property will increase more quickly than you can save to bridge the gap; reducing the opportunity for compounding capital growth. However, you need to feel that your investments are a manageable part of your life. If you are going through a major life change such as the birth of a child, change of career or retirement, you may be better off embarking on a second investment when your personal circumstances have settled. Seek professional advice about what is appropriate for your current overall situation.

Building your property portfolio—from one to two and beyond!

If you do decide to embark on a second investment and you want to look at property, speak to your lender to establish your financial situation. This basically involves the same process we outlined in chapter eight—an assessment of your:

- existing equity;
- wage/salary and rental income;
- debts; and
- living expenses.

Apart from any changes in your personal circumstances, the main difference this time will be that because you have a prime asset, you have considerably more equity for leveraging.

In fact, no matter how many investment properties you purchase, these key borrowing criteria remain constant. It is your ongoing accumulation of equity combined with cash flow from rental income and other sources that will determine if and when you can purchase subsequent investment properties. Your lender and accountant are best placed to help you structure your portfolio from a borrowings standpoint.

Once you know whether you can purchase property number two, and in which price range you can look, the acquisition process is very much the same as it was for your first property, but with one big difference. Property is like any other growth-based investment: to spread your risk and maximise capital growth it is vital to diversify. If you bought a two-bedroom 1960s to 1970s style unit in a particular suburb the first time around, don't go and buy the same style of property in the same or similar location just because you've become familiar with it. Consider a different style of unit in a different area, or, depending on your finances, a house, again in a different but equally well-performing location.

In any capital city, there will always be a range of property styles and locations that produces optimum investment performance. The most successful investors choose the best-performing property from all these sources—rather than buying the same kind of investment over and over again. They are not afraid to diversify and leave their emotions at the door!

> **Streetwise**
>
> *Purchasing different styles in a range of locations will help create a buffer against any localised fluctuations in value and build a strong base of equity to strengthen your financial position. At the same time, the combined rental income will go a long way towards meeting holding costs while you are still working, and replacing your salary or business income once you retire.*

What if your property isn't making the grade?

If you've assessed your property according to the criteria we've outlined and you're not happy with the results, don't panic just yet. There could be several reasons for the property's apparently lacklustre performance.

Compare your property's capital growth with the median price increase for each of the top five performing suburbs in your capital city. Remember to use the most consistently performing suburbs as your point of comparison, not new estates or inner city projects where prices are determined by the developer's premium and could temporarily skew the median value.

If the property is keeping pace with these growth levels or only doing slightly better, it is possible that external factors such as national economic fluctuations are at play. In this case, sit tight—the economic tide will turn eventually; it always does!

If your property is performing below these levels, ask yourself the following questions:

- *Is the suburb or pocket genuinely undervalued?* (Refer to chapter six for criteria.) If all indications are that prices in the area will begin to move within three to five years or slightly longer, it is probably best to hold on to the property. When prices do move, the capital growth relative to your modest buy-in price will have you smiling from ear to ear.

However, it may be that an area you thought was undervalued three to five years ago has actually turned out to be just plain cheap. Are there other areas showing signs of substantial capital growth where

FAQ: Should I sell my investment property?

If you have held your property for at least three to four years and it's averaging annual capital growth of at least 7 to 8% above the prevailing inflation rate, you should hold on to it for as long as possible! The ongoing capital growth and debt reduction will help you create net wealth and provide leverage to purchase further investments if you so desire.

If your property is not performing at these levels, there could be several reasons, as discussed in this chapter. Work through your options thoroughly before deciding whether to sell. But if selling is the only appropriate course of action, don't delay—it could cost you thousands as the gap between what you can sell an under performing asset for and what you'll need to spend on a top performing asset widens.

When you are close to retirement, rent becomes the income stream that replaces your wage or salary. If you have accumulated a portfolio of investment properties, it may be appropriate to sell one or two properties and retire the debt if you so choose.

you might be better off investing? If this is the case, you may need to consider selling the property and starting again elsewhere. If you are in any doubt, seek independent professional advice.

- *If the suburb is a good performer or genuinely undervalued, is the building style compatible with the rest of the streetscape?* If, say, you have purchased an ultra-modern apartment in an area otherwise replete with period homes, its contrast with the prevailing streetscape along with its appeal to a limited range of purchasers and tenants could hamper its capital growth prospects.

- *Is the property style compatible with the tastes of contemporary purchasers and tenants?* If your property is not stacking up in capital growth terms, it may be of a style that performed well before you bought it, but not in the years since. The inner suburbs of many Australian capital cities, for instance, are rife with examples of large blocks of utilitarian-looking flats that were built in the 1960s and 1970s but were not subdivided until the 1980s. During this time they became very popular with individual investors, because they could access investment property at affordable prices. After the first and second resales, however, the sheer number of these properties along with suboptimal locations in some cases made them less attractive to purchasers and tenants alike. Subsequently, some of these properties did not achieve the capital growth or rental income investors hoped for.

- *Have you spent your available capital wisely?* Remember what we said in chapter seven: Property in most suburbs varies considerably in terms of style, quality of construction, level of renovation and appeal to purchasers and tenants. Even in prime inner suburban areas and in streets where the architecture *appears* to be relatively uniform, not all properties are equal. Perhaps you have bought a couple of one-bedroom units in suburbs, streets or blocks with less than optimum capital growth potential. You may have been better off spending your capital on one well-located two-bedroom unit. Or maybe you bought a single-fronted period cottage in an area with a history of sketchy or minimal capital growth. You might have achieved better results by spending the same amount on a semi-detached house or two-bedroom unit in a prime capital growth location. And so on. You may want to look back at chapters six and seven to refresh your memory about choosing optimum locations and property styles.

If you have worked through these options thoroughly and it is becoming clear that your property's poor capital growth is likely to continue for the foreseeable future, do not be tempted to persevere. Owners of poorly chosen investment property inevitably find that the gap between the value of their asset and values in the wider market (particularly the prime investment areas) grows ever larger, creating a vicious cycle that diminishes their ability to get back on track and buy a really good asset.

A small matter of income ... retiring debt

THE SECOND (AND FINAL!) EXCEPTION TO OUR 'NEVER SELL' RULE!

If you have invested assiduously and wisely over a number of years, it is likely you will have a fair few assets—property and otherwise—together with the considerable debt that goes with them! As retirement nears and you wish to maximise your income, it may be appropriate to consult your financial and property advisers with a view to disposing of one or two assets so you can retire all your outstanding debt.

From a property investment viewpoint, you will need to undertake a review of your portfolio to ascertain:

- which properties have the highest level of equity;
- which combination of properties will provide the best stream of income and ongoing capital growth; and
- the smallest number of properties you need to sell to retire any outstanding debt.

So where to next if I really do need to sell?

While this book is not about selling property, an optimum sale result will help maximise the available capital regardless of why you are selling. So we'd be selling you short (pardon the pun!) if we didn't discuss a few issues associated with disposing of an asset.

Apart from general market conditions such as the relative balance of supply and demand, the key factors in determining the sale price of your property are:

- your choice of selling agent;
- method of sale.
- correct marketing;
- presentation; and
- astute negotiation.

When choosing an agent:

- Look for companies and individuals with long-standing expertise in your property's geographical area, as well as a sound track record in achieving good results for properties comparable to yours.
- Make sure you obtain value appraisals from several companies before choosing one—to give you a broad indication of the types of companies and levels of service you can expect. Don't automatically go with the agent who gives you the highest value appraisal! Go for the company and individual who can demonstrate a strong track record of achieving top results for comparable properties. If you know people who have sold comparable property in the area, ask them who they have used and what their experiences were.
- Similarly, do not assume that the agent who charges the highest commission will also deliver the best-quality service or the highest sale result.
- And do not be afraid to negotiate their fee within reasonable parameters. The aim should be to strike a balance between value for money from *your* point of view, and giving the agent adequate incentive to deliver a first-class result.

Be wary of agents who will readily discount their fee to minuscule levels just to win your business. It is likely they'll adopt the same approach to negotiating the sale price for your property!

When it comes to preparing your property for sale, remember what we covered in chapter seven. Cosmetic appeal is a key factor in determining market value, because it is the cosmetic aspects of a property that purchasers see and place importance on. Investors will size up your property in terms of appeal to tenants, while home buyers will try to imagine themselves living there and see if the picture fits.

We have also discussed cosmetic improvements in terms of preparing a property for lease—repainting, recarpeting, a good spring clean, garden tidy-up and perhaps a minor facelift to the kitchen and bathroom. Since tenants have a relatively minor financial stake in the properties they rent, this level of presentation is usually sufficient to attract them.

When you are selling a property, however, you will probably have to work harder to ensure a strong level of interest, not to mention recoup costs such as the agent's commission and advertising expenses. Cosmetic improvements in this case go a bit further—for example, polishing floorboards, repainting fences and outbuildings and planting trees, shrubs and flowers to bring the garden alive—or using indoor plants if the property is a unit. If the property is tenanted, ensure that your property manager requests the tenants' cooperation in keeping their possessions tidy and the property spotless. If the property is vacant, hire furniture and hang curtains to give it a welcoming feel.

If modest structural work is needed, for example, any repairs to fencing, plasterwork or guttering, this is the time to do it. These improvements are visible so they stand the best chance of being recouped in the sale price. If your suburb is more affordable than surrounding areas, home-buyers in particular will be attracted to a property they know has been improved in this way—rather than borrow extra money, pay the associated interest and do it themselves.

Once you've sold the property for the maximum possible amount within the context of local market conditions, you will be free to retire with little or no debt and live it up, or re-enter the market and, using the criteria for astute asset selection, start building an investment property portfolio that really will set you on the road towards financial independence.

Streetwise

Remember: this book is not just a blueprint for your first purchase—it should be your manual for each and every purchase. Reread chapters six to twelve every time you buy a property, and chapter thirteen once a year to evaluate the overall performance of your portfolio.

CHAPTER FOURTEEN
Adding Value

A SENSE OF ADVENTURE

Once you have got a few superb passive investments producing strong capital growth and rental income, and you are feeling a little more financially secure, you might like to consider a more adventurous approach to making money out of residential property. Adding value through improvements and land subdivisions can be very satisfying and rewarding pursuits for investors who have an entrepreneurial desire and sufficient financial resources.

This chapter is about showing you the differences in mindset, strategy and practice between a long-term, passive investment and actively adding value. We will be taking you through a range of scenarios to help you get your bearings and decide if, and how far, your comfort zone will take you down the adding-value path.

Before you decide whether adding value is really for you, you need to get comfortable with the idea of carrying a higher level of risk. A cool head, substantial financial resources, plenty of equity in other assets and patience (and believe us, you'll need the last one by the truckload!) are also essential if you are going to be successful.

Adding meaning to 'adding value'

When investors talk about adding value, many use the terms 'improvement' and 'redevelopment'. While the two terms are often used interchangeably, they mean very different things. So let's establish a few definitions before we go any further.

For the purposes of this chapter, we'll define **improvements** as *any alteration carried out to a building within the existing shell.*

There are two kinds of improvements—structural and cosmetic.

Structural improvements can be:

- *Remedial*—improvements to the property's structural integrity, for example, restumping or rewiring.
- *Lifestyle-enhancing*—improvements that increase the property's amenity, for example, creating outdoor living features or reworking the existing floor plan to bring it into line with contemporary living.

Cosmetic improvements can be:

- *Superficial* (non-invasive)—repainting, recarpeting or re-tiling.
- *Substantive* (somewhat invasive)—replacing benchtops and cupboard fronts, taking up carpets to expose and polish floorboards or remodelling the kitchen.

There is a good deal of overlap between cosmetic improvements carried out on the kind of passive investments we have focused on throughout this book and those carried out to add value for profit.

Because improvements are not very invasive and relatively inexpensive, there is less need to sell the property quickly to recoup the cost. This makes them suitable for investors who wish to adopt what is essentially a passive buy and hold strategy, but with a degree of entrepreneurial input.

By contrast, a **redevelopment** involves *adding to an existing dwelling, subdividing an existing property or building from scratch*. Because they are more expensive, and usually alter the property's basic structure and layout, redevelopments are better suited to on-selling at the completion of the project.

What is adding value—and why do it?

Whatever form it may take, adding value is about developing a residential building or site to its highest and best use—that is, increasing its market worth by spending money on amenity and lifestyle-enhancing features.

Yet many investors ignore these fundamentals and let emotion and ego cloud their judgement. Almost inevitably they are bitterly disappointed because they have grossly underestimated the cost of the improvements, grossly overestimated the market value of the completed project and spent too much money on all the wrong things.

Streetwise

Before you contemplate adding value to a property, ask yourself why you want to do it in the first place—and this is not a silly or rhetorical question! You should only contemplate this to substantially boost capital or market value or boost rental value and minimise the shortfall between outgoings and rental income. Keeping emotions out of your investment decisions is crucial, especially when it comes to adding value.

SO, HOW DO YOU ADD *TRUE* VALUE?

If you have ever been to a property inspection with an estate agent, you will be well acquainted with how a property's most appealing features are highlighted to engage the emotions and ensure the purchaser pays the highest price. However, consider what you would think if, instead of the fresh paintwork, new carpet or polished floorboards, a cosy living room and sparkling new kitchen and bathroom, you encountered new stumps, new wiring and an empty barrel of insecticide left over from pest prevention treatment to the sub-floor timbers! Which improvements would you go for?

The truth is that we like our creature comforts and are willing to pay for them. So, generally speaking, works with a direct and positive impact on lifestyle and aesthetic appeal are the ones that add tangible value. While structural improvements such as replacing a roof, restumping or treating a termite infestation may require considerable expenditure and are essential to securing the physical integrity of the property, they do not usually translate into added capital value. From an investor's point of view, if the cost of an improvement or redevelopment does not translate to a proportional increase in the property's value within a relatively short period, you have overcapitalised the property.

Remember, too, that the original architecture of the property and surrounding streets and suburbs should dictate the overall *style* of any works. Unsympathetic changes will have a detrimental effect on future value and show poor returns on the capital spent, even in a buoyant market or if the property is held for a reasonable period.

KNOW YOUR MARKET

No matter how straightforward—or how adventurous—your project is, before you go any further than the 'I'm *thinking* about adding value' stage it is vital to attend as many open-for-inspections as possible for recently completed projects that are similar to the one you propose and in the immediate vicinity.

For example, if your project will be purely cosmetic, take careful note of the colours and finishes used in the properties you visit. If you intend to add an extension, note how storage and living space, sleeping quarters and utility areas such as kitchens and bathrooms have been enhanced.

Track sale prices and take a careful note of which kinds of completed projects consistently attract the biggest crowds and fetch the highest prices.

You will also need to differentiate between meeting the market's standards and overcapitalising by trying to outdo the competition. Ask yourself whether you automatically stand to gain a higher profit by installing a European kitchen when most other properties in the area are selling perfectly well with excellent locally produced appliances. The local market may not be willing to bear the extra cost plus the profit margin that would make it worth your while.

On the other hand, if you have invested in a very prestigious suburb where the market expects and is routinely prepared to pay for the latest and the greatest Europe has to offer, and sales figures for properties that do not meet these standards are measurably lacklustre, the more expensive option may be justified. In the end, it all comes down to correctly aligning with the market in which you are investing.

Next, no matter how small or large the project you're contemplating, never buy a property you have earmarked for improvement or begin a redevelopment without undertaking a thorough building inspection. This is one way to minimise the possibility of unexpected delays and/or additional expenses during the works.

Furthermore, an exhaustive feasibility study is essential for any project that goes beyond the substantive cosmetic level. You'll find examples of feasibility studies later in this chapter. This will give you a solid grasp of the building's condition and the kinds of improvements that will produce the desired result—a finished property that is substantially more valuable than the one you started with.

SMALL STEPS FIRST: COSMETIC IMPROVEMENTS

The best way to get your feet wet is to start out with a small-scale, straightforward project such as undertaking cosmetic improvements to a unit or a small house.

Find a property that has all the right attributes: good inner suburban location, timeless architecture and one that is priced within financially comfortable parameters. If your budget restricts you to a unit, make absolutely certain you buy one that is optimally positioned. If you need to, revisit chapters six and seven for a refresher on choosing locations and building styles.

For this first project, choose a property that is structurally sound, even if you are a qualified builder or a very handy layperson. There are two very good reasons why:

- Even if you only have to pay wholesale rates for structural work, you will not see the cost reflected in the eventual sale price or market value. Money spent on invisible structural work is dead money.
- It is vitally important that you have an enjoyable, relatively trouble-free and profitable first experience. Your underlying confidence often determines your level of success with future projects.

Dipping your toes in the water—superficial cosmetic improvements

The most straightforward and commonly attempted adding value scenarios are Levels One and Two.

Level One—existing unit or small house in sound structural order, with good floor plan but looking tired. Only small-scale cosmetic improvements needed.

Level Two—existing house structurally sound, with adequate accommodation and good floor plan but in need of a more extensive overhaul, for example, needs the kitchen freshened up in addition to repainting and recarpeting.

Many budding developers choose to cut their teeth on these sorts of projects because they produce a sense of accomplishment quickly with relatively little risk, while allowing them to learn the basics as they go along. Improvements at these levels typically consist of repainting, recarpeting or polishing floorboards that are in good order, or perhaps replacing floor coverings, splashbacks and cupboard fronts in the kitchen and bathroom. When choosing colours and materials, be sure your choices reflect the tastes of prospective buyers in the area and are consistent with what you'd expect to see in the neighbourhood.

If you want to undertake improvements at these levels, be sure that the property you choose can be made to look appealing without having to undo a lot of pre-existing renovations that are still current. You would be surprised how often investors will go in and spend several thousand dollars undoing someone else's perfectly acceptable renovation before they begin their own works. Such unnecessary expenditure is driven by personal tastes, not business sense, and is seldom recouped by a commensurate increase in capital value.

Wading in waist deep—substantive cosmetic improvements

Level Three—existing house, basically in sound order but in need of substantive cosmetic remodelling to meet modern lifestyle requirements.

Typically, a Level Three property requires a new kitchen, new bathroom, built-in wardrobes and other storage facilities in addition to the cosmetic improvements required in Levels One and Two.

Many properties that require improvements at this level have outside toilets and laundries. Don't be put off by this, as long as the property is otherwise structurally sound. These facilities can usually be brought inside easily and inexpensively using existing plumbing.

Diving in ... to redevelopment

Once you get beyond Level Three it becomes important to seek out a team of well-credentialled, reputable professionals, including:

- a property adviser, for valuable advice on timing and the correct choice of property for your purpose and ensuring you don't overpay for the site or property;
- an architect, builder, possibly a surveyor and specialist tradespeople, such as cabinetmakers, for the design and construction phase;
- an estate agent, for an important grass-roots insight into local buyers' preferences; and
- a lawyer and accountant, for advice on legal and tax issues affecting your entitlements and responsibilities during the works and on the profits and proceeds of the sale.

Each person will play an integral role in advising you, protecting your interests and minimising risks that go hand in hand with a major redevelopment.

If at all possible, convene regular meetings with members of your team. Getting your team talking directly to each other rather than through you will encourage them to share mutually beneficial information—saving you countless telephone calls and one-off meetings with individual providers. You will also be helping *them* to establish new business networks—a win all around.

This done, the next step is to engage in some serious number crunching with the help of your team. Feasibility studies are an essential part of project management and will save your bacon many times over in the face of the inevitable ups and downs. If the project involves anything more than substantive cosmetic improvements and repairs, *always* do a feasibility study and *always* very conservatively, based on a worst-case scenario.

Level Four—small to medium–size block of units all on one title, or each on its own title, requiring:

- modernisation of the kind described under Levels Two and Three;
- cosmetic improvements;
- possibly provision for individual courtyards for ground floor units, general landscaping, garaging; and
- subdividing, if the units are all on one title.

Level Five—existing house requiring extensive structural and cosmetic works—the classic 'renovator's delight'.

It may come as a surprise that we rate the 'renovator's delight' among the riskiest propositions in the redevelopment stakes, especially when it is one of the most common forms of adding value. The reason lies in the amount of structural work required before any cosmetic work can even be contemplated. Often, the amount of time and money required to bring a building back to a structurally sound state substantially exceeds the property's ability to increase commensurately in value in the short term.

If you are contemplating improving a stand-alone renovator's delight as an investment, the short answer is be wary! This may be feasible if you are going to rent it out in a basic but liveable state for a few years afterwards to help reduce debt and recoup your expenses, then further enhance the property with a view to occupying it as a principal place of residence thereafter.

Streetwise

Choosing a run-down property or buying below market value, spending money on improving it and having it revalued so that you can borrow against the extra equity you have theoretically created is a very common strategy, often lauded by those who purport to show you how to 'create instant wealth'. But it is rife with risk.

This approach assumes that quality investment property can readily be bought for a song, and that any expenditure will automatically translate to a commensurate increase in capital value. The result? Overcapitalisation.

The reality is that if a property sells for considerably less than ostensibly similar properties it is very likely that it lacks the fundamental characteristics that confer strong capital growth. And there is little point spending money if you are not going to make money through strong demand driven capital growth.

Improving a property, having it revalued and using the mounting equity to acquire further assets is fine, provided you allow sufficient time between acquisitions for the overall market to rise and your strategy includes regular debt reduction along the way so that you are not overexposed.

Building from scratch

Level Six—vacant land or a demolition site, possibly with two street frontages, suited to a single dwelling, dual occupancy, townhouse or unit development.

Redeveloping a vacant site to its highest and best use is the most challenging way to make money out of residential property. If you want to go down this path, you will get the best results by subdividing a large block into smaller parcels. This will maximise site coverage without adversely affecting the quality of life for the end-users. You must ensure that the proposed dwelling or dwellings are in keeping with the surrounding architecture and that local planning regulations and guidelines are met.

Here are the major steps you will need to complete when adding value at this advanced level:

- Finance the project—see your banker and work out what you can afford to borrow, buy and repay.
- Time the acquisition and refurbishment carefully.
- Select the site and undertake feasibility studies.
- Enlist professional expertise—architect, accountant, property adviser, selling agents and others to advise you.
- Appoint and supervise builders and other tradespeople.
- Time the resale correctly, appoint a selling agent, and generate a budget for advertising the property.

Let's look at some of these steps in more detail.

SITE SELECTION

You will need to select a building site that is either vacant or has an existing property on it of little intrinsic value and of no architectural significance to the area. Do not choose a site in an architecturally significant or heritage area with an old building that, if demolished, would raise bitter objections from local residents and lengthy, expensive delays for you—unless, of course, you like the idea of sleepless nights!

Within a general context, there are a number of broad-based guidelines that can help when it comes to site selection in a Level Six project.

1. *A fairly level site is preferable.* The last thing you want is expensive excavations for which you won't see a cent in return.

2. *A dual street frontage* can be advantageous, though not mandatory, especially if you propose subdividing the block into two or more separate titles and building two or more dwellings.

3. *Great street, inappropriate house for the street and area.* Very often you will come across a street in a superb location that meets all the criteria for top-class investments and is reasonably architecturally uniform, except for one house that is the thorn amongst the roses! In this situation you could be face to face with a wonderful redevelopment opportunity provided you design and build something that will enhance and blend in with the street's predominant architecture.

4. *An undervalued, underutilised site* in a previously industrial or commercial area that is currently being rezoned and reassigned to residential use.

Choosing such a site may require some mental gymnastics. The characteristics of these sites are often the antithesis of those we would normally recommend as long-term investments. They are often found on busy roads and, in the short term at least, will not look like an idyllic living environment given the amount of surrounding development activity. If you opt for this scenario, your degree of success will depend on your ability to correctly anticipate the locality's potential to become desirable in the immediate future, and certainly within your project's completion and resale timeframe.

In this instance, because you are interested in a short-term turn-around and profit, *not* long-term capital growth potential, a main road location will not necessarily be out of the question as long as the dwelling's design and orientation significantly enhances quality of life for residents and minimises the impact of a busy location. This is one of the very few instances in which residential investment property in a main road location may be a worthwhile option.

5. *Make sure there is existing basic infrastructure close by*—transport, shops, educational facilities—with clear potential for desirable amenities to develop further as the area becomes more established.

6. *Most of all, you will need to negotiate a competitive purchase price based on your conservative feasibility study* (see pages 276–78), given that your timeline, objective and profit all need to converge within a relatively short period.

The purchase price of the site is the key to the entire viability of a development. This is because the value of a site is subject to highly variable market forces. Under no circumstances should you significantly exceed the projected purchase price for the site as independently assessed by a professional who is working for you. Doing that is a surefire recipe for blowing your budget and that all-important profit margin.

BUILDING FROM SCRATCH—WHEN TIMING DOES MATTER

Unlike the more passive forms of property investment, undertaking a major redevelopment requires careful timing to maximise profit.

FAQ: I want to renovate a property to achieve capital growth. What do you suggest?

Despite what some advisers tell you, you don't need to actively add value to a property to achieve good capital growth. If you buy in a location with limited market supply and high demand from a broad range of buyers, this *alone* will generate a substantial amount of growth. On the other hand, if you buy a poorly located property, you'll rely largely on renovating to achieve growth—running the risk that the property may not appeal to a sufficiently broad range of buyers, *and* it will be eating into your profits.

If you do want to renovate, you may be better off choosing a well located property and confining your work to cosmetic improvements that add tangible value.

Many investors sit back for a year ... or two, or three and watch everyone else scooping the pool. Based on tall tales of glory from those who have profited from a redevelopment, they finally decide to act. Little do they realise that it takes 12 to 18 months to get from acquiring the site to the sale of the completed project. This amount of lead-time is necessary to obtain building and town planning permits, source and engage a reputable builder and architect—and complete the construction, marketing and sale processes.

Ultimately, many developers end up trying to sell their finished project at a time when new dwellings are in full supply. As a result, the project competes with innumerable others for the attention of a limited quantity of purchasers. Bad move—not to mention expensive, when you factor in all the costs associated with holding and promoting a languishing development that should have sold shortly after completion.

Ideally, a redevelopment project should hit the market at the peak of buyer demand, and certainly before the local building cycle tops out.

Enlisting professional advice

Good old-fashioned number crunching comes into its own when you are contemplating a Level Five or Six redevelopment. In over 20 years of property advisory experience we have observed that lack of attention to the financial feasibility of a proposed project is the number-one mistake investors make.

Under no circumstance should you skip your feasibility study on the basis that 'She'll be right mate!' Believe us, *'she'* won't be. Such a high-risk undertaking requires a careful and considered approach.

The first step in conducting your feasibility study is to spend considerable time in the market in which you intend to invest. Note the types of redevelopments that are coming on to the market and, of these, which locations, styles and characteristics are achieving the best resale results. Inspect as many properties as you possibly can to ensure you are conversant with the design, styling, materials, workmanship and buyer responses to the projects in your target areas. Focus exclusively on the projects that most closely mirror a realistic construction budget and resale price for your purposes.

It is also worth noting which estate agencies appear to be best equipped to manage the eventual sale of your project. Invariably, one or two will crop up as the most consistent performers and the most knowledgeable in handling the specialised marketing of redevelopment projects. You will find a similar pattern emerges when it comes to choosing an architect and builder—some will have considerable experience in small- and medium-scale redevelopments and will be an invaluable source of advice and information. Builders and architects almost always display their contact details via on-site signage.

FEASIBILITY CASE STUDIES

Once you have identified a suitable site or property, you need to generate several feasibility studies based on different levels of improvement or redevelopment. This will help you work out how to maximise your profit.

Streetwise

The benchmark against which to assess the feasibility of each option should be based on the current market value of the site at the time you undertake your feasibility study. For the project to be feasible, you must end up with a balance in excess of the current site value after all costs and your profit are deducted.

Take a look at the following sample feasibility studies which are modelled on real-life situations. The most important figure is the percentage profit each scenario yields—and that's nothing below 20 per cent.

As you read, keep in mind that the actual figures don't matter because they will vary depending on where in our great land you happen to be reading this. It's the strategy behind the numbers and the attention to every last detail of materials, fees and services associated with the project that's important. Ready?

Sample property

Address: 100 Rompitin Road, Superville

Site area: 765 square metres: 17 m x 45 m (55 ft x 150 ft = 8250 sq ft approx.)

Aspect: north/south.

Current status of site: two rather run-down, although structurally sound, two-bedroom/one-bathroom duplex units built in the 1950s, each with garage, occupy the site. The two units are both on the same title. The units have been tenanted since the purchase to offset holding costs and aid debt reduction.

Financial status: Bought for $350 000 and tenanted since the acquisition.

Current site value: $500 000—now debt-free.

Objective: Improve and sell for maximum profit.

OPTION 1: SUBDIVIDE THE TWO UNITS AND UNDERTAKE COSMETIC WORKS

Construction
Modernise kitchens and bathrooms	$15 000
Landscape to create courtyards	$10 000
Reinstate existing fencing	$3000
Total construction	**$28 000**

Interior finishes
Flooring i.e. carpets, lino, tiles	$8000
Window finishes i.e. blinds, curtains	$4000
Paint throughout interior and exterior, timber and metal fixtures as required	$10 000
Total interior finishes	**$22 000**

Professional and other fees
Stamp duty on purchase (based on Victorian rates at the time of purchase)	$16 660
Architect and project management	$nil
Surveyor	$2500
Solicitor—conveyancing/subdivision and sale: 2 x $1000 (original acquisition and resale)	$2000
Real estate agent commission on resale @ approx. 2% of resale price	$17 500
Municipal permits	$1000
Marketing for resale	$4000
Total professional and other fees	**$43 660**

Subtotal—construction, finishes and fees	*$93 660*

Finance
Borrow	$93 660
Bank fees	$500
Interest rate @ 7% pa over 6 months including up to 90-day settlement	$3296
Contingency	$10 000
Total cost of project	**$107 456**

Resale details
Two refurbished units, each on its own title @ a conservative market value of $350 000 ea	$700 000
Total projected gross realisation	$700 000
Less	
Percentage profit (loss) 20%	$140 000
Total cost of project	$107 456
Balance	**$452 544**

Is this project feasible, based on current site value of $500 000?	*No*

OPTION 2: DEMOLISH EXISTING BUILDING AND ERECT TWO NEW 210 M² HOUSES

Construction
Demolition of existing structures	$6000
Two dwellings @ $210 000 ea (based on a cost of $1000 per square metre)	$420 000
Driveway and two double garages	$25 000
Landscaping and fencing as required	$28 000
Total construction	**$479 000**

Interior finishes
Flooring i.e. carpets, polished floorboards, lino, tiles	$20 000
Window finishes i.e. blinds, curtains	$8000
Paint throughout interior and exterior, timber and metal fixtures as required	$15 000
Light fittings	$4000
Total interior finishes	**$47 000**

Professional and other fees
Stamp duty on purchase	$16 660
Architect and project management	$52 600
Surveyor	$2500
Solicitor/conveyancing/subdivision and resale, two @ $1000 (original acquisition and resale).	$2000
Real estate agent's commission on resale @ 2%	$32 000
Municipal permits	$3000
Marketing for resale	$7000
Total professional and other fees	**$115 760**

Subtotal—construction, finishes and fees	*$641 760*

Finance
Borrow	$641 760
Bank fees	$500
Interest rate @ 7% pa over 18 months including up to 90-day settlement	$67 437
Contingency	$30 000

Total cost of project	**$739 697**

Resale details
Two new 210 m² houses conservative market value of:

(front dwelling)	$820 000
(rear dwelling)	$780 000

(Front units in tandem projects like this are generally assumed to realise a higher sale price because their street frontage theoretically affords greater appeal)

Total projected gross realisation	$1 600 000
Less	
Percentage profit (loss) 20%	$320 000
Total cost of project	$739 697
Balance	**$540 303**

Is this project feasible, based on current site value of $500 000?	Yes

OPTION 3: THREE NEW 160 M² UNITS

Construction
Demolition of existing structures	$6 000
Three dwellings @ $160 000 ea based on construction cost of $1000 per square metre	$480 000
Driveway and three garages	$40 000
Landscaping and fencing	$28 000
Total construction	**$554 000**

Interior finishes
Flooring i.e. carpets, polished floorboards, lino, tiles	$25 000
Window finishes i.e. blinds, curtains	$10 000
Paint throughout interior and exterior, timber and metal fixtures as required	$20 000
Light fittings	$5 000
Total interior finishes	**$60 000**

Professional and other fees
Stamp duty	$16 660
Architect and project management	$52 600
Surveyor	$2 500
Solicitor/conveyancer, three @ $1000	$3 000
Real estate agent commission on resale @ approx. 2% of resale price	$27 800
Municipal permits	$3 000
Marketing for resale	$7 000
Total professional fees	**$112 560**

Subtotal—construction, finishes and fees	**$726 560**

Finance
Borrow	$726 560
Bank fees	$500
Interest rate @ 7% pa over 18 months including up to 90-day settlement	$76 341
Contingency	$30 000
Total cost of project	**$833 401**

Resale details
Three new 160 m² houses with a market value of:
Front dwelling	$480 000
Middle dwelling	$450 000
Rear dwelling	$460 000

(Front units in projects like this are generally assumed to realise a higher sale price because street frontage theoretically affords greater appeal. Middle units are the least favoured and rear units are considered to be the most private, though they don't offer the street appeal of front units.)
$1 390 000

Total projected gross realisation	$1 390 000
Less	
Percentage profit (loss) 20%	$278 000
Total cost of project	$833 401
Balance	**$278 599**

Is this project feasible, based on current site value of $500,000?	**No**

Now that you are well aware of the risks associated with adding value and you have an insight into how to crunch the numbers, you can decide if this specialised area of property investment is really for you.

Whichever direction your property investment journey ultimately takes you, have courage, plan carefully and, most of all, enjoy the process!

APPENDIX A
Glossary of Property Investment Terms

Throughout this book we have thrown a number of unfamiliar terms and concepts your way. For easy reference, we have extracted the key ones and summarised them here.

Body corporate An entity comprised of the owners of individual units or apartments in a block. The body corporate is responsible for insuring and maintaining 'common property' such as the external portions of the building like shared laundries, courtyards and walkways.

Capital gains tax (CGT) The Federal Government levies this tax on investment properties purchased on or after 20 September 1985. The tax is calculated at 50% of your marginal tax rate on the total capital gain (capital growth) you make during the time you hold a property, but is only payable if you *sell*.

Capital growth The dollar amount or percentage by which a property's capital value—as distinct from *rental income*—increases over a certain period. Capital growth can come from inflation or a high level of market demand in relation to supply. Inferior investment properties rely heavily on inflation, which fluctuates, while prime properties derive their growth from ongoing high demand.

Capital growth compounds annually, so the amount of growth in one year is added to the previous year's growth, rapidly increasing the property's value and your equity.

Cash rate The rate at which major players in the financial markets, such as banks, lend money 'at call' to each other. The cash rate is set by the Reserve Bank of Australia, and acts as a benchmark for other important rates, such as the standard variable rate for home and investment loans.

Comparables Properties that have a similar location, building style, level of renovation, number of bedrooms and, if applicable, land size, to the one you wish to purchase. Researching comparables is the most accurate way of assessing a property's likely market value.

Contract of sale A legally binding written agreement between the seller and buyer of a property which sets out the terms and conditions of the sale.

Conveyancing The process of transferring property from one owner to another. Given the legal and administrative complexities of conveyancing, it is preferable to engage a professional practitioner.

Depreciation Capital assets such as carpets and curtains that provide a benefit over a number of years are said to depreciate or decrease in value as they reach the end of their useful life. Owners of investment properties that produce income can write off the cost of these assets over time as tax deductions.

Diversification The practice of purchasing property of different sizes, styles and locations to spread risk and increase the long-term viability of a property portfolio.

Due diligence The scrutiny of information *assumed* to be factual in order to fully establish its credentials, veracity or legitimacy.

Equity   The proportion of a property's value that you *own*, as distinct from the proportion you *owe*. Equity is comprised of three elements: your deposit, inflation-driven and demand-driven capital growth, and the principal component of your loan repayments.

Gearing   Borrowing money to purchase an investment property. In the early years, your property may be negatively geared, i.e. the interest on your loan repayments, along with your holding costs, will exceed your rental income. As time passes and the property grows in value, you may choose to repay principal. At some point your rental income will exceed the interest on your loan repayments and your holding costs, and the property will become 'positively geared' (ie it will generate an increase in excess of all your holding costs).

Goods and services tax (GST)   The GST is levied on a wide range of goods and services. As a property investor, you will pay GST on the purchase price of brand-new property and on the cost of renovations to established property. GST is also payable on a range of holding costs, e.g. insurance, repairs and maintenance and property management fees.

Inflation   Refers to increases in the Consumer Price Index, which is used to measure changes in the cost of living.

Land tax   Levied annually in all states and the ACT. Land tax is based on the combined unimproved land value of the total number of investment properties you own. As an ongoing holding cost, land tax is tax deductible.

Leveraging   The practice of accessing a portion of the equity in one property, for first time investors this is usually your home, to purchase an investment property or other asset. Residential property gives you a considerable degree of leverage because lenders see it as relatively secure.

Median value When all the sale prices of properties across a particular location and timeframe are arranged in ascending order, the middle sale price is the *median value*. Median values can provide a *general* guide to long-range price movements in a particular geographical area.

Mortgage protection insurance Insurance you pay on settlement to protect *the lender* in the event that you default on loan repayments.

Negative equity When the outstanding debt on a property is greater than its market value.

Passive income Rent—income you don't earn through your own exertions (unlike your wage or salary).

Productive and non-productive debt Productive debt is incurred to purchase assets that grow in capital value, e.g. investment property. Non-productive debt is incurred to purchase assets that generally *decline* in capital value, e.g. cars, furniture and household items.

Rental return Refers to the rental amount as a percentage of a property's capital value. Contrary to popular belief, a high rental return does not indicate a prime investment. The *higher* the rental return, the *lower* the capital value; and the *lower* the rental return, the *higher* the capital value.

Return on equity In general terms, this refers to the amount of capital growth over a particular period, relative to the initial equity you put into the property (e.g. the deposit). Return on equity can be a useful measure of the success of your investment.

Scarcity value A characteristic of property styles and location that demonstrate strong growth patterns. It refers to rare architectural styles and locations that are strictly limited in supply and cannot be readily replicated in the market place.

Stamp duty   A one-off cost payable on settlement. Stamp duty is payable on the value of the property transfer and the value of the mortgage. Unlike land tax, stamp duty is not tax-deductible because the Federal Government considers it to be an acquisition cost, not a holding cost.

Undervalued   An undervalued suburb or precinct is one in which property values are relatively modest in comparison with established prime investment locations, but which has many of the same characteristics that confer long-term capital growth potential. These include attractive streetscapes, uniform architecture with scarcity value, proximity to amenities like schools, shops and public transport and an absence of industry in the immediate vicinity.

Vendor bidding   The somewhat controversial practice whereby a vendor can bid at the auction of their property, or nominate someone to bid on their behalf to encourage bidding from genuinely interested buyers.

APPENDIX B
Useful Contacts

A number of statutory and industry bodies provide useful information on issues associated with investing in property. Some can also refer you to reputable practitioners in specialist fields. The key contacts are listed below.

DEMOGRAPHIC AND ECONOMIC DATA

Australian Bureau of Statistics
Ph 1300 135 070 or www.abs.gov.au
The ABS provides useful statistics on a range of demographic and economic factors that impact on property investment.

Departments of infrastructure and planning (or similar)
Most State governments have a department responsible for analysing economic and demographic trends, and planning infrastructure such as roads, schools and hospitals.

Victoria
Department of Infrastructure
Ph: (03) 9655 6666

Northern Territory
Department of Infrastructure Planning and Environment
Ph: (08) 8935 2610

Queensland
Director for the Infrastructure and Major Projects Public Works Department
Ph: (07) 3225 8248

Western Australia
Department for Planning and Infrastructure
Ph: (08) 9216 8877

New South Wales
Infrastructure Coordination Unit
Ph: (02) 9228 3200

Australian Capital Territory
Department of Urban Services
Ph: (02) 6207 5111

Tasmania
Department of Infrastructure, Energy and Resources
Ph: 1300 135 513

South Australia
Department for Transport, Urban Planning and the Arts
Planning SA
Ph: (08) 8303 0777

PROPERTY DATA

Real Estate Institute of Australia and State real estate institutes
The REIA and its State member affiliates are the peak bodies representing the real estate industry. They can also be a useful source of statistics on property sale prices, based on information provided by members.

Real Estate Institute of Australia
Ph: (02) 6282 4277 or www.reiaustralia.com.au

Real Estate Institute of NSW
Ph: (02) 9264 2343 or www.reinsw.com.au

Real Estate Institute of Victoria
Ph: (03) 9205 6666 or www.reiv.com.au

Real Estate Institute of Queensland
Ph: (07) 3891 5711 or www.reiq.com.au

Real Estate Institute of South Australia
Ph: (08) 8366 4345 or www.reisa.com.au

Real Estate Institute of Tasmania
Ph: (03) 6223 4769 or www.reit.com.au

Real Estate Institute of Western Australia
Ph: (08) 9380 8222 or www.reiwa.com.au

Real Estate Institute of ACT
Ph: (02) 6282 4544

Real Estate Institute of Northern Territory
Ph: (08) 8981 8905 or www.reint.com.au

Valuer-general's department (or similar)
Since every property transaction involves a land transfer, these State government bodies can provide comprehensive data on sale prices across particular localities and timeframes.

Victoria
Valuer General
Ph: (03) 8636 2515

New South Wales
Office of the Valuer General
Ph: (02) 8258 7470

Queensland
Cadastral Information and Valuation Policy
Department of Natural Resources Landcentre
Ph: (07) 3896 3798

ACT
Australian Valuation Office
Ph: (02) 6216 8157

Northern Territory
Office of the Valuer General
Ph: (08) 8946 0651

Western Australia
Valuer Generals Office
Ph: (08) 9429 8411

South Australia
Department for Administrative and Information Services
Land Services Group
Ph: (08) 8226 4003

Tasmania
Office of the Valuer General
Ph: (03) 6233 3714

TAXATION

Australian Taxation Office
www.ato.gov.au

The ATO administers federal taxation laws and can provide information on federal tax issues that impact on your investment, e.g. income tax, Capital Gains Tax, Goods and Services Tax, depreciation.

State revenue office (or similar)
These organisations administer State taxation law and can provide information on State tax issues that affect your investment, e.g. stamp duty and land tax.

Office of State Revenue NSW
Ph: 1800 061 163 or www.osr.nsw.gov.au

State Revenue Office Vic
Ph: (03) 9628 6312 or www.sro.vic.gov.au

Office of State Revenue Qld
Ph: (07) 3227 8733 or www.osr.qld.gov.au

Office of State Revenue Western Australia
Ph: (08) 9262 1200 or www.srd.wa.gov.au

ACT Revenue Office
Ph: (02) 6207 0028 or www.revenue.act.gov.au

Revenue SA
Ph: (08) 8226 3750 or
www.treasury.sa.gov.au/revenuesa

Territory Revenue Management
Ph: (08) 8999 7949 or www.nt.gov.au/ntt/revenue/index.html

Department of Treasury and Finance Tasmania
Ph: (03) 6233 3068 or www. treasury.tas.gov.au

CONVEYANCING

State law institutes or societies
www.lawcouncil.asn.au/links.html
These are the peak bodies for legal practitioners and can refer you to suitable providers.

Law Society of New South Wales
Ph: (02) 9926 0333 or
www.lawsocnsw.asn.au

Law Institute of Victoria
Ph: (03) 9607 9311 or www.liv.asn.au

Queensland Law Society
Ph: (07) 3842 5888 or www.qls.com.au

Law Society of the Australian Capital Territory
Ph: (02) 6247 5700 or
www.lawsocact.asn.au

Law Society of South Australia
Ph: (08) 8229 0222, or www.lssa.asn.au

Law Society of Tasmania
Ph: (03) 6234 4133 or
www.taslawsociety.asn.au

Law Society of Western Australia
(08) 9221 3222 or
www.lawsocietywa.asn.au

Law Society of the Northern Territory
Ph: (08) 8981 5104 or www.lawsocnt.asn.au

RENOVATIONS, REDEVELOPMENTS

Master builders associations

These State and Territory-based associations can refer you to reputable builders.

Master Builders Association of NSW
Ph: (02) 8586 3555 or www.mbansw.asn.au

Queensland Master Builders Association
Ph: (07) 3404 6444 or www.qmba.asn.au

Master Builders Association of Victoria
Ph: (03) 9411 4555 or www.mbav.com.au

Master Builders Association of South Australia
Ph: (08) 8211 7466 or www.mbasa.com.au

Master Builders Association of Western Australia
Ph: (08) 9322 5133 or www.mbawa.com.au

Master Builders Association of ACT
Ph: (02) 6247 2099 or email canberra@mba.org.au

Territory Construction Association
Ph: (08) 8922 9666 or email mbant@ozemail.com.au

Index

Adelaide
  property values 56, 60
  urban zones 108
advice, property investment 18–20, 22
advisers, financial 20
advisers, property investment
  accountability 26
  questions to ask of 23–6
agents 21–3, 203–4
apartments *See* units
architectural style
  blending with streetscape 118, 126
  broad-ranging appeal 123
  reproductions of period-style 124–5
  timelessness 81, 124
  ultra-contemporary 123

asset classes 5–7
assets
  reviewing 242
  security 15–16
auctions 205–15
auctions vs private sales 215

banks 8, 146
bidding, vendor 207, 209, 212
bonds 231
Brisbane
  inner city housing 66
  property values 56, 59
  top performing suburbs 102
  urban zones 107
building, new, on vacant land
  site selection 269–71
  steps to follow 268–9
  timing 271–3

building inspections for construction and defects 169–73
buyers
  first home buyers 48, 50, 73, 187
  types of 48–9
buying investment property
  auctions 205–15
  auctions vs private sales 215
  off-market transactions 205
  private sales 202–5
buying subject to finance 152

Canberra
  property values 56, 58
  urban zones 112
capital cities *See also* names of cities
  median house prices 53, 56
  median unit prices 56
  reasons for choosing 97
  where to buy in 99, 102–3
capital gains tax 33, 188–9
capital growth
  assessing 239–40
  compounding 86–90, 91, 93
  and equity 7–8, 13
  and inflation 47
  performance benchmark 86, 246–7
  potential for 7–8, 78–9
  vs rental income 17, 96
capital loss 9
cash rates 39–41
CBD, proximity to 65, 80–1

certificate of title 176
CGT *See* capital gains tax
commercial property, economic factors influencing 35
compound growth 87
consultants, financial 20
contract of sale 175–6
control, personal, in property 15
conveyancing 169–70, 173–8
cooling-off period 152
courses, property investment 20–1

Darwin
  property values 56, 59–60
  urban zones 110
debt
  household 41–2
  non-productive 151
  productive 151
  reduction 94
  retiring 253–4
demand for property 16–17, 39, 47, 49, 71, 126
demographic data 61–2
depreciation 193
diversifying property holdings 144, 249–50
dummy bidding 207, 209, 212

economy
  cycles 34–5, 37–8, 50
  global 42
  historical stages 36–7
economy, Australian, link to US economy 42–3

Index

equity 7–8, 13, 149–51, 239–40
estate agents 21–3, 203–4

finance *See* loans
financial advisers 20
first home buyers 48, 50, 73, 187
Flemington (Vic.) 121
floor plans 81, 140

GDP *See* gross domestic product
gearing 191–3
goods and services tax 185–8, 234–6
gross domestic product 37, 43
GST *See* goods and services tax

Hobart
   property values 56, 60
   urban zones 111
holiday homes, as investment 100–1
home buying
   considerations 69–70, 74–5
   emotional factors 69
   as financial springboard 73–4
   as personal security 69–70
   vs investment property 68–9, 74–5
home ownership 69–70, 72
honeymoon rates 163
houses vs units 124, 132–4
housing activity 46

improvements, building
   to achieve capital growth 272

cosmetic 259, 263–5
structural 136–7, 259, 261
income, rental *See* rental income
income tax 189
indexation 33, 188
inflation
   causes 43–4
   effect on property values 31–3, 44–5
inflation target 39–40
inner city units 64, 127, 131
inner suburbs 64–6, 71, 99, 103
inspections
   building, for construction and defects 169–73
   property, open for viewing 197–201
insurance
   building 180–2
   contents 180–2
   cover note 180
   importance of 169–70, 178
   income protection 183
   landlord protection 182–3
   life 183
   mortgage protection 149, 156, 183
   public liability 182
   reviewing 244
interest rates
   fixed vs variable 159–60
   for investment property loans 148
   set by Reserve Bank 39–41
investment alternatives 5–7
investment portfolio

beginning investing 85–6, 90–1
building 248–9
delaying investing 90–1
diversifying property holdings 144, 249–50
investment property
  adding value 138–9, 259–79
  advantages 7–9, 14–17
  age of property 125, 132
  assessment sheet 197, 199–200
  benefits of 72
  choosing right building 92, 122–45
  disadvantages 9
  evaluating performance 89–90, 237–47
  features of good investment property 78–81
  keeping 93
  location 97–9, 102–3, 117–19
  low-performing 250–3
  managing 219–35
  new vs established 94–6, 129
  prices 94–6
  rating 197, 199–200
  reasons for buying 75, 78
  returns 96
  selling 52–4, 93–4, 251, 254–7
  vs home buying 68–9, 74–5
  vs shares 27–31

Kensington (Vic.) 121

land, vacant, as investment 143, 144–5
land tax 190–1

land values 132
leases 230–1
legal procedures *See* conveyancing
leveraging 8, 149–50
lines of credit 163
loans
  bank 8, 146
  buying subject to finance 152
  choosing a package 148, 156–64
  finding a lender 153–4
  honeymoon rates 163
  how much you can borrow 154–6
  lines of credit 163
  mortgage broker 147–8
  mortgage offset facilities 161
  pre-approved 153
  raising 149
  redraw facilities 162–3
  repayments, principal or interest 156, 158–9
  repayments, weekly or fortnightly 164
  reviewing 164–5, 242
location, choosing 97–9, 102–3, 117–19

maintenance, building 88, 134–7, 138–9
median values 31, 50, 113–16
Melbourne
  inner city housing 63, 65–6
  property values 51, 56, 57–8
  top performing suburbs 102
  urban zones 106

monetary policy 41
mortgage *See* loans
mortgage broker 147–8
mortgage market 146–7
mortgage offset facilities 161
multi-unit developments 64, 66–7, 127–31

National Tenancy Database 221
negative gearing 192–3
negotiation 201–2, 204
New Farm (Qld) 65, 66
Newtown (NSW) 65

off-market transactions 205
orientation 140, 143
ownership, home 69–70, 72

parking 137, 140
Perth
  property values 56, 60
  top performing suburbs 102
  urban zones 109
population size and density, impact on property values 62–3
Port Melbourne 114–15
private sales 202–5
private sales vs auctions 215
private treaty 202–5, 215
property *See* investment property
property assessment sheet 197, 199–200
property inspections, open for viewing 197–201
property managers
  accountability 223–6

advantages 220–2
  fees 222–3
  finding 223–5
  questions to ask of 225–6
  reviewing 243–4
  role 227–34
property values
  and the economy 46–50
  effect of inflation on 31–3, 44–5
  effect of population size and density 62–3
purchasers *See* buyers

rating, investment property 197, 199–200
real asset security 15–16
redevelopment 260, 266–7
  feasibility studies 273–8
redraw facilities 162–3
regional centres 98
renovations
  to achieve capital growth 272
  cosmetic 259, 263–5
  structural 136–7, 259, 261
rental guarantees 10, 130
rental households, percentage of 16–17
rental income 8–10, 17, 79–80, 96, 227–8
rental market 10
rental returns 10–13, 80
repayments, weekly or fortnightly 164
Reserve Bank of Australia
  interest rates, setting 39–41
  role in managing economy 49

297

residential property
  cycles 38–42, 61–7
  demographic factors influencing 61–7
  economic factors influencing 35, 38–42
residential tenancies tribunal 233–4
retirement, funding 4–5, 85
return on equity 239–40
Richmond (Vic.) 65–6
rural areas 98

sales *See* auctions; private sales
sales results, tracking 116–17, 208
scarcity value 123, 126
security, asset 15–16
seminars, property investment 20–1
settlement 175, 178, 204
shares vs investment property 27–31
shortfall, funding 157
solicitors 169, 173–8
stamp duty 129, 177, 178, 189–90
standard of accommodation 135–6
structural soundness 81, 125, 172–3
style, architectural *See* architectural style
suburbs
  inner 64–6, 71, 99, 103
  middle-ring 71
  undervalued 119–21

superannuation 4–5
supply and demand for properties 10, 39, 49, 71, 126
Sydney
  property values 51, 55–7
  top performing suburbs 102, 103
  urban zones 104–5

tax
  buying investment property for tax reasons 14–15, 195
  capital gains tax 33, 188–9
  goods and services tax 185–8, 234–6
  income tax 189
  land tax 190–1
  stamp duty 129, 177, 178, 189–90
tax benefits, of property 14, 244–5
tax deductions 193–4
tenants
  accommodation expectations 135
  disputes with 233–4
  selecting 221, 229–30
timing the market 39, 52–5

undervalued suburbs 119–21
units
  choosing the right kind 134
  inner city 64, 127, 131
  multi-unit developments 64, 66–7, 127–31

position in block 143
  vs houses 124, 132–4
urban consolidation 71
urban drift 63–7
US economy 42–3

vendor bidding 207, 209, 212
vendors
  auction 206, 210
  off-market transactions 205
  private sale 203–5

Wakelin Property Advisory

You've read *Streets Ahead* and want to invest in top notch residential property, but don't know where to start?

Company Services

Wakelin Property Advisory provides a comprehensive and totally independent advisory service for residential property investors. We can help with the planning, searching, selection, evaluation negotiation or bidding at auction, advise on rental management and ongoing performance monitoring of your investment property portfolio.

Courses

Streets Ahead—Introductory

A two hour introduction to the principles of successful residential property investment, including where and what to buy, how much to pay, pitfalls to avoid and how to finance.

Streets Ahead—Advanced

Spend a full day in the property market with Richard Wakelin and Monique Wakelin and put their tried and tested formula to work. In addition to learning more about economic cycles, tax, finance and rental management, Richard and Monique will take you 'on site' to assess real life case study properties which bring everything you've read about in this book to life!

Please call us at Wakelin Property Advisory on 03 9859 9595 or email us at info@wakelin.com.au. Our website is at www.ownproperty.com.au